"Spector disentangles the dilemmas of
works?' – a question he answers on leve
tions to human psychology. Corruption is often a process of negotiation,
and this book shows how we can help such negotiations fail. In these pages,
reformers, scholars and citizens will find new challenges and fresh perspectives on age-old problems."
— *Michael Johnston, Charles A. Dana Professor of*
Political Science, Emeritus, Colgate University, USA

"Spector brings his decades-long experience in combating corruption to
produce an impressive analysis of why reform efforts to eradicate corruption have had only minimal success. It is a must-read for policymakers
concerned with finding new pathways to sustainably tackle corruption."
— *Shaukat Hassan, former Senior Policy Advisor,*
Canadian International Development Agency

"Fighting corruption is incredibly hard. Few have more experience designing, implementing, and assessing anti-corruption programs than Dr. Spector. Students of governance, reformers, and anti-corruption practitioners
should keep this book nearby to chart their course through treacherous
waters."
— *Juhani Grossmann, Team Leader, Basel Institute on*
Governance, Switzerland

Curbing Corruption

Many anti-corruption efforts have had only a minimal effect on curbing the problem of corruption. This book explains why that is, and shows readers what works in the real world in the fight against corruption, and why.

Counter-corruption initiatives often focus on the legal, institutional, and contextual factors that facilitate corrupt behavior, but these have had only nominal impacts, because most of these reforms can be circumvented by government officials, powerful citizens, and business people who are relentless in their quest for self-interest. This book argues that instead, we should target the key individual and group drivers of corrupt behavior and, through them, promote sustainable behavioral change. Drawing on over 25 years of practical experience planning, designing, and implementing anti-corruption programs in over 40 countries, as well as a wealth of insights from social psychological, ethical, and negotiation research, this book identifies innovative tools that target these core human motivators of corruption, with descriptions of pilot tests that show how they can work in practice.

Anti-corruption is again becoming a priority issue, prompted by the emergence of more authoritarian regimes, and the public scrutiny of government responses to the COVID-19 pandemic. Straddling theory and practice, this book is the perfect guide to what works and what doesn't, and will be valuable for policymakers, NGOs, development practitioners, and corruption studies students and researchers.

Bertram I. Spector has more than 40 years of experience conducting and directing research, training, and technical assistance programs internationally, specializing in the anti-corruption and international negotiation fields. For the past 25 years, he has focused his attention on designing, implementing, and researching practical programs to fight corruption and strengthen good governance and integrity in developing countries. Dr. Spector directed the Transparency and Accountability Practice Area at Management Systems International (MSI), an international development consulting firm that implements programs for the United States Agency for International Development (USAID) and the United Kingdom's Department for International Development (DFID), among others. In recent years, he provided day-to-day technical guidance to in-country teams implementing multi-million dollar, multi-year anti-corruption projects in Ukraine, Afghanistan, Indonesia, Mali, Liberia, and Mexico. Dr. Spector has authored and edited three books on fighting corruption, several program papers and handbooks currently in use by the US Government, and many scholarly articles in the anti-corruption field.

Routledge Corruption and Anti-Corruption Studies

The series features innovative and original research on the subject of corruption from scholars around the world. As well as documenting and analyzing corruption, the series aims to discuss anti-corruption initiatives and endeavors, in an attempt to demonstrate ways forward for countries and institutions where the problem is widespread. The series particularly promotes comparative and interdisciplinary research targeted at a global readership.

In terms of theory and method, rather than basing itself on any one orthodoxy, the series draws broadly on the tool kit of the social sciences in general, emphasizing comparison, the analysis of the structure and processes, and the application of qualitative and quantitative methods.

Corruption and the Lava Jato Scandal in Latin America
Edited by Paul Lagunes and Jan Svejnar

The Conundrum of Corruption
Reform for Social Justice
Michael Johnston and Scott A. Fritzen

Comparing Police Corruption
Bulgaria, Germany, Russia and Singapore
Leslie Holmes

The Politics of Anti-Corruption Agencies in Latin America
Edited by Joseph Pozsgai-Alvarez

Curbing Corruption
Practical Strategies for Sustainable Change
Bertram I. Spector

For more information about this series, please visit: www.routledge.com/
Routledge-Corruption-and-Anti-Corruption-Studies/book-series/RCACS

Curbing Corruption

Practical Strategies for Sustainable Change

Bertram I. Spector

Routledge
Taylor & Francis Group

LONDON AND NEW YORK

First published 2022
by Routledge
4 Park Square, Milton Park, Abingdon, Oxon OX14 4RN

and by Routledge
605 Third Avenue, New York, NY 10158

Routledge is an imprint of the Taylor & Francis Group, an informa business

© 2022 Bertram I. Spector

The right of Bertram I. Spector to be identified as author of this
work has been asserted in accordance with sections 77 and 78 of the
Copyright, Designs and Patents Act 1988.

British Library Cataloguing-in-Publication Data
A catalogue record for this book is available from the British Library

Library of Congress Cataloging-in-Publication Data
A catalog record has been requested for this book

ISBN: 978-1-032-14792-5 (hbk)
ISBN: 978-1-032-13560-1 (pbk)
ISBN: 978-1-003-24111-9 (ebk)

DOI: 10.4324/9781003241119

Typeset in Times New Roman
by codeMantra

For my wife, Judy

Contents

PART III
Practical implementation   123

Preface

For the past 25 years, I have conducted research on corruption and implemented practical anti-corruption programs along with many excellent colleagues in over 40 countries. Always, the goal has been to make corruption fail. This quest has certainly consumed the talented efforts of many generations of researchers and implementers before me. We have not succeeded – but we are getting closer. There have been many twists and turns in what have been considered the "right" strategies to follow to disincentivize corrupt behaviors. Would reforms to the legal structure be enough? Maybe the anti-corruption objectives of existing governmental institutions need to be adjusted or new agencies need to be established. How can corrupt behaviors be prevented? Does there need to be more transparency and accountability for government officials? And what about civil society and business groups that are complicit with corrupt officials? What can be done to engage them actively in the strategic equation to reduce corruption? It is not an easy social landscape.

Over the years, we have piloted many creative ideas and learned from past efforts. We have always questioned whether we are approaching the problem correctly. We always ask, *Are we missing important cues?* I think progress has been made, but more needs to be done.

Thanks to programs sponsored around the world by the United States Agency for International Development (USAID), the United Kingdom's Department for International Development, the World Bank, and many other agencies and organizations, my colleagues and I at Management Systems International (MSI) have had the opportunity to consider, analyze, and pilot many innovative approaches to reduce corruption. We were able to test many ideas, observe the results, monitor them systematically, and compare options. Short case studies of many of these anti-corruption pilot tests are presented throughout this book to illustrate what is possible and what might be effective in the right context if there is the will, resources, and commitment to sustainability.

Many of these ideas worked, but the longevity of their impact is unknown and their spread throughout the targeted country was limited. Unfortunately, in many situations, country- and donor-sponsored programs to fight corruption are short-lived and if rapid results are not detected, the funding is pulled back before it is possible to assess whether the efforts are significant or not and before it is possible to scale up the intervention throughout the country.

In an ideal world, people would always do the right thing based on ethical principles, and act to achieve social justice and the greater good. But human tendency is to pull in the opposite direction – to act out of self-interest, with little thought for the implications of our behaviors for others and the society at large. This inclination toward corruption seems to be built into our DNA and it would take very deliberate and targeted initiatives to turn us around. Maybe that is why human behavior is not so impacted by the typical anti-corruption initiatives – political, legal, and economic solutions – that result in stronger laws, regulations, policies, and institutions. These are too remote from the drivers that really motivate our thoughts and actions. Instead, corruption needs to be fought as one would fight a disease that attacks one's body – at a very personal level. Attempts to modify individual behaviors that visibly demonstrate the benefits of those adjusted ways of behaving may be the most powerful agents of change when it comes to corruption.

This book explores the range of anti-corruption initiatives that have been tried over the last 30 years or so and examines some areas and strategies where more attention might yield better payoffs in terms of making corruption fail. I am convinced, as are others, that fighting corruption is an evolutionary task. It cannot be conquered quickly or by one unique approach. It requires multiple layers of strategies, situationally conceived and implemented, over several generations to succeed.

Based on this theme of looking at the corruption problem with fresh eyes, I have been surprised by how well some research I had done at the beginning of my career – in graduate school and in early consulting assignments – fits into the theme of this book. My research on ethical behavior and moral development in the legal profession, and on achieving beneficial outcomes through negotiation processes adds new insights into making corruption fail.

I would like to recognize the great creativity and practical implementation of my colleagues at MSI for many of the tools and approaches discussed in this book, especially Svetlana Winbourne, who has been my principal partner in designing and implementing new anti-corruption initiatives in many countries. Also, many others served as major idea-makers and implementers on-the-ground for our projects in developing countries, including Juhani Grossmann, Shaukat Hassan, Larry Held, Daud Omari, Barbara James, Sarah Dix, Gerard Mosquera, Emil Bolongaita, and Phyllis Dininio. I also acknowledge Edward Weisband and Thomas Franck for their guidance and advice related to my research on the moral development of lawyers, the results of which contributed to their book, *Resignation in Protest: Political and Ethical Choices between Loyalty to Team and Loyalty to Conscience in*

American Public Life (Grossman Publishers 1975). I worked together with Joseph Moskowitz on the experimental research for that book. And the wisdom I have received over the years from I. William Zartman and Daniel Druckman concerning negotiation processes has proven invaluable to my thinking about the linkages between bargaining theory and corruption for this book.

I also owe many thanks to MSI and USAID for the opportunities and challenges of conducting research on corruption and anti-corruption reforms throughout the world, as well as designing, implementing, and monitoring new and innovative initiatives aimed at fighting corruption, many under very complex and difficult circumstances.

1   Since the dawn of humankind

I was driving to the office on a weekend after returning from a three-week assignment overseas where I provided technical support to a donor-funded anti-corruption project. There was little traffic on the parkway and my mind began reliving highlights of the advocacy training for civil society organizations that I had conducted and next steps for the project, and less so to the pressure of my foot on the car's gas pedal. A siren and flashing lights behind my car immediately brought me back to reality, and I slowed down, pulled over to the shoulder of the road and awaited the policeman. I was traveling 12 miles over the speed limit, he said. He also commented on my bright red car, saying that I probably liked to drive fast in this sporty looking car! (It was only a Volvo.)

The policeman went back to his vehicle, did some checking, and came back to my car to talk. He handed me a speeding ticket and then alerted me to two ways I could handle the fine. My mind immediately rushed back to my recent anti-corruption project and how traffic police typically deal with citizens in other countries. I remembered being in a car in Vladivostok, Russia not long before, traveling to a meeting with an official of the local prosecutor's office, and we were pulled over by a traffic policeman. We did not appear to be doing anything wrong. But before the policeman could say anything, the official in the car flashed his government ID and the policeman waved us on.

Having been pulled over on the parkway now, I was sure about the two options that I would be presented with: (1) pay a bribe to the policeman right now and it will all go away or (2) pay the ticket, which would cost more than the bribe. I was wrong. The policeman did offer me two options: the first was that I could pay the ticket by sending a check through the mail and the second was that I could appeal the fine by going to traffic court. Was I relieved! But I knew that most of the people I know in other countries where I worked on anti-corruption programs would not have been so lucky.

The way this anecdote would have played out in many other countries is an example of *petty corruption* – low-level exploitation of ordinary citizens by low- to mid-level civil servants who use their positions of power and authority for their own self-interest rather than the people's interest. Growing

DOI: 10.4324/9781003241119-1

up and living their lives in countries where corruption is an integral part of the national culture, many civil servants approach their jobs as a means to benefit themselves, their friends, and their families, rather than ensuring quality services to the public they are meant to serve. Many times, corrupt practices are used by civil servants just to provide themselves with a living wage. In some situations, they ask citizens for bribes to get what they are otherwise entitled to for free, while enriching themselves. In other cases, they steal government funds directly, approve government contracts for friends or relatives from whom they receive monetary kickbacks, or develop legislation or regulations with hidden loopholes that allow them to profit. The latter cases can easily up the ante to *grand corruption* levels, where larger sums of money and influence pass hands from government coffers to private bank accounts.

Corruption can be defined as the abuse of entrusted power for private gain.[1] At its heart, corruption depends on those government officials – public servants – who are willing to take advantage of their position and authority to do what is good for them, their family, and their friends, at the expense of the rest of the population. It draws upon a deep self-interested instinct in humans to benefit themselves. Citizens who do not hold government office can also participate in corruption for their own benefit. They can initiate an offer to those in office – a bribe or kickback, for example – for making a decision that favors the engaged citizen at the expense of others, for instance, money or gifts to the public official in exchange for a lucrative government contract or speedy admission to a university for their children. What is always missing is an understanding of the impacts of these special actions and empathy for those that do not benefit – or suffer – from the corrupt act. If special advantage is given to the official or the complicit citizen, others in the community will likely be the losers. The government budget will be plundered, government programs will have less funds to deliver services, and the quality of those services will be diminished. Public servants will not be acting to serve the public as a whole, but a smaller and engaged corrupt community instead, and the general public will suffer the consequences.

Corrupt officials believe they can act as they do because of insufficient accountability mechanisms and inadequate oversight of their decisions. Laws may be on the books that outlaw corruption, but neither law enforcement nor auditors nor parliament nor citizens conduct adequate monitoring of their actions to detect or prosecute them for corruption. Corrupt officials invariably believe that they can stay below the radar and not get caught, even in the face of examples of others who have been called out, prosecuted, and convicted. They believe they are smarter than others and can commit the crime without the punishment. In fact, they often believe they are not doing anything illegal. They are doing what everyone does: they are doing what's needed to benefit themselves and those close to them.

But we cannot always blame government officials alone for corruption. Corruption is almost always a two-way street. There are the government officials who abuse their authority and initiate the corrupt action, but there must also be others who agree to participate and pay the price so that they can get the services they need. These victims of corruption may not like the transaction, but they go along with it to get the services. Any time there is an opportunity for a face-to-face interaction between government officials and citizens, there is an opportunity for a corrupt transaction. The transaction is most likely to be initiated by the officials in their role as the authority providing the services sought. But it can just as easily be initiated by the citizen who knows how the game is played and can try to set the price paid to get the services needed. Those who cannot pay the price suffer.

Many people in many countries live their lives either employing corruption themselves or being surrounded by corruption. In everyday life, corruption can happen when you need to access health care or enroll your children in school – which are supposed to be provided to citizens for free or for a set price. But you are asked to pay extra or provide a gift to receive it; otherwise the service is not provided or is delayed. Or you are a businessperson and need a license or a citizen seeking to renew a driver's permit; again, you are confronted with the quid pro quo of paying an extra fee or not getting what you are entitled to. Worse yet, you are a taxpayer and have heard that the city is building a new school in your district or purchasing life-saving medicines for your local hospital. Sounds good, but school construction is never completed and only expired drugs are available to the public because hefty kickbacks had to be paid to certain city officials by the vendors to win the public procurements.

These episodes of corrupt transactions have been an integral part of human existence since the beginning of social interactions. Ancient Greek and Roman literature describe the role of corruption in everyday life and the Old Testament includes proscriptions against corruption. Bribery, corruption's principal manifestation, is as old as recorded history and is mentioned in Psalm of David 15 as one of those basic volitional actions that will prevent one from "dwelling upon Thy holy mountain." Those in a position of power or authority feel they are entitled to benefit themselves, their families, and their friends, regardless of how their actions impact others. It is a part of human nature. Moreover, culture and tradition often serve to deeply embed these behaviors as being acceptable from generation to generation. Even when nations enact laws that criminalize corrupt transactions, these activities still endure. Corruption is not only pervasive and widespread but very resistant to change. Overall, success stories are few and far between. Corruption is a hard nut to crack.

This book is not so much about describing corruption and its impacts on governance, the economy and the lives of everyday citizens. That's been analyzed in many other research efforts.[2] Instead, this book examines why reform efforts that have been tried to reduce corruption over the past 6,000 years – since the dawn of civilization – have had minimal effects on eradicating this "plague," and what new paths policymakers may want to try that could yield better outcomes to make corruption fail. Corruption is a deeply engrained human instinct, and to reduce or eliminate it, we have to delve deeper into the basic human motivation to find out what reforms might result in its demise – or close to it. First, let's take a bird's-eye view of the problem.

Corruption and development

Corruption is a worldwide phenomenon, largely prevalent and unchecked in countries undergoing transitions, modernization, and development.[3] But that does not stop corruption scandals in highly developed countries from being reported on almost a daily basis. Certainly, one cannot be attentive to current events today without being inundated by the many reports of corruption in *both* the developing and developed worlds.

Evidence of corruption has exploded in relation to government responses to the COVID-19 pandemic in 2020 and 2021: public procurements of COVID-19 relief items and vaccines have been riddled with fraud, many purchases have gone missing after being purchased, high-level government officials have jumped the queue to get their vaccinations quickly, transparency regulations have been eased in public contracting for pharmaceuticals, and lack of public trust in government due to embedded corruption has resulted in vaccine hesitancy among the population, among many others.[4]

In 2016, the leaked documents, known as the Panama Papers, revealed extensive fraud, corruption, money laundering, and tax evasion by public officials and wealthy individuals from hundreds of countries going back to the 1970s. The great damage and loss of life in major earthquakes in Turkey in 1999 and India in 2001 have been attributed not so much to acts of God, but to pervasive corruption; it is common practice in these countries for government inspectors to turn a blind eye to building code violations in return for bribes from construction firms. In Salt Lake City, a big scandal revealed how bribery and gifts were intimately involved in the selection of sites for the 2000 Olympic Games. In Brussels, department heads in the European Commission had to resign in 1999 due to allegations of fraud and corruption.

In Ukraine, surveys conducted prior to the Orange Revolution found that 35% of companies pay bribes frequently, an average of 6.5% of annual corporate revenue is paid in bribes as unofficial taxes, and over 30% of households claim that they are confronted by some form of corruption every year.[5] While corruption remains a real and constant phenomenon that plagues all countries, the difference between developing and developed countries is in the extent to which institutions and processes have been implemented to keep opportunities for corruption checked and under control, and predictable punishment meted out, when corruption is exposed.

The bribery transaction has two basic variants – the demand and the offer. It can be initiated by officials who use their position to extort payments and favors from citizens who are eligible to obtain services for no extra fee whatsoever. Alternatively, it can be offered by citizens who seek special dispensation or service by paying off or providing a gift or favor to an official who is otherwise entrusted with upholding the law. Whether or not the quid pro quo, in fact, occurs after the corrupt transaction is initiated depends upon the ethics, desperation, desire for gratification, and fear of punishment by both sides in the transaction.

What makes corruption so prevalent in development situations? Corruption is more than just a function of personal greed or cultural predisposition.[6] It tends to prevail where the *rule of law* is not clearly elaborated and public officials have wide authority to act; under these circumstances, officials can make decisions that benefit themselves with impunity, free from the risk of certain detection. Corruption thrives when officials are not held *accountable* and there is minimal *transparency* in the decision process. Weak and ill-conceived *incentives* also make societies vulnerable to corruption – when civil servants are not paid a living wage, when there are few rewards for good performance, and when there is little fear of punishment for wrongdoing. Countries with *weak institutions* that are over-politicized and cannot enforce their decisions are also prone to corrupt practices. When there is a lack of *political will and commitment* to make reforms among society's leadership, corruption prospers. An underdeveloped *civil society* also contributes to corruption, because this is the sector of society that typically serves as the external watchdog of government operations and decisions; without their active role in pressuring officials, government can often proceed unchecked. Finally, in developing countries where *citizen loyalties* to the state are still in a formative stage and may be more strongly focused on personal, tribal, or clan relationships, corruption in the state can grow because accountability is not enforced.

Wide discretion, limited accountability, and limited transparency in government decision-making open the doors to bribery transactions.[7] Wide discretion provides government officials with the opportunity to interpret laws, regulations, and processes, and makes negotiation concerning how they are implemented possible. Limited accountability provides government officials with practically free agency; they can negotiate on terms that will yield personal benefit with little risk that they will be caught and punished for overstepping the public trust. Limited transparency offers both the public official as well as their negotiating partner the relative secrecy that is required to conduct their extra-legal transaction. The opposite of each of these conditions that make bribery negotiations possible can be rectified by the effective rule of law. In such situations, what is expected of public officials is clearly prescribed, their ability to interpret is circumscribed, and government decision-making is predictable to all parties and open to inspection by all. These are circumstances that reduce the opportunity for negotiation and hence for bribery.

What makes corruption so counterproductive to development? First, it impairs the possibilities for economic growth.[8] Corruption scares off private investment from domestic and foreign sources that fear the risks, unknown costs, and harassment involved in highly corrupt systems. Corruption also encourages the growth of a shadow economy, where taxes and fees are not paid to the state but rather as unofficial payments to corrupt bureaucrats. Second, corruption reduces the ability of the state to govern. It undermines the rule of law and replaces it with a personalistic and changeable set of informal relationships. It also reduces the capacity of the government to deliver quality public services; with funds siphoned off from the public treasury into the pockets of corrupt officials, there is less money available to provide citizens with the services that their government is supposed to provide. Finally, corruption demoralizes the public and results in a loss of confidence and trust that government is there to serve the people and develop the country.

Given the prospects of these negative consequences, international donors, as well as developing and transitioning countries themselves, have become extremely sensitive to the existence and growth of corruption and many have sought aggressively to implement anti-corruption campaigns. But leakage of donor development funds, especially surrounding large public construction projects, major procurements, and humanitarian crises, has caused donors to be cautious in their granting and lending programs and has resulted in the imposition of conditionality clauses that require countries to diagnose their corruption problems and implement active and realistic national anti-corruption strategies before new funds are released.[9]

Corruption's daily impacts

To put things into perspective, let's quickly assess how corruption hurts. The 2018 World Economic Forum estimates that the global cost of corruption is at least $2.6 trillion, or 5% of the global gross domestic product (GDP). The World Bank calculates that businesses and individuals pay more than $1 trillion in bribes every year.[10] On October 15, 2020, the United Nations Secretary-General Antonio Guterres, in the face of the COVID-19 pandemic crisis, issued a statement in which he made an urgent call for more robust systems of accountability, transparency, and integrity.[11] Especially in this health crisis, he targeted corruption as a betrayal of public trust that is most potent when governments respond to the pandemic unchecked. Officials and businesses have new opportunities to commit fraud and abuse that accrue to their personal benefit while diverting resources from the general population that is suffering.

A few examples of how corruption has become embedded in the cultures and lives of peoples around the world make this problem all too real. I draw on two very different countries where I have conducted on-the-ground research: Mozambique and Ukraine. While these assessments were developed several years ago and reform programs have been conducted since then to reduce the corruption vulnerabilities identified, it is not uncommon for such corruption problems to persist. As well, these findings are rather familiar in other countries.

Mozambique (2005)

In Mozambique, corruption is culturally tolerated due to resignation, fear, or a general feeling of not complaining about corruption – "letting it go" and "not making waves" because of a fear of retribution and a desire to avoid problems.[12] Further, with the extended family at the core of people's lives, many behaviors that might be considered to be conflicts of interest, nepotism, or favoritism are not generally viewed as corrupt practices. Instead, Mozambicans who achieve positions of authority and influence are often expected to use their position to help family members and friends get jobs, avoid red tape, and circumvent the system. There are pervasive institutional and procedural weaknesses that contribute to inescapable corruption at the administrative level – the near-daily bribes required to pass through police roadblocks, register a child in school, deal with various inspectors, or get faster treatment at a clinic. At the same time, there is a broader political and economic context that discourages accountability and presents limited incentives to leaders to change the status quo.

A prominent area where grand corruption is prevalent is the judicial sector. The courts in Mozambique are seen not only as a main venue for corruption but also as a key bottleneck in efforts to sanction corrupt behavior. Corruption manifests itself in the buying and selling of verdicts, the exertion of political control over judicial outcomes, "losing" evidence or case files as directed or paid to do, intimidation of witnesses, and freeing of key suspects. Political control and manipulation of the judiciary from above are at the root of these critical failures of the state. Criminal investigators may use their knowledge to do favors for a price (for example, letting the accused know they are under investigation or warning them of an upcoming search) or extort bribes by refusing to investigate a complaint until paid or demanding payments from potential suspects. Bribing investigators to "lose" critical pieces of evidence reportedly is common.

Another sector rife with corruption is public health care. Major corruption and mismanagement problems in the public health system stand as obstacles to continued improvement in health care delivery. Corrupt behaviors range from diverting, stealing, and/or reselling of drugs and supplies, using public facilities for private gain, and requests for unofficial payments for services that are supposed to be provided at no cost. The very poor suffer the most from this corruption when they fail to receive the services they require or are forced to pay a greater percentage of their income to access services that should be provided free or at a lower fee. While there are certainly many honest and hard-working health care providers in Mozambique, there are reports of many doctors, nurses, pharmacists, laboratory technicians, administrative staff, and maids who are involved in "wage enhancement" activities to supplement low salaries. Many of these persons do not consider their activities to be corrupt behaviors, which include charging bribes to provide regular services or to speed up the provision of services, stealing drugs and selling them on the open market, using access to patients in public hospitals and clinics to transfer them to private clinics, and manipulating the drug registration and procurement process. Often patients or their families offer bribes to health care workers to seek better or faster service.

Corruption in the education sector is also widespread and weighs most heavily on children, young girls, and the poor. It also has a pernicious impact on the country's future development prospects. While corruption in this sector tends to deal with small amounts of money, it affects almost the entire population. School construction – where larger sums of money are involved – is procured at the provincial levels. Corruption enters in here as simple fraud due to lax controls and accountability mechanisms. The human resources and public financial management systems are generally weak. To encourage bribe-giving from parents, school administrators often assign girl students to the evening shift – generally viewed as unsafe – in anticipation of bribes to change shifts. Girls are also often pressured into sex with male teachers for grades, amounting to sexual corruption. The full assessment report for Mozambique continues on with analyses of corruption in public financing and budgeting, public procurement, customs, inspections, municipalities, and political parties – primarily in the realm of grand corruption.

Ukraine (2017)

While corruption is pervasive at all levels, many Ukrainians still do not equate some common behaviors and transactions as being corrupt.[13] For example, providing gifts or cash to speed up service delivery from governmental authorities or bribing officials to look the other way are commonly accepted modes of transacting with government by citizens and businesses, and often not perceived as corruption. This "culture of corruption" results in a popular mindset that excuses or tolerates this behavior, because it is seen as a way to satisfy personal and private interests or the only way to get things done in a failing system of service delivery.[14]

Citizen are often complicit in "greasing the wheels" at a petty corruption level, for instance, with a bribe or gift to get needed health care, and at a grand corruption level, businesses are complicit in giving kickbacks to government officials to win public procurements.[15] While public opinion surveys indicate that citizens believe corruption is growing in Ukraine and express negative reactions toward corruption, those beliefs reflect primarily on what high-level officials or oligarchs are doing, not what ordinary citizens do at a personal level to benefit themselves and their families. Tolerance for corruption runs deep in the everyday lives of Ukrainians. At the same time, citizens have started benefiting from a growing range of electronic and centralized services, including e-governance and one-stop shops for administrative services, that reduce the need for direct contacts with multiple public officials and therefore reduce opportunities for corruption.

Corruption is a two-way street – it can be initiated by the official and by the citizen – both well prepared by tradition and culture on how to get things done. Some public officials believe they can rightfully extort bribes to compensate for their low salaries. Citizens believe they can bypass laws and regulations to compensate for inadequate service, for example, paying to jump the line at a medical facility or "thanking" teachers for their services with a gift or bribe. In part, this tradition is a lasting legacy of the Soviet past, where taking from the collective good or property was not seen as something shameful.

Corruption is sometimes used as an "access to power" mechanism where payments are made to secure a position in a government institution which would then allow the civil servant to engage in rent-seeking behavior and retrieve the money paid for the position.

The two dimensions of corruption (petty and grand corruption) are not connected in the minds of most Ukrainians. Grand corruption is seen as evil, practiced by high-level officials and oligarchs. This high-level corruption (state capture by business elites) was challenged by the 2014 Euromaidan revolution, but the promise of full-fledged "de-oligarchization" has so far failed to deliver.

On the other hand, petty corruption is not even acknowledged as corruption, per se, because it is done in support of your own or your family's personal interests. In general, people know what is right and wrong, but the use of petty corruption is not equated with illegality in most people's minds. Moreover, the complexities of the anti-corruption regulatory regime make it a hard task to understand even for civil servants, let alone the ordinary citizen.

On the legal and regulatory front in 2017, domestic anti-corruption legislation had progressed and is becoming more prescriptive and detailed. While this is a positive step, it also stimulates creative thinking by those who it is supposed to limit or restrain – they find ways to circumvent the new laws to continue their corrupt transactions. For example, more stringent regulations on declaring assets, including assets of spouses, have led to a growing number of fictitious divorces; assets of high value have also been given to grandparents to avoid declaration.

International peer review mechanisms that Ukraine subscribes to, for example, the Council of Europe's Group of States against Corruption (GRECO), the United Nations Convention Against Corruption (UNCAC), and the Organization for Economic Cooperation and Development's Anti-Corruption Network (OECD ACN) Istanbul Anti-Corruption Action Plan, offer guidance and recommendations for "bulletproofing" anti-corruption regulations and access to good practices worldwide. At the same time, recommendations of these bodies have to be adapted to the Ukrainian context and backed up with strict implementation practices.

While Ukraine has recently made unprecedented progress toward transparency and data openness, the lack of effective investigation and prosecution quickly reduces expectations of punishment and creates an atmosphere of cynicism among citizens. For instance, while journalist investigations may uncover corruption-related cases through open registries and digital databases that have become available since the Euromaidan, official action to prosecute these cases is often slow or suspended. Additionally, e-declarations have exposed excessive levels of wealth and savings among officials, but formal investigations into illicit enrichment have yet to produce any indictments.

Thus, the public is often made aware of corruption in their midst, but they have low expectations of any quick or adequate official response. They expect corrupt officials to enjoy impunity. This spiral leads to reduced trust in government and promotes beliefs and behaviors by ordinary citizens that corruption is acceptable because perpetrators won't get caught.

Fast forward to April 2019 when Volodymyr Zelensky was elected president of Ukraine, running on an anti-corruption platform. The newly elected parliament quickly passed several anti-corruption laws – ending immunity for sitting members from civil lawsuits, targeting illegal enrichment by government officials, and addressing corruption in land reform, among others. Several anti-corruption institutions were reinvigorated. But by the latter half of 2020, Ukraine's anti-corruption infrastructure came under serious attack by the parliament; the constitutionality of the High Anti-Corruption Court and the National Anti-Corruption Bureau was questioned. As well, other critical anti-corruption mechanisms came under assault, such as electronic asset declarations, illicit enrichment prohibitions, and lifestyle monitoring. Corruption and anti-corruption in Ukraine remain a very dynamic situation.

Next steps

While there is no vaccine yet that is proven to eliminate the human corruption pandemic, recent efforts have demonstrated that there are ways that courageous individuals, communities, and nations can respond to corruption that will mitigate its occurrence and its impacts. Policymakers are looking for more than just research on the nature of the corruption problem; they need guidance on reform strategies that are likely to succeed based on lessons learned from practical implementation. The focus of this book is to highlight the motivating and demotivating factors surrounding corruption, and to put forth practical findings of what has worked and what has not worked in different countries under certain conditions.

The next five chapters look at a wide range of initiatives that have been implemented in recent history in attempts to reduce corruption in many countries, and how well they have fared. Some of these programs display promise, but most show only moderate to minimal impact on corrupt behavior. One conclusion that can be drawn is that we may not be on the right track. Maybe past anti-corruption efforts are not working because they are targeting the wrong motivators. So, in subsequent chapters, we examine several potential paths that can lead policymakers to more impactful anti-corruption reforms – either through motivating anti-corruption behaviors or demotivating corrupt instincts. The goal is to find the drivers that will yield sustainable behavioral change. Theory and real-life examples are explored. In the end, we offer recommendations on how best to organize national and international responses to corruption, looking to achieve more effective and viable results in the future.

Notes

1 Transparency International. At: https://www.transparency.org/en/what-is-corruption.
2 For in-depth analyses of corruption, its causes and consequences, see Bertram Spector, editor (2005). *Fighting Corruption in Developing Countries.* Bloomfield, CT: Kumarian Press; Arnold Heidenheimer, Michael Johnston and Victor LeVine (1999). *Political Corruption: A Handbook.* New Brunswick, NJ: Transaction Publishers; J. Edgardo Campos and Sanjay Pradhan, editors (2007). *The Many Faces of Corruption.* Washington, DC: The World Bank; Susan Rose-Ackerman and Bonnie Palifka (2016). *Corruption and Government.* New York: Cambridge University Press; Zephyr Teachout (2016). *Corruption in America.* Cambridge, MA: Harvard University Press; Sarah Chayes (2020). *On Corruption in America.* New York: Knopf.
3 Samuel Huntington (1968). *Political Order in Changing Societies.* New Haven, CT: Yale University Press; John Kramer (1999). *Anti-Corruption Research Concerning Eastern Europe and the Former Soviet Union: A Comparative Analysis.* Washington, DC: Management Systems International.
4 Daniela Cepeda Cuadrado (2021). "Covid-19 Corruption in 2021: January–April Developments," April 22. Bergen: U4 Anti-Corruption Resource Centre. At: https://medium.com/u4-anti-corruption-resource-centre/covid-19-corruption-in-2021-march-april-developments-c4a6dbee530b.
5 Management Systems International (2000). *Integrity Survey in Kharkiv, Ukraine.* Washington, DC: USAID (conducted by Kiev International Institute of Sociology, November-December 1999).
6 Daniel Kaufmann (1997). "Corruption: The Facts," *Foreign Policy* 107 (Summer): 114–131.
7 USAID (1999). *A Handbook on Fighting Corruption.* Technical Publication Series. Washington, DC: Center for Democracy and Governance, Bureau for Global Programs, US Agency for International Development.
8 Paolo Mauro (1997). "The Effects of Corruption on Growth, Investment and Government Expenditure: A Cross-Country Analysis," in K. Elliott, ed., *Corruption and the Global Economy.* Washington, DC: Institute for International Economics: 83–107.
9 Jonathan Sleeper (2003). "How USAID Safeguards against Corruption Can Be Used by the Millennium Challenge Account," Issue Brief #3 (PN-ACT-341), Washington, DC: US Agency for International Development (June).
10 United Nations Security Council (2018). "Global Cost of Corruption at Least 5 Per Cent of World Gross Domestic Product, Secretary-General Tells Security Council, Citing World Economic Forum Data." At: https://www.un.org/press/en/2018/sc13493.doc.htm.

11 Official Statement of the United Nations Secretary-General Antonio Guterres, October 15, 2020, United Nations. At: https://www.un.org/en/coronavirus/statement-corruption-context-covid-19

12 Many of the findings reported here were drawn from Bertram Spector, et al. (2005). *Corruption Assessment: Mozambique.* Washington, DC: USAID. At: https://pdf.usaid.gov/pdf_docs/PNADF937.pdf.

13 These are updated findings drawn from Bertram Spector, Svetlana Winbourne, et al. (2017). *Anti-corruption Dynamics in Ukraine: A Political Economy Analysis.* Washington, DC: United States Agency for International Development.

14 M.I. Khavronyuk (2017). *Executive Summary of the Shadow Report on Evaluating the Effectiveness of State Anti-Corruption Policy Implementation.* Kyiv: Centre of Policy and Legal Reform and Transparency International Ukraine.

15 Sean Roberts and Robert Orttung (2015). *Changing Corrupt Behaviors Assessment.* Washington, DC: USAID. At: https://www.usaid.gov/sites/default/files/documents/1863/Changing%20Corrupt%20Behaviors%20Assessment%20Oct.%202015.pdf.

Part I

Lessons learned

Anti-corruption programs have been implemented in countries worldwide over many years. They include efforts to strengthen enforcement of anti-corruption laws and regulations, innovative approaches that streamline and simplify government processes to prevent corrupt actions in the first place, and the education and engagement of civil society, businesses, and the mass media to apply greater pressure on the authorities for anti-corruption results. Lessons learned from these initiatives can support improvements in future programs to make them more impactful and sustainable. Where do we stand? Are we moving in the right direction?

DOI: 10.4324/9781003241119-2

2 Are we on the right track?

Over the past 30 years or so, a great deal of attention has been paid by policymakers in countries around the world on how to reduce or eliminate the problem of corruption. Especially starting in the early 1990s, governments and international donor agencies began to actively reassert their opposition to corruption by implementing a variety of reform programs. These efforts progressed through three waves.

The first wave in the mid-1990s sought to expose the importance of dealing with the corruption problem by measuring the extent to which it existed and the impact it was having on countries worldwide. Indexes of a country's level of corruption were ranked against other countries and publicized to indicate any progress and apply social pressure on governments. Technical support was also provided to countries to develop strategies and action plans to fight corruption, with an emphasis on strengthening law enforcement and catching, prosecuting, and convicting corrupt officials.

The second wave of activities began in the 2000s to implement reforms. The greatest emphasis was on developing significant legal and regulatory frameworks that address the corruption threat and building enforcement capacity to investigate and prosecute corrupt officials. In addition, institutional reforms were begun, including establishment of anti-corruption commissions and strengthened supreme audit institutions. Major public awareness campaigns to spread knowledge of the negative impacts of corruption and to build civil society groups to advocate for reforms were also pursued.

The third wave in the 2010s refocused anti-corruption programs toward preventive reforms: building stronger accountability and control mechanisms that would have the power to avert corrupt behavior. More attention was placed on government auditing and oversight activities, as well as citizen-based social auditing, to detect and collect evidence about corruption. In addition, more emphasis was placed on anti-corruption initiatives in specific sectors other than the judicial sector, like education, health, energy, environment, agriculture, and the private sector, where tactics to fight corruption might have to be honed to address corruption's particular inroads in those areas. Programs that address corruption have become more

DOI: 10.4324/9781003241119-3

comprehensive, multi-method and coordinated across institutions and policy areas, while engaging all key stakeholders from government, business, the mass media and civil society.

A lot has been written about corruption and its impacts on economic, social, and political development in countries, but we are still learning about the particular initiatives that can control corruption effectively. While there has been much progress in recent years, the global problem of corruption is still very much with us. Many approaches that have been tried have had some impact, but some have not, and a lot has to do with the context within which they are implemented, the actors targeted by these initiatives, and the strength of the incentives to change behavior.

A look at the United States

Most of this book examines anti-corruption reforms that have been implemented and tested in developing countries. But let's start with a look at the history of how a developed country has attempted to tackle the problem to see if there are some lessons that can be applied elsewhere. Let's start with the United States.

Most countries that were once considered developing countries, but have now graduated to developed country status, went through long periods of endemic corruption that seemed intractable. Looking back at the history of corruption in the United States between 1865 and 1941 – from the beginnings of the industrial revolution to its entry into World War II – research studies reach several conclusions about the path of anti-corruption initiatives and reforms in the United States that show that what may seem as an entrenched culture of corruption can be reversed to the point where public corruption is viewed as an aberration.[1]

Even before the country's beginnings – before the American Revolution – political corruption, bribery, fraud, and influence peddling were the way things got done. These many years later, while the United States has clearly not solved its corruption problem entirely, corruption is not seen as the country's primary operating system. The US example clearly shows that systemic corruption cannot be eliminated through just a few clever and highly targeted strategies; it is a slow and evolutionary transition.

In the case of the United States, the path to reduced corruption, in part, relied on a major growth in government's reach and power to adopt and activate regulations, institutional safeguards, and oversight, along with leadership from high level champions for reform, though with some backsliding along the way. Initially, laws were enacted to prohibit bribery of members of Congress, limit private lobbying, reform the collection of customs duties, conduct greater oversight of railroads, and introduce civil service reforms to reduce the spoils system. But when cases were brought to court, there were few convictions initially, and the states were reluctant to pick up on these anti-corruption laws and regulations. Over 76 years, in a process of fits and

starts, these laws gradually became stronger and covered more civil servants at all levels of government, criminal prosecutions of corrupt officials
became more certain, tougher regulations on political finance and lobbying
were enacted, and independent regulatory commissions gained traction as
overseers of a wider array of government institutions and economic sectors.
While political champions of these reforms came and went, resulting in delays and some relapses of these changes, progress was made in an incremen-
tal fashion.

One critical actor that promoted this movement for reform was the mass
media and their investigative journalists – or muckrakers, as they were
called – that exposed corruption scandals and built up public awareness of
systemic corruption in government and industry in the early 1900s. With
greater public understanding of the extent and impacts of this corruption
came increased citizen outrage, thus providing incentives to the political
champions of reform to push forward stronger legislation, regulations, and
institutional reforms. This time period, spanning three generations, changed
the public's perceptions of corruption in the United States from being the
prevalent way to get things done to a rather unusual occurrence, although
one that did not disappear by any means. Certainly, headlines about home-
grown corruption continue to persist in the American media.

If the US case is to be meaningful to current day developing countries, it says that effective and sustainable change is feasible, but probably cannot take place as a quick revolutionary push; to take hold and be
successful at adjusting past habits, the reforms must be evolutionary and
multi-generational. Monitoring and enforcement of punishment strategies,
combined with other preventive strategies, seemed to yield the best results.
There needs to be a combination of aggressive law enforcement to serve as
a deterrent to corrupt behavior, as well as institutional changes and reforms
that provide incentives that seek to shift political and social norms, prevent
corrupt behavior, and increase obedience to the rule of law. And the public
needs to be actively engaged, with the help of the media, to maintain pressure on political leaders to enforce and ramp up anti-corruption reforms to
sustain effective results.

What does success look like?

Policymakers, international donors, and researchers are all intensely interested in finding out what initiatives work successfully to combat corruption.
We may be just getting to the point of finding answers backed up by evidence, but there are still limitations to what we know. As indicated, since
the mid-1990s, there have been many interventions conducted worldwide –
some explicitly anti-corruption, some using other terminology but implicitly
focused on corruption, and some subsumed under larger programs. However, there is no single database that gathers together the results of these
efforts and no integrative and systematic analysis of what actions promote

effective anti-corruption reform. Even if there were such a database, most of these programs employed inadequate techniques of measuring, assessing, and evaluating their impact on corrupt practices. As a result, much of the existing literature on these anti-corruption interventions is anecdotal by nature, presenting the outcomes of single case studies to demonstrate impact, or based on shaky measurement and statistics.

What does success in fighting corruption look like and how can it be measured? One can look at both the short-term and long-term results from anti-corruption initiatives. Short-term successes – over the course of three to five years, for example – are usually the outcome of specific programs and might demonstrate some visible changes in the way government operates and how citizens respond to government. It may not be possible to detect actual reduced corruption over the short term, but one might be able to detect important changes that could lead to reduced corruption. On the other hand, over the longer term, the success of anti-corruption initiatives should be able to demonstrate reductions in the occurrence of corrupt behaviors and resulting anti-corruption benefits.

Project-specific, short-term successes of enforcement initiatives can be measured by monitoring the number of investigations, prosecutions, and convictions achieved, new laws passed and regulations adopted, and new anti-corruption institutions established. Short-term results of preventive initiatives, also at a project level, can be observed by monitoring the number of oversight and audit activities conducted by government and civil society, changes in administrative procedures, increased transparency and openness of government decision-making processes, and reductions in citizen complaints about government corruption, for example. Governments and donor organizations are most appreciative of these short-term success measures because they provide indications of visible changes, they can increase public confidence and trust in government, and for donors, they provide some recognition that their initiatives and funding have been well planned and spent.

To understand long-term success, the focus needs to be different. It needs to monitor the results of many projects and initiatives over a longer period of time and assess their combined impact on corruption levels. Most available are annually updated indices of corruption, such as Transparency International's Corruption Perceptions Index and the World Bank's Control of Corruption Index, among others. But researchers have many methodological issues with these types of broad indices[2] – they focus on citizen perceptions, not on actual behavior; they aggregate survey data from many sources that are not always compatible; they incorporate a time lag – data released in the 2020 index may reflect data collected a year or two earlier; and many other issues. On the other hand, these indices do correlate fairly well with other measures that are related to reduced corruption. While there are objective measures that can demonstrate reductions in corrupt behavior – increased conviction rates, the results of financial audits, and the results of procurement and budget expenditure analyses – they typically reflect only a partial view of corruption that is project- or sector-specific, and may not represent the overall national standing regarding corruption.

After so many years of anti-corruption programming, USAID, DFID, and other international donors commissioned several systematic studies in the early 2010s to find out what works. These studies use the data that exists – typically case studies, program evaluations, and qualitative research – to assess what initiatives have proven to be most effective.[3] They analyzed reporting from those interventions where sufficient measurement exists or conducted comparative case analyses of similar interventions to determine if there is a firm foundation to guide future anti-corruption programming based on past results.[4] Unfortunately, the impact measurement for most of these interventions is faulty. Quantitative data, if it exists, is scant and limited. Data collection usually ends soon after the intervention is implemented. And it is often difficult to determine actual anti-corruption results in the short-term. Further, the data is typically collected and analyzed by the implementing agent and thus might be biased.

Despite these failings, we can get some general direction from these initiatives. We examine here the findings from these meta-analyses to identify early takeaways from this research. Our focus is on the results that suggest effective outcomes for specific types of anti-corruption interventions. There are many more findings that suggest how best to assess the situation, how to select goals and strategies, how to identify effective entry points, and how to design programs; these can be found in the full study reports. Many findings indicate mixed results, that is, some interventions showed success in some countries, while the same interventions failed or showed inconclusive results in other countries. Moreover, because of the widespread absence of well-measured impact data, the findings presented here are based on only a small subsample of actual interventions that have been attempted over the past 20–30 years.

Broad trends

An analysis of 107 USAID projects from 2007 to 2013, where sufficient data were available, reveals some broad but useful recommendations for future program design and the contexts within which they are implemented. The results are based on improvements or weakening of anti-corruption outcomes over the period of project duration.[5]

Small and nonexplicit anti-corruption interventions can have negative effects. If anti-corruption is only a small component of a larger program, corruption levels are most likely to remain the same or increase (62.8% of cases). If there are no explicit anti-corruption objectives in the program, corruption is likely to remain the same or increase (58%).

Strong political will does not necessarily yield success. The political will to fight corruption by government is often viewed as a critical precondition for success, but other factors can impair that outcome. When the government has strong political will to fight corruption, but the anti-corruption intervention is only a small element in a large program or not an explicit objective of the program, corruption is likely to remain the same or increase (in 66.6% and 61.6% of cases, respectively). And when there is strong political will, but the beneficiary lacks resources or capacity, corruption is likely to remain the same or increase (53.3%).

These results are intensified when examining the role of civil society. When civil society has strong political will to fight corruption, but the anti-corruption intervention is only a small element of a large program or not an explicit objective, corruption is likely to remain the same or increase (in 75.8% and 69.7% of cases, respectively). And when civil society's political will is strong, but the country is in a state of political-economic instability or transition, corruption is likely to remain the same or increase (77%).

More complex interventions appear to fare better at achieving sustained reductions in corruption. Reform efforts are more effective when they are conducted in combination with other reform efforts – like strengthening audits *plus* publicizing sanctions or decentralization activities, along with CSO capacity building in oversight to keep local officials accountable. So, achieving effective anti-corruption results appears to benefit from judiciously designing initiatives in a "checks and balances" fashion. For example, if you are trying to reform governance practices to reduce their vulnerability to corruption, it benefits to do so in combination with promoting negative sanctions if officials abuse their authority. Or if you are trying to reduce corruption by reducing the concentration of power in the central government, it is wise to simultaneously ensure that local officials know that their actions will be closely monitored by watchdogs.

Challenging country contexts can impact anti-corruption programs negatively. If the host country is experiencing political-economic instability or is in a state of transition, corruption is likely to remain the same or increase (64%). When programming interventions, it is crucial to consider the conditions under which they will be implemented. Capacity, sustainable funding sources, political will, freedom of the press, and community engagement, among others, play important contextual roles in supporting and strengthening the focused intervention. Conducting and revising political economy analyses (PEA) on a regular basis will support implementers to understand the complex situational dynamics that can influence accomplishment of goals.

Another condition that impacts effective results is the sector within which the intervention is implemented. Success depends on the readiness of the sector – its leadership, legal framework, institutional setup, practices and procedures, interface with citizens and business, resources, capacity, and so on – to accept the implemented reform. Again, periodic PEAs will be able to inform implementers on these conditions.

The types of corruption targeted can impact success or failure. Fifty percent of cases targeting petty corruption resulted in reduced corruption. Of the remaining petty corruption projects, 35% showed an increase in corruption and 15% showed no change. Precisely 62.5% of cases that targeted grand corruption resulted in increased corruption. For programs targeting administrative corruption, there is approximately the same percent that result in reduced, as increased, corruption outcomes.

The type of targeted stakeholder can affect the results. Precisely 61.1% of programs where civil society was the primary stakeholder resulted in increased corruption. For programs where the judiciary, local government and central executive branch were the primary stakeholders, the outcome is a draw; approximately the same percent result in reduced corruption as result in increased corruption.

The findings from this small sample of USAID projects suggest more about *what to avoid* than what works in designing anti-corruption programs. But that can be very useful advice too. In summary:

- Strong political will of stakeholders by itself is not sufficient to yield positive project results; other factors can intervene to reduce project success.
- When anti-corruption projects are designed, they should be implemented clearly and primarily as anti-corruption projects; playing down the prominence of anti-corruption goals is not helpful over the long term.
- Country context is a very important factor; instability and transition can intervene to reduce anti-corruption program success.

A more detailed review of the results of actual anti-corruption programming – broken down by the particular type of intervention – provides many practical takeaways that have helped policymakers design workable approaches.[6] In the next chapter, we examine initiatives focused on reforming laws, institutional structures, and anti-corruption enforcement. Then, in the following chapter, we present findings of initiatives that seek to prevent corruption; these are often not framed as anti-corruption efforts, but rather as reforms that will strengthen the processes and functions of government, through improvements to governance, accountability, and transparency. We also look at sector-specific approaches to fighting corruption which target tightening governance processes so that they do not become vulnerable to fraud or abuse. Then, in subsequent chapters, we review initiatives that have been tried to promote civil society's engagement in fighting corruption, and how best to implement anti-corruption approaches in post-conflict situations.

Notes

1 Mariano-Florentino Cuéllar and Matthew Stephenson (2020). "Taming Systemic Corruption: The American Experience and Its Implications for Contemporary Debates," (September 4). *Harvard Public Law Working Paper No. 20–29.* At: https://ssrn.com/abstract=3686821.

2 Alex Cobham (2013). "Corrupting Perceptions: Why Transparency Internation-al's Flagship Corruption Index Falls Short," July 23. At: https://www.cgdev.org/ blog/corrupting-perceptions-why-transparency-international%E2%80%99s-flagship-corruption-index-falls-short; Paul Heywood (2014). "Measuring Cor-ruption: Perspectives, Critiques, and Limits." At: https://www.ceu.edu/sites/ default/files/attachment/event/9385/heywood-measuring-corruption.pdf; Paul Heywood and Jonathan Rose (2014). "Close but no Cigar: The Measurement of Corruption," *Journal of Public Policy* 34, 3: 507–529.

3 Four meta-analysis studies serve as the basis for our assessment: Management Systems International (2015). *Practitioner's Guide for Anti-corruption Programming*. Washington, DC: USAID; DFID (2015). *Why Corruption Matters: Under-standing Causes, Effects and How to Address Them: Evidence Paper on Corruption (January)*. London: DFID; R. Hanna, S. Bishop, S. Nadel, G. Scheffler, and K. Durlacher (2011). *The Effectiveness of Anti-corruption Policy: What Has Worked, What Hasn't, and What We Don't Know–A Systematic Review. Technical Report*. London: EPPI-Centre, Social Science Research Unit, Institute of Education, University of London (supported by DFID); and Jesper Johnson, N. Taxell and D. Zaum (2012). *Mapping Evidence Gaps in Anti-corruption: Assessing the State of the Operationally Relevant Evidence on Donors' Actions and Approaches to Re-ducing Corruption*. Bergen, Norway: U4 Issue No. 7 (supported by DFID).

4 Other recent reports have claimed to review what interventions work, but have employed more anecdotal, less systematic methodologies; they are not included in our assessment. These include studies sponsored by the Group of States against Corruption (GRECO), the World Bank, the Norwegian Agency for De-velopment Cooperation (NORAD), and the Organization for Economic Coop-eration and Development (OECD).

5 Increased or decreased corruption outcomes are measured by change in the World Bank Governance/Control of Corruption indicator score from the year of project startup to one year after project completion. See Svetlana Winbourne and Bertram Spector (2014). *Analysis of USAID Anti-corruption Programming Worldwide (2007–2013)*. Washington, DC: USAID.

6 See Winbourne and Spector, op.cit., and its annexes, as well as other sources. Practitioners should also refer to various anti-corruption toolkits that can of-fer additional ideas, such as the *Transparency International Corruption Fighters' Toolkits*. At: http://www.transparency.org/whatwedo/tools/corruption_fighters_ toolkits_introduction/2/; *UN Global Compact Anti-Corruption Tools Inventory*. At: http://www.business-anti-corruption.com/resources/anti-corruption-tools-inventory.aspx; and *UN Anti-Corruption Toolkit*. At: http://www.unodc.org/pdf/ crime/corruption/toolkit/corruption_un_anti_corruption_toolkit_sep04.pdf. In addition, programming options on a sectoral basis can be found in Bertram Spector, editor (2005). *Fighting Corruption in Developing Countries: Strategies and Analysis*. Bloomfield, CT: Kumarian Press, and J. Edgardo Campos and Sanjay Pradhan, editors (2007). *The Many Faces of Corruption*. Washington, DC: The World Bank.

3 Legal and institutional reform programming

What works?

Many anti-corruption reform initiatives are not labeled as explicitly seeking anti-corruption results. Depending on the context, there is fear that such clearly defined efforts might incur the wrath of powerful officials who participate in corrupt transactions, and these reforms might be sabotaged as a result. But if the political situation allows, explicitly anti-corruption initiatives are implemented that typically work directly with dedicated anti-corruption agencies or other institutions of accountability. By far, most of these programs seek to develop new or adjust existing anti-corruption laws and regulations, or implement and enforce anti-corruption laws, regulations, policies, and procedures within governmental agencies. Here are four very different cases from Indonesia, Armenia, Afghanistan, and Liberia that have had varying levels of success.

Support to Indonesian Anti-corruption Institutions (2011–2016).[1] The five-year USAID Strengthening Integrity and Accountability Project (SIAP-1) focused on supporting the Corruption Eradication Commission (KPK), the Supreme Audit Body (BPK), and several other anti-corruption institutions in Indonesia. For the KPK, the project conducted extensive training to strengthen the staff's investigative capacities, developed an e-learning module on gift regulations for civil servants nationwide, provided strategic communications support to strengthen KPK's public outreach, conducted training for fraud examiner certification, and supported anti-corruption court monitoring and analysis to draw lessons for future prosecutions. For BPK, the project conducted practical training on performance audits, and developed and implemented a comprehensive Fraud Risk Assessment system to allow major government departments to self-assess their vulnerabilities to corruption and design action plans for improvement.

What happened in the short run? Parliament and the police were always at odds with these anti-corruption institutions because legislators and police have been the prime targets of their investigations. The withdrawal by the police of their investigative staff that had been seconded to the KPK resulted in a rapid and major shift in emphasis by the project to train newly recruited staff to take on those investigative functions. Then, by the middle of the project, political campaigns for parliamentary and presidential elections

DOI: 10.4324/9781003241119-4

led to an almost complete transformation of government leadership, along with major changes among the commissioners who direct the KPK and BPK. This created a situation where, in midstream, the project needed to reconfirm the political will and cooperation of these key beneficiaries.

Mobilizing Action Against Corruption in Armenia Project (MAAC) (2006–2011).[2] This USAID-sponsored project worked with the government's Chamber of Control on drafting a manual for detecting tax fraud and assisted in training auditors on investigations of such corruption-related fraud, helped the government prepare its compliance report for the OECD on progress made to combat corruption, cooperated with the Human Rights Defender in conducting several public events, assisted the government with the development of a new national anti-corruption strategy, and provided assistance to the National Assembly and several ministries. On the demand side, the project supported a network of 11 Advocacy and Assistance Centers (AAC) that provided legal assistance to victims of alleged corruption, and awarded grants to NGOs conducting public awareness activities and engaging with youth.

What were the results of this project? Despite pre-project consultations between USAID and the government, MAAC was perceived suspiciously by the government which resulted in weak cooperation from several governmental agencies, delays, and activity modifications. Attempts to switch the focus to other agencies were unsuccessful. Several factors contributed to these challenges. The mid-term evaluation pointed to deficiencies in the project design, as well as to implementation shortcomings. At the same time, growing citizen unrest against corruption in neighboring countries, such as in Ukraine, Georgia, and Kyrgyzstan, likely impacted the Government's attitude toward donor programs working in the governance area, particularly those supporting civil society. While there were difficulties working with the government, MAAC's program with the demand side showed positive results, in particular, with the AACs that registered citizen complaints and achieved resolution for many of them via administrative and judicial action.

Support to the Afghan High Office of Oversight (2010–2013).[3] Corruption in Afghanistan is entrenched and extremely well-organized through patronage networks, imposing a staggering impact on the daily lives of Afghans. Mindful of these developments, the Government of Afghanistan created the High Office of Oversight (HOO), mandated to coordinate and oversee the implementation of the National Anti-Corruption Strategy, register citizen complaints, conduct preliminary investigations, track financial assets of government officials, reduce opportunities for corruption, help government agencies develop their own anti-corruption initiatives, and promote public education and awareness about corruption and anti-corruption programs.

To support this initiative, USAID launched a three-year Assistance for Afghanistan's Anti-corruption Authority (4A) Project in 2010 with the goal of equipping the HOO to effectively deliver on its mandate and building the capacity of other stakeholders to fight corruption. The 4A project helped to develop a new three-year Anti-corruption Strategic Plan for the government, strengthened the High Office's organizational structure and functions, established an asset declaration and verification system, and reinforced the citizen complaint system. The project also worked with several government ministries to conduct "vulnerability to corruption assessments" that helped them detect their corruption risks and implement appropriate sectoral anti-corruption reforms.

As well, the 4A project worked closely with civil society organizations, the parliament and the mass media to develop awareness, motivation, and skills necessary to become effective and sustainable partners with government and maintain demand for anti-corruption reform. The project provided support to a newly created women-led anti-corruption caucus in the lower house of parliament to develop their skills of executive oversight and strengthen their legal analysis of corruption impacts in draft laws. This caucus also promoted the establishment of similar anti-corruption caucuses within provincial assemblies. 4A worked closely with the CSO community which created the Afghan Coalition Against Corruption with about 70 member organizations that conduct advocacy and public awareness activities throughout the country. And the project supported establishment of a Citizen Legal Advocate Office (CLAO) in Kabul, a nongovernmental group that provides pro bono legal support to hundreds of corruption victims.

What happened? Afghanistan is a challenging political and security terrain in which to seek anti-corruption reforms. The project was able to provide some capacity enhancement to the HOO, but for many reasons, the agency fell short of fulfilling most of its mandates. Moreover, changes in the HOO's leadership in mid-project slowed down cooperation. The project's early pivot to work with demand-side groups instead was a positive adjustment.

Legal Professional Development and Anti-Corruption (LPAC) Activity in Liberia.[4] This five-year project sponsored by USAID from 2015 to 2020 provided technical assistance to strengthen legal educational institutions and the Liberian Anti-Corruption Commission (LACC). Focusing on the anti-corruption component, the project made notable progress toward building capacity and professionalism among the Commission's investigators and prevention officers.

Much of this assistance consisted of specific training support on the investigation of complex corruption cases and operations and ensuring that the skills were applied effectively. Extensive training and day-to-day coaching resulted in an increase in the average number of cases investigated by LACC and submitted to the Ministry of Justice (MOJ) for prosecution from one to eight cases annually. The training improved the quality of investigations by upgrading the planning and execution of investigations as well as the use of new investigatory techniques. Follow-up mentoring by the project's expert staff served as an extra stimulus that motivated the use of new skills and the sustainability of these approaches beyond the classroom.

The project's training of other enforcement agencies in corruption investigative techniques led to the Commission becoming the hub of multiagency investigation efforts on complex corruption cases. LPAC also delivered trainings in trafficking-in-persons (TIPs) investigations, sensitive witness handling, and data analytics, and conducted a comprehensive assessment of Liberia's draft Whistleblower Law.

Significant efforts were made in building overall institutional capacity and strengthening corruption prevention and public education functions. The project trained Commission staff on how to conduct detailed corruption risk assessments in governmental agencies, enforce conflict of interest policies, and improve the Commission's ability to collect and verify public official asset declarations.

What were the results? Despite changes in leadership at the Commission which introduced substantial political obstruction to corruption investigations toward the end of the project, windows of opportunity did present themselves, allowing for several major cases to be brought before grand juries and prosecuted on an expedited basis. As LPAC concluded operations in 2020, US government officials informed the project that its comprehensive training of Liberia's legal community on TIPs, coupled with the Commission's use of corruption risk assessments for TIPs, played an instrumental role in Liberia maintaining Tier 2 status on the US State Department's TIPs Watchlist.

Key takeaways

An analysis of these and other explicitly anti-corruption initiatives that are primarily focused on legal, enforcement, and institutional strengthening approaches offers many takeaways.

Government institutions of accountability can be effective if they have independence and resources.[5] There are no silver bullets in fighting corruption. Some anti-corruption agencies are successful but others are not, largely explained by the extent of their mandate, the degree of independence and resources they are given, the extent of staff professionalism and skill, and basic elements of the rule of law.[6] Even well-resourced and independent anti-corruption agencies can face stiff political resistance. A study of eight anti-corruption agencies points to several tactics they can use effectively to outmaneuver opponents and achieve their anti-corruption objectives[7]:

- Strong internal controls and accountability mechanisms help to preserve the independence and integrity of anti-corruption agencies and protect them from being subverted or discredited.
- Alliances developed between anti-corruption agencies and state institutions, but also with citizens, the mass media, civil society, and international actors, can help them mount counterattacks if threatened, resulting in better anti-corruption outcomes.

• Anti-corruption agencies can show long-term gains when they exercise corruption prevention initiatives aimed at disrupting corrupt networks, together with implementing public education efforts that reshape public norms and expectations.

Combining accountability mechanisms and sanctions for getting caught can be effective. Government monitoring programs, such as government audits, can help to reduce corruption if they simultaneously increase the probability that corrupt officials will get caught and will incur some cost for engaging in corrupt activities. Monitoring and sanctions may be implemented separately, but a comprehensive review[8] finds that monitoring on its own is ineffective and, similarly, increasing the threatened sanctions for corruption has no effect when the probability of getting caught is too small. This review draws these lessons from a total of 14 interventions that used rigorous methodologies to gauge their impact. In four cases, governments successfully implemented monitoring programs combined with nonfinancial sanctions such as publicizing municipal audit records prior to mayoral elections or terminating the bureaucrat's position. In another three cases, community monitoring combined with a mass media or other information dissemination strategy (and accompanying social sanctions) proved effective in lowering corruption, whereas less-focused information dissemination efforts in two further cases were unsuccessful. Mixed results for community monitoring used alone in two additional cases suggest its effectiveness may be heavily reliant on the cohesiveness of the community to respond to corruption findings. Finally, two interventions combining monitoring of absenteeism with financial sanctions in the form of fines taken from employees' wages concluded that the schemes can work if managers support the efforts of monitors.

In a case from Brazil, audit results that uncovered corrupt politicians were used most effectively when reported widely to the population.[9] Taking advantage of a federal anti-corruption program that randomly assigned municipalities to be audited, researchers in Brazil compared the electoral outcomes for mayors in two groups of municipalities: those that were audited before and those that were audited after the 2004 election. This provided an opportunity to observe whether voters' access to information prior to the election about politicians' corruption levels affected reelection rates for incumbent mayors.

The results of this case found that publicly released audits reduced the reelection of corrupt incumbent mayors and this effect was more severe in municipalities with a local radio station. In municipalities where two corruption violations were reported, the release of information reduced the incumbent's likelihood of reelection by 7 percentage points. In municipalities where two violations were reported and a radio station existed, the release of information reduced the incumbent's likelihood of reelection by 11 percentage points. When corruption was not found in a municipality with a

local radio station, audits increased the likelihood that the mayor was ree-
lected by 17 percentage points.

*Successful anti-corruption program initiatives must be tailored to the exist-
ing context.* A literature review points to the importance of tailoring interventions to specific contexts.[10] The review analyzed direct anti-corruption
interventions in six areas, including public sector reform, oversight institutions, civil society support, general budget support, donors' own systems,
and multilateral agreements on international anti-corruption standards.
The evidence shows that the same interventions work in some cases but not
in others, suggesting that context matters for the efficacy of these reforms.
Findings suggest a number of situational factors that influence the effectiveness of specific reforms, including:

- The impact of support to supreme audit institutions depends on the independence and political composition of parliamentary committees.[11]
  When parliamentarians are independent of the executive and hail
  from the opposition or a rival political faction, they have more incentive to follow up on audit recommendations and pursue those under
  investigation.
- Support for anti-corruption laws is only likely to have an impact when
  the country has a well-functioning judicial system.[12] Getting the laws in
  place can be seen as an interim step in such a context, but are unlikely to
  have an effect on corruption levels independent of other reforms.
- Civil service reforms are more effective where patronage-based systems
  are weak, which may prevail in a post-conflict or transitional situation,
  for example. However, some reforms are more politically risky than
  others. Whereas downsizing is likely to trigger resistance from within
  the civil service, organizational reforms that alter staff assignments and
  compensation reforms that provide bonuses for performance may succeed even where patronage systems are in place.[13] Further, establishing
  job qualifications only for new applicants is less likely to trigger resistance than requiring current employees to meet such qualifications.
- The effectiveness of anti-corruption agencies depends on a number of
  conditions, including adequate staffing, training and remuneration, political independence, and basic elements of the rule of law.[14] But even
  well-resourced and independent anti-corruption agencies can often face
  stiff political resistance.

*Rule of law initiatives tend to be successful in establishing the first-line
measures that can result in reduced corruption.*[15] Having a sound legal framework that supports the rule of law and combats official abuse is an important first step to controlling corruption. The extent to which such statutes
are enforced in practice demonstrates the government's political will and
commitment. Laws that identify specific behaviors as being corrupt and
itemize punishments if convicted offer a basic first line of defense against

corruption. Laws that govern conflicts of interest, anti-money laundering, and public procurement, for example, allow the state to pursue corrupt public officials for more complex abuses of power. These laws also announce to the public that such activities are not acceptable.

Based on the analysis of recent USAID anti-corruption initiatives, more than 70% of all programs targeted at reforming the rule of law achieved outcomes that would likely reduce corruption to some extent.[16] These initiatives range from putting in place a sound legal framework to prevent and combat corruption, strengthening investigative and prosecutorial capacities, improving professionalism, and implementing systems to prevent corruption within the justice sector.

A typical example of such a project is the Rule of Law Program (ROLP) in Jordan[17] that strengthened the oversight of case management and court administration processes, designed and implemented efficient and transparent case management procedures for all courts, and enhanced and expanded nationwide automated case management and information data resources. The project assisted with improving and institutionalizing the training of court staff in court administration and specialized training within the Judicial Institute. With the support of the project, criminal and civil procedure codes were amended to reduce delays, increase transparency, and enhance capacity to deal with complex cases.

Another example is the Combating Corruption and Strengthening Rule of Law project in Ukraine, which assisted in implementing controls to ensure that the judicial system becomes more accountable to the public through instituting strengthened court automation, judicial testing, and judicial discipline.[18] The project established a registry of court decisions, developed and implemented a uniform random case assignment system in selected courts, established an effective and transparent process of judicial appointment and disciplinary procedures, and created an operating system for administrative courts in the regions. Although public perception of widespread corruption in the judiciary still increased, the project resulted in a small decrease in extortion by court administration staff and an increase in citizen trust in the judiciary.

There are many other examples of how projects can strengthen the capacity and professionalism of justice sector institutions, standardize their procedures, and implement modern systems to reduce corruption. A USAID analysis provides a substantial overview of corruption risks associated with the justice sector and suggests approaches to address them.[19] But it should be noted that

> a changed institution should not necessarily be a goal in and of itself. Such programming often does not address the root causes of corruption within the rule of law system, such as distrust, systemic corruption or a lack of capacity – root causes that are all associated with power and culture.[20]

Supporting domestic stakeholders can help in advocating for passage of legislation and promoting local ownership. For example, programs in Albania and Malawi benefited from strong stakeholder involvement in the legislative process to strengthen anti-corruption laws. In Albania, legislation impacting the business community was languishing in Parliament. USAID engaged the business community by making it aware of the positive effects that the legislation would have, after which they became strong advocates for its passage. Similarly, part of the Malawi program related to developing strengthened laws dealing with financial crimes.

In Panama, the administration of justice at the community level is frequently tainted by arbitrary resolutions and corruption. A government-led initiative had been launched to address this issue, but it did not include comprehensive discussions involving stakeholders. Once the program overcame an initial lack of interest by some government agencies, it successfully gathered many stakeholders (for example, the Solicitor General's Office. Attorney General's Office, the Judicial Branch, and civil society organizations) and coordinated and expedited their discussions around the design and agreement of an Administrative/Community Justice Law.[21]

The vagaries of the legislative/political process can slow down passage of laws. As a foundational aspect of anti-corruption programming, the passage of laws is sometimes seen as a prerequisite to follow-on activities. Upon the adoption of new laws on public procurement, anti-money laundering, and conflicts of interest, for example, associated reforms to reduce corruption are often planned. However, realistically, a thorough legislative process in such complicated areas could legitimately last two to three years. Where programs run into legislative roadblocks, implementers usually find productive ways to instill good practices that could be codified later. Thus, delays in legislative processes to strengthen the legal framework do not have to forestall implementation of rule of law good practices.

Enhancing domestic capacity to investigate and prosecute crimes of corruption is paramount as exposure and awareness increases.[22] Awareness about corruption grows as reforms begin to take effect and corrupt practices and individuals are exposed. If there are no evident consequences, however, corrupt officials become emboldened and the general public becomes discouraged, thereby perpetuating the corruption problem. To avoid the suggestion that public officials are above the law, it is important to follow up the activities that expose corruption with thorough investigation and, where appropriate, prosecution. The impact of improved investigations and prosecutions of corrupt actors is wide-ranging. Enforcement action against high-ranking officials reinforces the principle of equality before the law, improving public trust in government. Uniform enforcement with demonstrable consequences (criminal, administrative, and/or civil sanctions) is also a strong deterrent for others.

Technical assistance to law enforcement in anti-corruption programs requires substantial investments in training and equipment. Corruption is among the most challenging of crimes to investigate and prosecute. Incidents of petty corruption can often be addressed at the administrative level. Law enforcement, however, has to be equipped to address complicated schemes camouflaged by complex money laundering operations in order to reach the grand corruption cases. Criminal defendants may be high level government officials, and organized crime with its vast resources is frequently involved. Consequently, the criminals are often better equipped than law enforcement, making prosecution virtually impossible.

Programmed initiatives in this domain have helped bolster enforcement by providing forensic laboratories and securing evidence warehouses, complete IT infrastructure, portable state-of-the-art digital recording equipment, surveillance and countersurveillance equipment, portable printers, laptops, portable scanners, digital audio recorders, long-range day and night cameras, and covert handheld mobile phone jammers, in addition to training officers on modern investigative techniques.

Investigating and prosecuting cases of grand corruption are also difficult because of the tremendous reluctance of witnesses to come forward for fear of reprisal. In many countries, this is addressed with plea bargaining and/or witness protection programs. The mere passage of legislation is insufficient. While the law may allow for the granting of protection, providing that protection after witnesses have endangered themselves by testifying is expensive and difficult.[23]

Checks and balances must be maintained to demonstrate the objectivity of the enforcement entity. Some countries opt for dedicated corruption investigation units, imbuing them with specific competencies and authority, allowing their staff to become specialists in anti-corruption investigation and prosecution areas. However, experience in Moldova serves as a reminder that the need for checks and balances is commensurately greater when powers are consolidated in a single entity. In Moldova, the intended public-private oversight of the central anti-corruption agency, the Center for Combating Economic Crimes and Corruption, proved to be problematic. From the outset, the ostensibly independent Civilian Oversight Board was beholden to the executive branch. The Ministry of Justice, itself a part of the executive branch, was authorized to appoint the board, giving rise immediately to questions about the Board's independence. Finally, the government failed to provide the Board with resources or oversight authority, as intended.

Alternatively, some countries utilize a decentralized approach. In Uganda, for example, they developed anti-corruption investigation capacity through units created within five ministries, each of them responsible for ferreting out corruption within their own ministry.

Punitive measures must be enforced upon convictions. If convicted officials are not subsequently punished, the prosecution may be viewed as disingenuous, further undermining anti-corruption efforts by reinforcing the notion that high level officials operate with impunity. Uneven application of the penal code can suggest that prosecutions are a sham, and the lack of consequences following convictions will bolster public belief that higher forces are impervious to the rule of law.

Notes

1 Management Systems International (2014). *Indonesia Strengthening Integrity and Accountability Project-1, Annual Report*. Washington, DC: USAID.

2 USAID (2010). *Mobilizing Action Against Corruption in Armenia Project, Mid-term Evaluation*. At: http://pdf.usaid.gov/pdf_docs/PDACR143.pdf.

3 Management Systems International (2013). *Support to the Afghan High Office of Oversight, Final Report*. Washington, DC: USAID. At: http://pdf.usaid.gov/pdf_docs/PA00JP3T.pdf.

4 Checchi Consulting (2020). *Legal Professional Development and Anti-Corruption Activity in Liberia (LPAC), Final Report*. Arlington, VA: Checchi Consulting. At: https://pdf.usaid.gov/pdf_docs/PA00XFM1.pdf.

5 Norwegian Agency for Development Cooperation (2011). *Joint Evaluation of Support to Anti-Corruption Efforts 2002-2009, Synthesis*. Oslo, Norway: NORAD.

6 Emil Bolongaita (2010). *An Exception to the Rule? Why Indonesia's Anti-Corruption Commission Succeeds Where Others Don't – A Comparison with the Philippines' Ombudsman*. Bergen: Chr. Michelsen Institute (U4 Issue 4). At: http://www.u4.no/publications/an-exception-to-the-rule-why-indonesia-s-anti-corruption-commission-succeeds-where-others-don-t-a-comparison-with-the-philippines-ombudsman/; USAID (2005). *USAID Anti-Corruption Strategy*. Washington, DC: US Agency for International Development.

7 Gabriel Kuris (2014). "From Underdogs to Watchdogs: How Anti-Corruption Agencies Can Hold Off Potent Adversaries," *Innovations for Successful Societies*, Princeton University. At: http://www.princeton.edu/successfulsocieties/content/data/policy_note/PN_id236/Policy_Note_ID236.pdf.

8 R. Hanna, S. Bishop, S. Nadel, G. Scheffler, K. Durlacher (2011). *The Effectiveness of Anti-corruption Policy: What Has Worked, What Hasn't, and What We Don't Know–A Systematic Review*. Technical Report. London: EPPI-Centre, Social Science Research Unit, Institute of Education, University of London. At: http://blog-pfm.imf.org/files/u4-paper.pdf.

9 Claudio Ferraz and Frederico Finan (2008). "Exposing Corrupt Politicians: The Effects of Brazil's Publicly Released Audits on Electoral Outcomes," *The Quarterly Journal of Economics* 123, 2: 703–745.

10 Jesper Johnsøn, Nils Taxell and Dominik Zaum (2012). *Mapping Evidence Gaps in Anti-corruption: Assessing the State of the Operationally Relevant Evidence on Donors' Actions and Approaches to Reducing Corruption*. Bergen: Chr. Michelsen Institute (U4 Issue 2012:7). At: https://www.cmi.no/publications/file/4624-mapping-evidence-gaps-in-anti-corruption.pdf

11 World Bank (2008). *Public Sector Reform: What Works and Why? An IEG Evaluation of World Bank Support*. Washington, DC: The World Bank. At: http://web.worldbank.org/WBSITE/EXTERNAL/EXTOED/EXTP. UBSECREF/00,,menuPK:4664077~pagePK:64829575~piPK:64829612~theSitePK:4663904,00.html.

12 Ibid.

13 Ibid.

14 USAID (2005), op.cit.

15 Ellen Seats and Samantha H. Vardaman (2009). *Lessons Learned Fighting Corruption in MCC Threshold Countries: The USAID Experience*. Washington, DC: USAID. At: http://pdf.usaid.gov/pdf_docs/pnads603.pdf.

16 Findings based on analysis of over 100 USAID programs implemented between 2007 and 2013.

17 United States Agency for International Development (2013). *Rule of Law Program (ROLP) in Jordan, Final Report.* At: http://pdf.usaid.gov/pdf_docs/PBAAA435.pdf.

18 United States Agency for International Development (2009). *Combating Corruption and Strengthening Rule of Law in Ukraine, Final Report.* At: http://pdf.usaid.gov/pdf_docs/Pdacn921.pdf.

19 United States Agency for International Development (2009). *Reducing Corruption in the Judiciary: Office of Democracy and Governance – USAID Program Brief.* At: http://pdf.usaid.gov/pdf_docs/PNADQ106.pdf.

20 Adam J. Bushey (2014). "Second Generation Rule of Law and Anti-Corruption Programming Abroad: Comparing Existing U.S. Government and International Best Practices to Rachel Kleinfeld's Advancing the Rule of Law Abroad: Next Generation Reform," *Houston Journal of International Law* 37: 139.

21 United States Agency for International Development (2009). *Panama Strengthened Rule of Law and Respect for Human Rights Program, Final Report.* At: http://pdf.usaid.gov/pdf_docs/PDACW212.pdf.

22 Seats and Vardaman (2009), *op.cit.*

23 While, overall, law enforcement activities are typically outside of an international donor's mandate, it is an important component for anti-corruption reform and needs to be addressed. Donors need to seek out country and donor cooperation on law enforcement issues to complement its corruption preventive and awareness interventions.

4 Preventing corruption through accountability, transparency, and governance programming

What works?

In addition to fighting corruption explicitly, interventions can be selected to address corruption in indirect ways. Rather than targeting agencies whose mandate is to specifically address corruption issues, such as anti-corruption commissions, prosecutor's offices, audit agencies, and ombudsman offices, interventions can be designed to address government institutions with other mandates but that may be vulnerable to corruption and abuse, especially those that deliver public services or deal with public financial management. These programming options – to promote government accountability, transparency, and good governance – typically feature preventive activities that build capacity, professionalism, and integrity; generate information openness; and make officials more accountable to the public they serve. Two cases are described here, one from the West Bank and Gaza and the other from Russia.

Palestinian Authority Capacity Enhancement (PACE) (2008–2013).[1] The United States reengaged its support to the Palestinian Authority (PA) in mid-2007 after a newly created government made reform and development of the Palestinian Authority a key objective and had requested assistance from the international community in this endeavor. The creation of the Palestinian Reform and Development Plan (PRDP) was seen as a comprehensive strategy for the restoration of good governance and the rule of law in the West Bank. This demonstrated political will for change, in combination with strong mobilized donor commitment to support Palestinian reform initiatives, created a good entry point for USAID to initiate the Palestinian Authority Capacity Enhancement (PACE) project. The overall goals of the project were to help increase the transparency and accountability of the Palestinian Authority, improve its effectiveness and efficiency in the delivery of public services, bolster its capability to communicate with the public, strengthen its ability to incorporate public participation in government decision-making, and decrease corruption in the public sector.

PACE improved basic government services by using an integrated approach that included facility renovations, business process reengineering, information technology (IT) upgrades, training in customer service, and other interventions that produced measurable improvements in

DOI: 10.4324/9781003241119-5

transparency, efficiency, and consumer satisfaction. At the institutional level, PACE empowered civil servants with knowledge and skills for sustained ongoing government reforms through a Centers of Excellence (COE) framework. More than 380 COE team members from six ministries identified and implemented approximately 100 government reform initiatives. PACE also improved the capacity to regulate prices in the telecommunications sector, strengthened communications and training functions in government institutions, institutionalized methods to seek citizen feedback on government performance, removed barriers to women's access to services, and strengthened services and human resources procedures in the civil sector overall.

The project resulted in an increase of the weighted index of customer satisfaction at targeted service centers operated by several ministries by 21.5% between 2009 and 2012. Citizen satisfaction with civil affairs services increased by almost 20% at targeted offices, and the time required to receive some services dropped by as much as 50%. Similarly, the index of customer satisfaction with the car and driver licensing bureaus in targeted locations increased by 40%. 70% of the users of property tax services indicated improvement in their services. Streamlined procedures for procurement and warehousing resulted in reduced costs and fewer opportunities for corruption. Finally, PACE support to CSOs resulted in improved relationships between the PA and CSOs and engaged thousands of Palestinians in efforts to improve government performance and services.

The project was implemented in a complex and often unpredictable political environment, including the suspension of the Palestinian Legislative Council that limited interventions for policy reform, changes in ministerial leadership that placed additional challenges on project implementation, and excessive interest in quick fixes for service delivery at the expense of longer-term capacity building. Nevertheless, the project received strong cooperation from all partner organizations and achieved results in full and on time. The project was closely aligned with national program priorities and in close partnership with counterparts that contributed greatly to its success.

Community Participation and Regional Advocacy Project in the Russian Far East (2006–2009).[2] In the early 2000s, Russia began showing signs of slippage in its democratic reforms, while still maintaining its rhetoric about adherence to democracy and fighting corruption. Mixed messages sent from the central government were interpreted inconsistently in the regions by local officials who often relied on their instincts for choosing their policy path. The three-year USAID Community Participation and Regional Advocacy Project in the Russian Far East, also known as the *Our Rights* project, did not have an explicit objective of addressing corruption; instead, it dealt with corrupt practices implicitly by mobilizing communities to advocate for their rights and for better governance, while increasing their participation in local self-governance.

The project worked in two regions of the Russian Far East and engaged more than 400 civil society and business groups in about a hundred advocacy campaigns that sought to implement reforms in the budgeting process, small- and medium-sized business development, the environment, housing and communal services, health care, land use and urban development, education, government transparency, public engagement in decision-making, and support for vulnerable groups. As a result of these advocacy campaigns, new regulations were adopted to open government hearings and encourage public participation in policy development and planning; administrative barriers to the development of local business were removed; and public service providers were held accountable for providing quality services.

For advocacy campaigns to be successful, sought-after reforms needed to be enacted. This depends not only on the quality of the campaign and skills of the advocates but also on the willingness and readiness of the government to dialogue with citizens. With power consolidated at the center and little interest there in democratic reforms, there were few local officials who wanted to be associated with local civil society advocates. Any progress that was achieved in making government more accountable and transparent was visibly diminished by the end of the project and NGOs experienced growing resistance from the government to reforms that they were advocating for.

Key takeaways from streamlining and e-governance

Preventive initiatives can be very effective designs in fighting corruption.[3] When the program intervention is focused on corruption prevention, either by promoting greater government transparency or strengthened government accountability, success in achieving anti-corruption goals is very likely (in 73% of preventive initiatives conducted by USAID).[4]

Transparency mechanisms can include open budgets, open hearings, access to information, and legal drafting related to transparency issues, among others. Accountability mechanisms can include codes of conduct, asset declarations, administrative/procedural simplification, audits, complaints management, and legal drafting related to accountability issues.

Government accountability and monitoring programs (such as government audits and community monitoring) work to reduce corruption by increasing the probability of getting caught, while legal, administrative or societal sanctions work by increasing the cost to an official who is caught engaging in corrupt activities. Monitoring and sanctions may be implemented on their own, but a review of research[5] finds that monitoring on its own is ineffective and, similarly, increasing the sanctions for corruption has no effect when the probability of getting caught is too small. In other words, monitoring is usually effective only if a simultaneous and significant incentive for compliance is provided.

The same study found that the anti-corruption programs with the greatest chance of long-term success are those that "change the rules" of the game.

These policy interventions aim to change either an aspect of the government system itself by creating fewer opportunities or reasons to engage in corruption. Rule-changing programs bypass the risk that the monitors themselves may become corrupt or that the bureaucrats will find ways to skirt the newly instituted monitoring and incentives procedures. By attempting to align the bureaucrats' own incentives with those of society, rule-changing programs have the potential to be more sustainable in the long term.

Standardizing and streamlining government processes reduces corrupt behaviors. A review of USAID anti-corruption programs[6] concludes that streamlining and standardizing government agency operations and service delivery reduces opportunities for corruption by reducing the space for bureaucratic discretion. Automating such processes through e-government systems further diminishes vulnerability to corruption by eliminating direct interaction between public officials and customers, embedding internal control mechanisms, and making processes transparent to citizens by providing public access to systems.

One of the mechanisms that became popular in the 2000s were one-stop shops (OSS) for business registration; these have expanded in recent years to include other operations, such as business licensing and permitting, export/ import operations, and investor registration. Although the effectiveness and impact of OSSs can vary widely,[7] they largely result in reducing opportunities for corruption. Studies and surveys conducted in 2005, 2008, and 2009 in Ukraine to explicitly measure corruption in registration and permitting showed notable reductions in corruption due to one-stop shops.[8]

Incorporating the concept of tacit approval reduces an official's ability to extort constituents. One of the most powerful means of extorting bribes is to withhold service. A business left waiting for operating permits loses profits for each day of delay and may be exposed to liability under other statutes. In Albania, regulations were amended to provide a reasonable amount of time to process an application.[9] If the public official deems the application deficient, this decision must be justified in the established time frame. If the official fails to act, the application is considered granted upon the expiration of the proscribed time frame, effectively eliminating a very potent corruption lever.

E-government activities reduce opportunities for corruption and are often self-sustainable. Automating processes through e-government systems further diminishes vulnerability to corruption by eliminating direct interaction between public officials and customers, embedding internal control mechanisms, and making processes transparent to the public by providing public access to systems. These systems can also have a side-effect of making government processes more efficient, resulting in saved money, new revenues, and improved access to government services.

Deployment of e-government systems in various governmental operations has shown significant impacts in increased citizen confidence in the government and reductions in corruption. For example, in Albania, perceptions of frequent corruption in tax collection and bribery in business registration and procurement decreased significantly after e-government applications were introduced. Also in Albania, the launch of automated information systems in pilot hospitals to track and optimize patient flow processes created greater control over critical data and reduced the opportunity for committing medical fraud.

Case management systems are another e-tool that have shown great potential in reducing opportunities for corruption. They have been used extensively in justice sector programs, but have expanded to the health sector and other service delivery agencies, although only a few of these programs measure their impact on reducing corruption. In Georgia, implementation of new courtroom regulations and systems, deployment of automated case management systems and court audio recordings, and procedural streamlining resulted in reductions in bribery in pilot courts.

This e-government option tends to be widely used by the business community. Improvements in the business registration process have led to significantly increased corporate tax collections. These reform measures are also popular with the government because they have the potential of being self-sustaining over time. Sustainability of these measures is further ensured by increased public demand. Improved services stimulate increased demand for those services. As users become accustomed to more accessible and more reliable government services, it becomes increasingly difficult for governments to regress.

Two consecutive US-sponsored projects implemented in Albania between 2006 and 2011 were focused on introducing e-government technologies to reduce opportunities for corruption in government-business sector transactions.[10] Particularly, they developed e-government systems to streamline tax declaration and payment, register businesses and receive business license applications, and conduct public procurement. In addition, the projects assisted in developing a publicly available geographic information system (GIS)-based urban development system to facilitate transparent construction permit issuance. Implementation of these reforms in combination with an information campaign among businesses and engaging NGOs in monitoring and assessing the effectiveness of the reforms resulted in businesses experiencing and perceiving less corruption in tax collection, procurement, and business registration. For example, perception of frequent corruption in tax collection decreased from 42% to 19% and in procurement from 42% to 17%. It also resulted in decreases in the value of gifts expected to secure government contracts from 6.15% to 1% of contract value and decreases in bribery during business registration in the centers supported by the project from 19% to 0%.

Install IT systems early in a program to fully integrate into the country's procedures. Many US-sponsored programs have provided for substantial technical investment in software, hardware and sophisticated equipment. Courts were automated with case management systems, law enforcement agencies received state-of-the-art equipment, customs officials joined international transport databases, and various government services were made available online. Along with automation is the inevitable risk that rather than curbing corruption, the program is "putting speed to chaos." Two other risks relate to ensuring that the equipment is used for its intended purpose and that the technical programs will be sustained beyond the donor's presence.

Introducing technical systems early in a program can help minimize these risks. First, it provides the opportunity to work out the inevitable glitches and tailor the system to specific needs. Second, it provides more time to train personnel on the intricacies of the system. Most importantly, it promotes sustainability. Over time, users of e-government services will demand that the services be continued and expanded; government officials will gradually become dependent on the automated systems to meet the increased demand. When technical systems are up and running, it is easier to secure commitment from the government to allocate budget and personnel for maintenance of computers and upgrading of software into the future. The government can see the important reforms made possible with automation, as well as the likely reaction if the improvements were to be retracted.

Technology-related initiatives can only go so far. Technical fixes, such as new information technology systems, new procedures, and staff retraining, are often critical in strengthening controls, reducing discretion, and enhancing transparency, all of which are essential in the fight against corruption.[11] But technical fixes are far from sufficient. In the absence of strong leadership and a culture of integrity, these tools often yield only temporary gains, as corrupt practices soon shift into new and perhaps more subtle directions. Providing sufficient time for systems to become rooted in everyday government operations and to run smoothly will make it more likely that they will be sustained as vehicles that prevent corrupt and abusive behaviors.

Civil service reform takeaways

Civil service reforms should balance positive and negative incentives.[12] Donors should continually reinforce the importance of host governments undertaking civil service reform together with other anti-corruption measures. In many countries, it is beyond dispute that government officials are sorely underpaid and do not have a stable career path to pursue. While some government offices are luxuriously furnished, others are understaffed and lack the basic materials to function. Until governments compensate these positions reasonably, the temptation for low-level bureaucrats to solicit bribes appears to be officially sanctioned and the challenge of combating corruption is heightened.

Government officials respond to incentives. Hence, incentives that invite or support the abuse of public authority for private gain must be changed. Incentives are influenced by rules of conduct, rewards for integrity, effective penalties for abuse, and systems for detecting abusive practices. Equally important are measures that increase transparency and public awareness to alter the political climate of tolerance for corruption.

Civil service reforms are more effective where patronage-based systems are weak. Especially in post-conflict situations, where leadership structures are in transition, internal controls may be minimal and introducing civil service reforms may be a challenge. Downsizing government departments can trigger resistance from within the civil service, but organizational changes that adjust assignments and compensation may succeed, even where corruption networks thrive.[13]

Public financial management takeaways

Focus reforms on making public financial flows more accountable. A review of close to 200 anti-corruption studies[14] points to the effectiveness of reforms focused on public financial flows. Across 22 categories, this review finds solid evidence for the impact of interventions in three categories: public financial management, procurement, and tax reform. These effective interventions include public expenditure tracking surveys, open auctions, audits of procurement, reforming the value added tax refund system, and establishing a semiautonomous tax authority.

Another evaluation of more than 460 World Bank projects that focused on public sector reform has similar findings.[15] Improvements in a composite measure of governance were greater for Bank interventions in public financial management and revenue administration, but smaller in civil service reform, anti-corruption (focused on laws and prosecutions), and transparency. Bank projects for tax administration generally succeeded and benefited from strong government ownership, particularly by ministries of finance. Projects focused on budget formulation and reporting usually had more success than those focused on the downstream phases of the spending cycle, such as procurement and auditing.

The World Bank review posits that financial management and tax administration reforms are more effective because they are less politically sensitive than issues surrounding public employment and corruption. It also credits good diagnostic work and indicators with generating better outcomes in these areas. In particular, it cites public expenditure reviews, and public expenditure and financial accountability indicators as instrumental in guiding reforms.

Public expenditure tracking surveys (PETS) track how public money flows from central ministries to service providers (notably schools and health facilities) in order to identify how much is lost or diverted on the way.[16] PETS identify problems but do not address them. For this to happen, PETS findings need to be disseminated and used to inform reform efforts. In Uganda, for example, a PETS conducted in 1996 showed that, on average, only 13% of the annual capitation grant from the central government reached the schools. To remedy this, the government increased the information available for local stakeholders to demand accountability. The government published the monthly intergovernmental transfers of capitation grants in the main newspapers and on radio, and required primary schools to post information on inflows of funds. A repeat PETS study in 2001 revealed a great improvement, as 82% of the grants reached the schools. By contrast, a series of PETS conducted over a decade in Tanzania revealed consistent large-scale leakage in education funds; here, the government did not disseminate the findings or engage in a policy dialogue to address them and the leakage persisted.

Preventive sectoral anti-corruption programming

Integrating anti-corruption objectives within sectoral programs is another strategy.[17] Sectoral programs can address corruption directly or indirectly by promoting good governance, transparency, and accountability. Illustrative case studies are provided from Liberia, Ukraine, and Moldova.

Liberia Governance and Economic Management Assistance Program (2006–2010).[18] After more than a decade of war, Liberia began its long process of recovery in 2003 with the support of bilateral donors and multilateral lenders who soon became alarmed at the extent of corruption in government. In response, the Government of Liberia (GOL) initiated a broad good governance and anti-corruption reform program, drafting the country's anti-corruption strategy and plan, establishing an anti-corruption commission and other oversight institutions, and passing key legislation. In September 2005, the GOL signed a multiparty agreement with several key international donors to assist in establishing sound fiscal and budgetary management throughout government, resulting in the Governance and Economic Management Assistance Program (GEMAP). As part of this initiative, USAID launched a five-year project to assist GEMAP in creating and institutionalizing effective financial and asset management policies and procedures, containing corruption, and improving overall economic governance.

Working across 11 government institutions, GEMAP targeted the core fiscal, monetary, and procurement activities of the GOL, as well as the GOL's major revenue-earning sectors: mining and timber, airport and seaport tariff collections, and petroleum storage fees. The project supported improvements to the budget process making budget preparation and execution more transparent and accountable, worked with other donors to replace the Finance Ministry's existing Integrated Financial Management Information System, computerized the mining cadaster, improved contracting and concession processes and approvals standards so that concession awards would be transparent, developed an inventory and procedures for managing and monitoring government fixed assets, improved the financial management system at state-owned enterprises, and developed stronger internal controls, internal audit processes, transparent procurement procedures, and billing and collection systems.

GEMAP did not eliminate corruption, but it did institute new processes that made corrupt practices more difficult. The project raised the visibility of these abuses, improved the accuracy of the budget, provided a clearer picture of the government's use of resources, protected revenues, and exerted central control over governmental processes. A major factor in the success of GEMAP was the Liberian president's public blessing of the program and her personal support at many critical moments, although there also were instances where she was reluctant to intervene for political reasons. Cosignatory authority for embedded advisors was also important to GEMAP's success. It introduced checks and balances into the PFM process, requiring at least two management approvals for financial decisions to be carried out. As a result, it gave them leverage, changed the way financial processes were viewed, reined in uncontrolled procurements, and regularized budget procedures. It brought a measure of transparency and accountability. Information systems installed by the project, although sometimes overwhelming for counterparts, promoted transparency, hindered opaque activities and made processes formal and predictable.

Ukrainian Standardized External Testing Initiative (2007–2009).[19] A series of protests in Ukraine, known as the Orange Revolution in late November 2004 through January 2005, were ignited by election fraud and outrage over massive corruption in the outgoing administration. It brought to power new leaders who declared their commitment to reform and integration into the international community. Soon after, a US-sponsored agreement was drafted to assist Ukraine in fighting the prevalence of corruption. In particular, corruption in the university admissions process was widespread and Ukraine was already taking steps to prevent abuses in the process by introducing standardized admission testing. In support of this initiative, USAID sponsored the Ukrainian Standardized External Testing for University Admissions (USETI) project with the objective of reducing corruption in this particular function in the education sector.

Over the course of two-and-a-half years, USETI supported the development and implementation of standardized admission tests, assisted with drafting legislation to create and protect testing materials and sanctioning those violating testing security, improved test security through the development of tools and procedures, provided technical assistance to university departments in teaching education measurement and psychometrics, and conducted extensive public awareness of the new testing process. The project resulted in successfully implementing standardized university admission tests and systems that reduced corruption significantly compared with the traditional system of admission exams.

The project did not report any significant challenges during implementation. To a large degree, this is credited to the fact that the project was complementing and supporting an ongoing effort that was a key priority for the Ministry of Education. Early evidence of reduced corruption as a result of the standardized test was very encouraging for both the Ministry and USAID, and their cooperation and support was extended through two follow-on projects.

Moldova Business and Tax Administration Reform (2006–2011).[20] Progress in instituting regulatory reform in Moldova, although steady, remains very slow. Problems with the rule of law, transparency, corruption, and red tape continue to interfere with the promise of an efficient private market economy. Private investment is being stifled and economic growth and development has been restrained. With the goal of greater integration into the European Union, the Moldovan government placed increased emphasis on the adoption of policies to make Moldova more "European." In both the EU Action Plan and the Economic Growth and Poverty Reduction Strategy Paper, the Government committed to undertaking needed political, economic, and regulatory reforms. Also, in December 2006, the Government signed on to receiving technical support from the United States which targeted corruption, with a particular focus on police and the judiciary, health care delivery, and tax and customs administration. USAID consistently supported Moldova over the years and the new Business and Tax Administration Reform project (BIZTAR) that was launched in 2006 was organically aligned with previous assistance and country commitments.

The objective of the BIZTAR project was to support the Government's efforts to encourage investment by improving the business enabling environment, reducing opportunities for corruption and abuse, and lowering the overall burden of state regulation on private enterprise. The project focused on streamlining business-state interactions through regulatory reform and promoting more efficient administrative procedures for reporting requirements for tax and other business purposes. In particular, it reduced regulatory and administrative burdens on private enterprise, streamlined tax administration, curtailed opportunities for corruption, and improved access for citizens and businesses to government information. The project succeeded in streamlining business registration processes by reducing the number of steps and time required to complete registration. It supported the effort to reduce and simplify legislation regulating the business sector, implemented an online tax filing system, and supported the drafting of new legislation on one-stop shops for business licensing and permitting.

BIZTAR was well received by many local counterparts in the government and private sector with whom the project established and maintained close partnership. Closely aligned country priorities were additional key factors contributing to the timely, smooth, and effective implementation of the project and results achieved.

Analysis of these and other sectoral anti-corruption initiatives, which focus on the economic growth, health, and education sectors, offers some key takeaways.

Key economic growth takeaways

Reforms that promote economic growth and improve economic governance can also curb corruption. This conclusion and the following lessons were drawn from a comparative analysis of four case studies of economic growth (EG) interventions.

The private sector can be vital in promoting and facilitating reforms that curb corruption.[21] The private sector can be an important agent of change and help donors prioritize activities. More fundamentally, private sector interest groups can help transform the political dynamics in favor of more serious attention to the costs of corruption. At the same time, since many in the business community are complicit in corrupt practices, project designers must identify and mobilize coalitions for reform from within the business community, rather than expecting all business leaders to be willing agents of change.

Anti-corruption interventions often suffer from inadequate cooperation between government and promoters of economic growth.[22] The effectiveness of anti-corruption interventions can and should benefit from increased collaboration between these two groups.

One-stop shops, e-government, and regulatory simplification are effective in many cases.[23] As discussed earlier, analyzing the results of anti-corruption interventions across 43 economic growth projects funded by USAID, three initiatives stood out as particularly effective in reducing corruption: establishing one-stop shops for government-business transactions, implementing e-government applications that allow businesses to transact with government electronically, and streamlining excessive regulations on the private sector that promote rent-seeking and bribery. In many cases, where data were collected to monitor these specific initiatives, it was demonstrated that they contributed to reduced opportunities for corruption.

Health sector takeaways[24]

Increasing salaries for health sector workers does not guarantee reduced corruption. Despite the view that salary adjustments can solve corruption, the evidence suggests that while wage levels may play a role in controlling corruption, it is not guaranteed and other changes need to accompany higher earnings.

Community oversight offers a means of engaging citizens in health sector oversight to improve quality and integrity. Citizen oversight, such as citizen report cards, provides clear information on the shortcomings and failures of health services. With this evidence in hand, citizens can make health care authorities account for corrupt behavior and delivery of services. But this bottom-up accountability may not work if the stakeholders lack acceptability or legitimacy.

Contracting out for health care services can reduce corruption, partly because it is easier to hold contractors accountable than it is for public workers.

Governments can often exert greater leverage over contractors than they can over civil servants. However, taking the contracting path requires developing significant regulatory capacity and control to ensure adequate oversight and accountability of contractors.

Establishing clear procurement and contracting rules and conducting frequent audits with sanctions for staff reduces corruption. Evidence across several countries shows the effectiveness of establishing clear rules, effective oversight to detect problems, enforcement of rules, and rewards and punishments for good and unacceptable behavior in the health sector. The frequency of audits by the central government and the autonomy of local government increases immunization coverage, suggesting that local governments can benefit from exerting its authority, and auditing will further encourage responsible public performance. Sanctions for the misuse of funds lead to more systematic adherence to honest financial procedures. Frequent audits of financial records combined with consequences for staff are successful in reducing corrupt behaviors.

Education sector takeaways

Comparative monitoring of education sector interventions across four countries yielded a set of anti-corruption options that produced positive results.[25] These include:

- Conducting audits and using accountability systems to deal with absentee and ghost employees.
- Developing standard operating procedures and protocols to certify compliance with existing education laws and decreasing bureaucratic discretion.
- Implementing procurement reforms to reduce discretionary decisions and increase competition and adherence to law.
- Strengthening the public financial management system within the Ministry of Education.
- Increasing oversight and audit capacity of the education inspector general.
- Monitoring and enforcing a code of ethics for teachers and administrators.
- Conducting oversight and accountability for teacher certifications.
- Ensuring that schools agree to delegate some oversight functions to teacher organizations and that their scorecards employ evidence-based impact evaluation approaches.

Notes

1 United States Agency for International Development (2013). *Palestinian Authority Capacity Enhancement (PACE), Final Report.* At: http://pdf.usaid.gov/pdf_docs/PDACY026.pdf.

2 Management Systems International (2009). *Community Participation and Regional Advocacy Project in the Russian Far East, Final Report.* Washington, DC: USAID. At: http://pdf.usaid.gov/pdf_docs/PDACQ845.pdf.

3 Findings are based on analysis of over 100 USAID programs implemented between 2007 and 2013.

4 Ellen Seats and Samantha H. Vardaman (2009). *Lessons Learned Fighting Corruption in MCC Threshold Countries: The USAID Experience.* Washington, DC: USAID. At: http://pdf.usaid.gov/pdf_docs/pnads603.pdf.

5 R. Hanna, S. Bishop, S. Nadel, G. Scheffler, and K. Durlacher (2011). *The Effectiveness of Anti-corruption Policy: What Has Worked, What Hasn't, and What We Don't Know–A Systematic Review.* Technical report. London: EPPI Centre, University of London. At: http://eppi.ioe.ac.uk/cms/LinkClick. aspx?fileticket=9T7I1Z7LFw8%3D&tabid=3106&mid=5783.

6 Svetlana Winbourne and Bertram I. Spector (2014). *Analysis of USAID Anti-corruption Programming Worldwide (2007–2013).* Washington, DC: USAID. Annex 3.2.

7 World Bank (2011). *How Many Stops in a One-stop Shop? A Review of Recent Development in Business Registration (English).* Washington, DC: World Bank Group. At: http://documents.worldbank.org/curated/en/708751468149688644/ How-many-stops-in-a-one-stop-shop-A-review-of-recent-development-in-business-registration.

8 USAID (2005). "Reducing Administrative Corruption in Ukraine: Regulatory Reform." At: http://pdf.usaid.gov/pdf_docs/PDACG850.pdf; USAID (2009). *Corruption and Business Regulations in Ukraine: Construction and Land Transactions Permits. Comparative Analysis of National Surveys: 2008–2009.* Washington, DC: USAID.

9 Millennium Challenge Corporation (2011). *Albania Threshold Program, Stage II.* At: https://www.mcc.gov/where-we-work/program/albania-ii-threshold-program.

10 Svetlana Winbourne, Bertram I. Spector and Elena Ponyaeva (2013). *Anti-Corruption and Cross-sectoral Program Mapping: The Europe & Eurasia Region and Business Enabling Environment Programs Worldwide.* Washington, DC: USAID.

11 USAID (2006). *Anti-corruption Interventions in Economic Growth: Lessons Learned for the Design of Future Projects.* At: http://pdf.usaid.gov/pdf_docs/pn-adg601.pdf.

12 Ibid.; Seats and Vardaman (2009), *op.cit.*; USAID (2006), *op.cit.*

13 World Bank (2008). *Public Sector Reform: What Works and Why? An IEG Evaluation of World Bank Support.* Washington, DC: The World Bank. https://openknowledge.worldbank.org/bitstream/handle/10986/6484/ 448180PUB0Box310only109780821375891.pdf?sequence=1&isAllowed=y

14 Jesper Johnsøn, Nils Taxell and Dominik Zaum (2012). *Mapping Evidence Gaps in Anti-corruption: Assessing the State of the Operationally Relevant Evidence on Donors' Actions and Approaches to Reducing Corruption.* Bergen: Chr. Michelsen Institute (U4 Issue 2012:7). https://www.cmi.no/publications/ 4624-mapping-evidence-gaps-in-anti-corruption

15 World Bank (2008), op.cit.

16 Bernard Gauthier (2013). "Making Leakages Visible: Public Expenditure Tracking in Education," in Gareth Sweeney, Krina Despota and Samira Lindner, editors, *Global Corruption Report: Education, Transparency International.* New York: Routledge.

17 Bertram I. Spector, editor (2005). *Fighting Corruption in Developing Countries.* Bloomfield, CT: Kumarian Press.

18 USAID (2010). *Liberia Governance and Economic Management Assistance Program, Final Evaluation Report.* At: http://pdf.usaid.gov/pdf_docs/PDACR798.pdf.
19 USAID (2009). *Ukrainian Standardized External Testing Initiative, Final Report.* At: http://pdf.usaid.gov/pdf_docs/PDACQ648.pdf.
20 USAID (2011). *Moldova Business and Tax Administration Reform, Mid-term Evaluation.* At: http://pdf.usaid.gov/pdf_docs/PDACS244.pdf.
21 USAID (2006), op.cit.
22 USAID (2006), op.cit.
23 USAID (2013). *Anti-corruption and Cross-sectoral Program Mapping: Enabling Environment Programs Worldwide.* At: http://www.usaid.gov/sites/default/files/documents/1866/AnalysisUSAIDAnti-corruptionProgrammingWorldwide-FinalReport2007-2013.pdf.
24 Maureen Lewis (2006). "Governance and Corruption in Public Health Care Systems," Working Paper Number 78, Center for Global Development. At: https://www.cgdev.org/sites/default/files/5967_file_WP_78.pdf
25 J-PAL (2006). "Encouraging Teacher Attendance through Monitoring with Cameras in Rural Udaipur, India." At: http://www.povertyactionlab.org/evaluation/encouraging-teacher-attendance-through-monitoring-cameras-rural-udaipur-india.

5 Civil society engagement
What works?

A number of studies point to the finding that effective anti-corruption initiatives need to engage both government *and* civil society efforts in a comprehensive program to reduce corruption. A multi-donor evaluation commissioned by seven Development Assistance Committee (DAC) donors looks at 90 interventions to strengthen citizens' voices and state accountability.[1] It finds that donor initiatives often focus either on voice or accountability, but that both are needed to improve governance and development outcomes. Similarly, a World Bank evaluation of governance and anti-corruption interventions between 2008 and 2010 stresses that weak civil society/demand-side pressures and external accountability can undermine government/supply-side efforts.[2] It notes how such demand-side pressures as vouchers or community involvement in managing schools can buttress state accountability systems in the education sector. As well, external monitoring of expenditures and procurement – by competitors, contractor associations, or civil society – can reinforce state systems in road construction. Supporting these findings, research by the Development Research Center, drawing from more than 150 case studies over a decade, shows that citizen action in promoting good governance becomes most effective through strategies that build alliances, mechanisms, and platforms linking champions of change from both state and society rather than treating citizen action and government initiatives in isolation.[3]

A review of more than 330 USAID anti-corruption programs implemented between 2007 and 2013 also makes a similar recommendation.[4] It finds that the majority of programs working on the supply side had rather narrow impacts on the demand side because they were not well equipped for working with civil society. In some countries, standalone civil society programs filled the gap by engaging CSOs, businesses or the media in advocacy and watchdog activities. The results from these programs showed that a combination of top-down and bottom-up approaches was very effective for ensuring government accountability in carrying out reforms, as well as sustainability of those reforms. The review noted that if separate supply and demand programs are implemented, they should be coordinated with each other. For example, a program in the health sector working on the

DOI: 10.4324/9781003241119-6

supply side should be complemented with a civil society program focused on health issues that monitors healthcare service delivery to keep government accountable.

Key takeaways

Actively engage citizens. Researchers using randomized evaluations find that active community participation in public projects and services is more effective at improving governance and reducing corruption when people are given specific tasks and training.[5] In Kenya, for example, training of school committees improved how these committees handled teachers accountable to them. In India, a program that trained local volunteers to directly intervene in child learning was very successful, while general encouragement to participate was not. A successful Uganda program developed specific action plans for communities and health providers on how services would be improved. The programs that proved successful in this study provided training or organizational support to help communities take on specific tasks.

Engage citizens in the "upstream" as well as "downstream" stages.[6] When citizens are involved in helping to formulate policies, they are then more likely to engage in monitoring them. In fact, when citizens are engaged in the budget allocation process, for example, they are participating in core decision-making and this can be more effective than monitoring budget implementation after the fact. In any of these processes, transparency, accountability, and participation strategies are linked. Upstream participation encourages engagement in downstream accountability mechanisms.

Researchers used a randomized experiment to evaluate the impact of community involvement in health care in Uganda.[7] They collected data on service provision via report cards from users and convened a series of meetings to analyze the data and develop an action plan for improved services and reduced corruption. Trained facilitators led discussions first with community members, then with healthcare workers, and finally with both groups. The action plan established ongoing monitoring by community members of health facilities. One year later, the treatment facilities experienced a 13-percentage point decrease in absenteeism and a 33% reduction in infant mortality.

Promote linked initiatives and collective action. A number of studies show that transparency and accountability mechanisms gain more traction when linked to other mobilization strategies, such as advocacy, litigation, electoral pressure, or protest movements.[8] So, for example, transparency and accountability in the education sector can be promoted when using a range of strategies, including budget analysis, research, media, monitoring, and advocacy. In addition, collective action rather than individual user or consumer-based approaches is more likely to lead to positive gains. This is because collective accountability mechanisms are better suited to use by the poor and vulnerable and are more likely to result in improved public benefits as opposed to the private benefits that can be the outcomes of individual action. In particular, collective accountability is more likely to result in reduced corruption and increased empowerment of citizens. For example, in Ukraine, seven media and human rights organizations coalesced over several years, with the support of a USAID-sponsored project, to draft a new access to information bill, lobby parliamentarians, and see it through to formal adoption as law.

Strengthen widespread stakeholder dialogue to advance reforms.[9] Widespread support for change from a range of stakeholders is necessary to advance comprehensive anti-corruption reforms. For example, public-private partnerships that include government, the private sector, civil society, and the media have proven to be successful in identifying governance problems, agreeing on solutions and implementing reforms. In addition, campaigns by coalitions of civil society groups to raise awareness of corruption problems or mobilize the public to support specific reform agendas have been the starting point for developing political will in many countries.

Private sector-citizen-government coordination is essential for key anti-corruption reforms.[10] The Honduras Greater Transparency and Accountability of Government Program (GTAG)[11] found that it is important to establish dialogue between businesses and government over common issues of interest, not only about the classic claim of lack of transparency from one side and closing of spaces from the other one. By organizing around common interests – such as improved delivery of municipal services with fewer opportunities for corruption – businesses and government can join forces to find acceptable solutions.

The Georgia Business Climate Reform (GBCR) project also learned the need to support reform priorities that both the government and private sector can agree on. It fostered public-private dialogues to identify priorities and focus investment on the biggest obstacles to business growth.[12] In Nepal, citizen charter activities were successful ways for people to re-engage after a long period of mistrust. Once businesses better understood such processes as registering land or obtaining passports, they were more likely to feel that local government was not a complex entity serving only people with special connections.[13]

Ensure follow-up to citizen complaints. Crowdsourced IT systems, such as "IPaidABribe.com," have been implemented in more than 14 countries to effectively engage citizens in reporting instances of corruption that are then made public on the web (anonymously) and aggregated into a growing database of incidents. The risk in gathering this information is that public expectations will rise and be dashed if the corrupt officials are not brought to justice. While these systems are typically maintained by anti-corruption NGOs, not the police, there have been many instances where independent corruption investigators – from civil society organizations or the mass media – research these reported abuses of power and pass the evidence to the authorities. Follow-up and feedback on complaints increase the credibility of authorities entrusted with fighting corruption.

Public awareness campaigns generate understanding of corruption costs and promote citizen advocacy.[14] Corruption is a complex issue and therefore is difficult to package into a single message in anti-corruption awareness campaigns. Furthermore, corruption is often grounded in a country's social and cultural history, political and economic development, and bureaucratic traditions and policies. Since this yields different perceptions and practices with respect to corruption, acceptance of what is reasonable and appropriate differs widely. Corruption is also not exclusively the fault of individuals, meaning allocating responsibility and casting blame may create a problem.

To generate public support, an anti-corruption campaign should frame the issue in moral terms and demonstrate its negative impact on human life. Key messages should aim to make corrupt behavior unacceptable. A campaign should communicate the harm done by corruption, in particular the human consequences of corruption. It should also highlight the reactions that citizens can pursue, for example, the proper procedures to report corrupt activities.

It is best to present issue-specific tactics, rather than look at corruption as a whole. The mass media and the public often focus on grand corruption. But it is usually better to highlight that corruption occurs not just at the grand level, but also at the petty level that impacts most of the population personally. It is also important that approaches are culturally and country-specific and that continual evaluation and feedback of a campaign's impact is conducted.

To be most effective, such anti-corruption communication campaigns need to be tailored to the audience. First, the messages need to be accessible. Public awareness campaigns that are perceived as too technical are often dismissed as too difficult to understand. It is advisable to generate a shared understanding of corruption which can then form the basis of an awareness campaign and redefine issues, previously seen as highly technical, into problems which require public and political action. Second, the messages need to be tailored to cultural norms. Campaign messages need to be relevant to the local community and resonate within culturally accepted norms and existing values. And third, the campaign should look at corruption from the target audiences' point of view. Campaigns should develop targeted messages geared toward specific societal groups that resonate with typical behaviors and attitudes.

Generating community responsibility for reducing corruption in society should be the principal theme of these campaigns. Effective communications initiatives identify corruption as socially unacceptable. Demonstrating the negative impacts or costs of corruption on society can help make that behavior socially unacceptable, despite culture or tradition. Awareness campaigns have the potential for activating the community to react by demonstrating the negative impacts that corruption has on society and the economy. It is important that credible and accurate evidence be presented, rather than large sweeping statements not backed up by facts. Another way to strengthen the campaign's message is to identify the agents that promote corruption. Specifically, revealing a person or group responsible for fraud or corrupt practices can provide a focus for the campaign. Shaming serves a dual function by influencing the behavior both of the person being shamed and of the community that witnesses the shaming.

Such public awareness campaigns can be most effective if they strengthen citizen beliefs of their control over outcomes. Increasing people's sense of control can cause citizens to take action against an issue which they previously felt they could do nothing about. This can empower people to take action and removes a sense of powerlessness.

Support for anti-corruption coalitions can empower and sustain reform programs.[15] Coalitions must clearly define their target audiences, develop strategies to reach out to them and incorporate their interests in coalition planning and activities. An anti-corruption and transparency coalition essentially has two target audiences: (1) citizens of a community who will benefit from more transparent and accountable governance, and (2) the government, which will gain credibility and trust as a result of being responsive to coalition demands for more transparency and accountability.

Coalition members should reach out to their target communities to understand their concerns, fears and hopes, and then incorporate these inputs into coalition goal-setting and strategies. By having community members participate in the development of objectives and activities, the coalition will gain community support, enhance its legitimacy, and strengthen its will to tackle corruption issues.

National and local governments, including political leaders, represent additional constituencies to which an anti-corruption and transparency coalition can reach out to. They essentially are users of the products and services produced by the coalitions – tools and strategies to detect, prevent and fight corruption, and opportunities for public dialogue. Proactive engagement of government and political officials will open dialogue, increase political will, and build support for anti-corruption reforms.

One of the most important assets of any anti-corruption and transparency coalition is its reputation, which gives it the credibility to raise awareness, influence change, and promote reform. There are some common factors that can help achieve credibility:

- Avoiding politicization through careful membership selection using clear criteria; maintaining neutrality when targeting offices or officials for investigation; and strategically engaging political actors.
- Striving for early successes and strategically disseminating information on those successes.

- Achieving consistency in anti-corruption messaging and clarity of purpose.
- Pursuing activities and adopting management practices that are consistent with the values and objectives of an anti-corruption and transparency group.
- Seeking strategic relationships. A strong coalition should develop relationships with experts who can supplement the organization's capacity to carry out specific tasks and build its credibility. Maintaining strategic relationships with the donor community, the government and other coalitions is also important in achieving the coalition's objectives to curb corruption.

Support for transparency and access to information programming are prerequisites for vital civil society engagement.[16] Transparency and access to information are indispensable prerequisites that enable civil society to identify and report corruption. Without public access to information about government decision-making processes, anti-corruption efforts are likely to fail. Programming initiatives that support greater openness, transparency, and access about information on government policies, programs, budgets, fees for public services, and performance permit citizens to oversee government, hold it accountable, and ensure that their rights are respected.

Access to information can contribute to improved government decision-making, public understanding, enhanced public participation, and increased trust.[17] Public requests for information can contribute to greater responsiveness by public officials, though not always, and is highly dependent on the status of the person submitting the request and civil society pressure. Community-based freedom of information strategies, which go beyond simple information and disclosure, can be instrumental in leveraging other basic human rights.

Transparency measures must be accompanied by activities that appropriately utilize the additional information made available.[18] Activities designed to increase transparency and, simultaneously, promote civic monitoring of government by civil society, media, or joint initiatives contribute to the goal of revealing appropriate or inappropriate government decision-making.

Transparency-enhancing measures generate information and provide broader access to information. Financial asset disclosure forms, internal audit reports, and published judicial decisions and dockets are examples of transparency measures. But merely expanding access to information can be seen as superficial and does nothing to address the corruption issue if there are no accompanying processes, whether internal or external, for reviewing and validating the information. For example, it is important to combine asset declaration directives with verification provisions and public access to the information needed to test veracity of the disclosures. Likewise, when hotlines and citizen complaint mechanisms are promoted, it is also important to ensure that there is visible follow-up to these complaints or else rising expectations will be quickly squashed.

Social accountability mechanisms are critical tools for citizen engagement.[19] There are several social accountability approaches that citizen groups use to monitor and oversee the delivery of public services that are often vulnerable to corrupt practices. For example, public expenditure tracking surveys, when linked to public information campaigns, can contribute to reducing leakages in service sector budgets locally. Citizen report cards can identify consumer complaints about the corrupt delivery of public services. Similarly, social audits and community oversight can contribute to exposure of corruption and effectiveness in program implementation. Community scorecards can point to corruption vulnerabilities and contribute to more responsive service delivery and greater user satisfaction.

However, by itself, community monitoring does not have the power to change the situation; proper incentives must be available, along with community-government partnerships, to turn information into visible reforms. Complaint mechanisms can contribute to the reduction of corruption by linking citizens directly to systems that can hold managers to account. And community-based information campaigns can have positive impacts on the level of citizen engagement in initiatives to keep local school systems accountable to the public they serve, for instance.

Case study: Sierra Leone

At the end of 2016, a DFID-supported anti-corruption reporting mechanism was brought online in Sierra Leone to engage citizens actively in registering bribe requests from government officials when citizens are seeking basic social services – education, health, water, energy, and security.[20] The Sierra Leonean public typically faces challenges when accessing these basic services, and is typically confronted with demands for bribes. The poorest are usually the ones who are hit the hardest, as demands for bribes can make entitlements, such as free healthcare or medicines, unaffordable.

The system, called "Pay No Bribe (PNB)," can be accessed on the web, on a smartphone app, and via a telephone hotline, and complaints are registered anonymously. It is similar to a system in India, called "IPaidABribe.com," except that the version in Sierra Leone is managed by the Anti-Corruption Commission, rather than an NGO. This accelerates the processing of each reported transaction from being a mere data entry to an active complaint that is pursued and resolved by the Commission directly or by the relevant government agency through administrative actions and system or policy reforms. With the Commission responsible for responding, PNB avoids raising citizen expectations without having any direct path to resolving the complaint. In addition to the PNB system, technical support was provided to the Commission, as well as to the government agencies that deliver public services, to conduct extensive public education campaigns about what constitutes corrupt behavior, citizen rights related to such requests, and how to employ the PNB system.

A baseline survey was conducted at the time the system was implemented and an endline survey was conducted two years later in late 2018. Comparison of these surveys demonstrates significant improvements in reduced petty corruption. Those who said that they paid a bribe over the last six months declined sharply over the two years since the system went online: when accessing services in the water sector (from 42% to 6%) or the energy sector (from 42% to 12%), and when dealing with the police (from 65% to 16%). However, surprisingly, the occurrence of bribe requests increased when seeking services in the health sector (from 25% to 36%) and the education sector (from 20% to 43%). Explanations for these two negative results could be that public education campaigns in these sectors started later and may not have had time to make a major impact on public thinking. As well, traditionally, giving small gifts for health or educational services in Sierra Leone has not been considered bribery until recent PNB campaigns sought to shift perceptions.

Overall, people credited the program with their increased knowledge of public services they should receive and how much they should cost. As well, when the public sees their complaints acted upon, they are convinced that citizens can make a difference in the fight against corruption. Comparing the baseline to the endline surveys, the perceptions that citizens can play an important role in fighting corruption increased from 32% to 68%, and the belief that government will act on reported cases increased from 39% to 73%.

Notes

1 Alina Rocha Menocal and Bhavna Sharma (2008). *Joint Evaluation of Citizens' Voice and Accountability: Synthesis Report.* London: DFID.
2 World Bank (2011). *Country-Level Engagement on Governance and Anti-corruption: An Evaluation of the 2007 Strategy and Implementation Plan.* Washington, DC: The World Bank.
3 Nicholas Benequista (2011). "Blurring the Boundaries: Citizen Action across States and Societies," Brighton, UK: The Development Research Center on Citizenship, Participation and Accountability. At: https://opendocs.ids. ac.uk/opendocs/bitstream/handle/20.500.12413/12499/cdrc_2011_blurring. pdf?sequence=1&isAllowed=y.
4 Svetlana Winbourne and Bertram Spector (2014). *USAID Anti-corruption and Cross-sectoral Program Mapping: Enabling Environment Programs Worldwide.* Washington, DC: USAID. At: http://www.usaid.gov/sites/default/files/ documents/1866/AnalysisUSAIDAnticorruptionProgrammingWorldwideFinal-Report2007-2013.pdf.
5 "Community Participation," on Poverty Action Lab website. At: https://www. povertyactionlab.org/evaluations
6 R. McGee and J. Gaventa (2010). *Review of Impact and Effectiveness of Transparency and Accountability Initiatives.* Brighton, UK: Institute for Development Studies. At: https://www.transparency-initiative.org/wp-content/ uploads/2017/03/synthesis_report_final1.pdf

 7 Martina Bjorkman and Jakob Svensson (2009). "Power to The People: Evidence From a Randomized Field Experiment on Community-Based Monitoring in Uganda," *The Quarterly Journal of Economics* 124, 2: 735–769.
 8 McGee and Gaventa (2010), *op.cit.*
 9 US GAO (2004). "U.S. Anticorruption Programs in Sub-Saharan Africa Will Require Time and Commitment," GAO-04-506 (April). At: http://www.gao.gov/products/GAO-04-506.
10 USAID (2006). *Anti-corruption Interventions in Economic Growth: Lessons Learned for the Design of Future Projects.* At: http://pdf.usaid.gov/pdf_docs/pn-adg601.pdf.
11 Management Systems International (2009). *Greater Transparency and Accountability of Government Program (GTAG), Final Report.* Washington, DC: USAID. At: http://pdf.usaid.gov/pdf_docs/PDACP996.pdf.
12 USAID (2009). *Georgia Business Climate Reform (GBCR), Final Report.* At: http://www.chemonics.com/OurWork/OurProjects/Documents/Georgia Business Climate Reform Final Report.pdf.
13 USAID (2009). *Transition Initiative: Nepal, Final Report.* At: http://pdf.usaid.gov/pdf_docs/PDACQ596.pdf.
14 Catherine Mann (2011). "Behaviour Changing Campaigns: Success and Failure Factors," U4 Expert Answer, (21 February: 270). At: http://www.transparency.org/files/content/corruptionqas/270_Behaviour_changing_campaigns.pdf.
15 USAID (2005). "Anti-corruption and Transparency Coalitions: Lessons from Peru, Paraguay, El Salvador and Bolivia," (August). At: http://pdf.usaid.gov/pdf_docs/PNADD813.pdf.
16 US GAO (2004), *op.cit.*
17 McGee and Gaventa (2010), *op.cit.*
18 Ellen Seats and Samantha H. Vardaman (2009). *Lessons Learned Fighting Corruption in MCC Threshold Countries: The USAID Experience.* Washington, DC: USAID. At: http://pdf.usaid.gov/pdf_docs/pnads603.pdf.
19 McGee and Gaventa (2010), *op.cit.*
20 Coffey International (2019). "Pay No Bribe – Endline Survey Report," Support to the Anti-Corruption in Sierra Leone Project. London: Coffey International. At: https://www.anticorruption.gov.sl/slides/slide/endline-survey-report-186.

6 Anti-corruption programming in post-conflict societies

Post-conflict situations pose special and complex conditions for anti-corruption programming that are both opportune and sensitive. Rebuilding political, social, and economic frameworks in the aftermath of conflict provides the chance for reformulating laws, institutions, and relationships to reduce the impact of traditional cultures of corruption. Corruption may have been among the major initiators of societal conflict and finding ways to eliminate it in the peacebuilding period should become high priority for the host country and donor community alike. But post-conflict situations are also extremely fragile and making significant changes in traditional political and economic structures by which the country operates could do harm in the short run.

Fragility and vulnerability to corruption in post-conflict countries are often traced to weak institutions, large inflows of foreign aid, and ongoing struggles for power. However, policymakers have yet to identify the best ways to approach anti-corruption programming in these settings. Research on six post-conflict countries offers some insights into the directions anti-corruption interventions should take under these contexts.[1] This research points to the relative success of interventions in post-conflict settings to strengthen audit and control, financial management, civil society, media support, and the private sector. The research also points to moderate success for initiatives that reform local governance, the judiciary and law enforcement among these six cases. Finally, disappointing outcomes resulted from attempts to support anti-corruption institutions, electoral strengthening, and parliamentary assistance in the face of political interference. These results are more fully described below.

Early anti-corruption interventions in post-conflict countries can help sustain the peace, but require special forethought to avoid doing harm[2]

Starting with mapping out the problem. Corruption risk assessments should be incorporated into doctrine and training, and integrated into operational planning and procedures. A corruption-focused political economy analysis

DOI: 10.4324/9781003241119-7

(PEA) should be completed to examine the actors, institutions, and political dynamics that support or oppose democratic reform, and to determine what the priority issues are in light of political feasibility.

Starting early and seeking early successes. In post-conflict settings, there is often a tension between focusing on short-term immediate objectives, such as promoting access to health and education, versus longer term governance and institution building objectives. Dealing with corruption is often relegated behind more pressing issues. However, experience demonstrates the critical importance of addressing corruption and governance issues from the outset so corruption does not become reinstitutionalized, undermining early state legitimacy.

At the same time, quick and visible wins will help gain citizen support for reform and send a strong signal of change. This can include, for example, the conviction of officials thought to be untouchable. Similarly, reforms should be prioritized in areas where they are likely to meet the least resistance, thus offering quick payoffs. Early successes should be widely publicized to build trust and restore confidence.

Integrating anti-corruption elements in peace agreements.[3] Corruption needs to be recognized as a serious impediment to reconstruction from the onset. Experience shows that the few countries which integrated anti-corruption provisions in the peace agreements that ended their civil conflicts experienced improvements in their governance indicators within five years after the agreement was signed. In addition to indicating promising levels of political will, this approach allows for rapid provision of resources and assistance to the parties to implement negotiated provisions. Such provisions should be as detailed, specific, and targeted as possible to translate them into actionable anti-corruption programs.

Sequencing and prioritization. While not providing specific guidance on sequencing, key priorities are identified for donor support to post-conflict countries to ensure that: basic public services are delivered, adequate legal frameworks are developed, the civil service is trained and professionalized, accountability is established through internal and external checks and balances, public finance systems are established and monitored, and regulations for business are simplified. In addition, experts warn against the risk of generating high expectations through awareness campaigns or political interventions, such as the development of an anti-corruption strategy or the establishment of an anti-corruption agency, as long as the state lacks the capacity to deliver. Emphasis should rather be put on the need to generate openness and transparency, and promote community involvement in oversight of reconstruction projects.

Tailoring anti-corruption programs to corruption patterns and quality of leadership. While sharing common features, post-conflict countries are also very diverse, especially with regard to the quality of their leadership, with fragility fueled by lack of capacity, lack of willingness, or a combination of both. Some states are weak but willing, whereas others may appear weak to external actors in terms of resources and institutional capacity, but may be repressive internally. Thus, there is a need to differentiate between the concept of state fragility (lack of power) versus state predation (abuse of power), and anti-corruption interventions need to be tailored accordingly, based on a careful assessment of the situation.

Supporting anti-corruption champions and islands of integrity. Even in challenging contexts, it is possible to identify and support groups or individuals within the public sector or specific institutions that can champion anti-corruption and accountability reforms. To achieve this, it is critical to discover and empower actors that have a genuine interest in anti-corruption reform.

Sanctions by external actors. Sanctions by external actors, for example, embargos or aid withdrawal, can also be used as a way of countering corruption, illicit trafficking, and corrupt resource agreements. However, there are some risks associated with such approaches, as sanctions can have a humanitarian impact on nontargeted civilian populations and reinforce illicit trade. This is reinforced by the "do no harm" principle, which warns against the potential impact of sudden withdrawals of aid and recommends harmonized and graduated responses to serious human rights and corruption cases, rather than sudden aid withdrawal which can exacerbate poverty and insecurity. In practice, these risks can be taken into account and sanctions can be increasingly targeted at specific actors with measures such as travel bans and asset freezes.

Program options need to be adjusted to take fragility of the state into account[4]

Strengthening rather than circumventing government institutions. There is a need to find the right balance between state and nonstate capacity development. There is often a temptation for donors to circumvent inefficient state structures and deliver more effective public services using nonstate actors or creating parallel structures for service delivery. While this approach may improve access to public services in the short or medium term, it will have little impact on building the government's capacity. In addition, relying exclusively on nonstate actors for anti-corruption sends a strong signal that government structures cannot be trusted and can undermine their accountability and the long-term sustainability of reforms.

Strengthening financial management systems. Most recommendations to address corruption in fragile states call for the establishment of transparent regulations and procedures, and emphasize the need to strengthen public finance management (PFM). Approaches that are reported to have achieved some success include strengthening audit and control capacity, budget monitoring, procurement processes, cash and debt management, and financial management information systems.

A comparative study in eight post-conflict countries demonstrates that PFM reforms were positively associated with gains in state "resilience" and control of corruption. Strengthening instead of bypassing local financial management systems is considered good practice, including the intensification of monitoring activities. Ensuring a sustainable and legitimate government revenue stream and preventing tax evasion is essential to strengthen the accountability line between citizens and the government. Related corruption risks involve revenues from natural resources and illicit goods, state control of public institutions through patronage networks, or the "purchase" of key ministries.

Strengthening public service delivery. Building or restoring effective governance is an essential element of post-conflict reconstruction, as a way to restore the government's legitimacy and gain the support of fractionalized constituencies. The peace-building process can be undermined by ineffective, incompetent, or corrupt civil service, lacking the resources to effectively deliver public services. As a result, addressing corruption in service delivery is an important aspect of post-war reconstruction. Early institutional and civil service strengthening programs can contribute to re-establishing effective service delivery, with measures aimed at eliminating red tape and inefficiencies, and building stronger and more capable public administration with barriers to cronyism and nepotism. But some authors argue that such programs, while bringing immediate results in controlling petty corruption, often neglect to take into account the systemic nature of corruption.

Strengthening political and legislative processes. It is also important to strengthen government accountability through transparent and accountable political processes. Such measures are typically neglected by anti-corruption policies. While programs tend to focus on the executive, little attention is typically paid to strengthening the capacity, transparency, and accountability of parliaments. As a result, MPs may have little capacity to perform their oversight role or be subject to influence peddling.

Civil society and the private sector can play a major role in rebuilding with sensitivity to corruption[5]

The role of civil society and social accountability mechanisms. Mobilizing nongovernment actors for anti-corruption reform is essential to build support for reform, as civil society has been found to play the most effective role in areas such as protection monitoring and advocacy in post-conflict settings. In particular, community-based approaches sometimes represent the only feasible option in the post-conflict setting for controlling corruption in service delivery through mechanisms such as participatory monitoring of expenditures, scorecards, and independent media. Similarly, in states affected by high levels of state capture, promoting horizontal accountability by reinforcing nongovernment actors is likely to be more effective than focusing on the executive which may be the source of the problem. However, engaging with civil society in post-conflict countries is associated with a set of specific challenges. The starting point should be to identify existing resources and actors that can provide a solid foundation upon which to re-build. In addition, as corruption can also affect CSOs, transparency in these groups should be promoted.

Privatization and economic development. Some argue that privatization can boost economic development and fight corruption, while others argue that privatization may not improve service delivery and, in fact, risks rein-forcing cronyism if state assets are not allocated through competitive and transparent bidding processes. As the privatization of assets is highly vul-nerable to corruption and has the potential of raising corruption from petty to high levels, some researchers recommend postponing privatization until a reasonable regulatory system is in place and/or supported by credible in-ternational agents.

Notes

1 Bertram Spector (2011). *Negotiating Peace and Confronting Corruption: Chal-lenges for Post-Conflict Societies.* Washington, DC: United States Institute of Peace Press.
2 Marie Chêne (2012). "Lessons Learned in Fighting Corruption in Post-conflict Countries," U4 Expert Answer 17, Number 355 (December). At: http://www.u4.no/publications/lessons-learned-in-fighting-corruption-in-post-conflict-countries/downloadasset/2995.
3 Spector (2011). op.cit.
4 Chêne (2012). op.cit.
5 Chêne (2012). op.cit.

Part II

New strategies

Are we on the right track? Past efforts to reduce and eliminate corruption have had only minimal impacts and backsliding is frequent. It resembles the Greek myth of Sisyphus who was punished by having to push a huge stone up a mountain only for it to roll down as it reached the top, and repeating this for eternity. But new strategies that refocus reform programs on motivating individual and group actors stand a better chance of producing sustainable results.

DOI: 10.4324/9781003241119-8

7 Activating behavioral change initiatives

By far, most of the anti-corruption initiatives and outcomes analyzed in previous chapters have been aimed at establishing a legal framework and institutional structure strong enough to recognize, detect, and prosecute corruption, broadly and in particular sectors, as well as strengthening processes by which government services are provided. These approaches create new laws, regulations, strategies, policies, action plans, institutions, and mechanisms meant to put a halt to corrupt behaviors. The assumption is that corruption happens primarily due to insufficient legal frameworks and institutions, and weak oversight. In many cases, stricter laws and regulations have been enacted detailing what are considered to be corrupt acts by public officials and citizens, with stronger penalties if and when caught and convicted. In addition, many new anti-corruption commissions and agencies have been established to manage and oversee the implementation of these new laws and regulations, to investigate and prosecute offenders, and to increase public awareness. The purpose of these stricter laws and institutions is to instill fear of punishment for wrongdoing. To a lesser extent, civil society engagement in anti-corruption efforts has also been promoted by these programs, largely sponsored by international donors. The concept here is to actively involve the victims of corruption in standing up for their rights and sustain strong demand for change.

Have these efforts provided sufficient motivation to incentivize actors to comply with the law and not engage in corrupt actions? To some extent they have, but it's clearly not enough. Perhaps these legalistic and institutional approaches, and the negative incentives they offer, are just the first steps toward reducing corrupt behavior and more needs to be done to get at the deeper driving factors of corruption, for example, embedded ethical, social, cultural, and psychological frameworks. These new lenses will switch our focus from the institutional level to the individual and group drivers of behavior. Personal motivation to "do the right thing," comply with the law, and desist from corrupt behavior may require more than just fear of punishment. In this and subsequent chapters, we expand the literature review to consider other frameworks and motivational factors that may lead people to obey the rule of law or not. Based on this examination, we may find some

DOI: 10.4324/9781003241119-9

new and helpful approaches to reduce corruption by activating behavioral change at a much more personal level, rather than at an institutional level.

Many past initiatives have been motivated by international donor organizations that promise funding only if such anti-corruption frameworks are put in place. The World Bank, the International Monetary Fund and bilateral donors, for instance, frequently made loans available to developing countries contingent upon them establishing anti-corruption agencies, whether or not they were properly funded, trained, and sustained.[1] The basic assumption is that the existence of anti-corruption laws, regulations, and institutions, by themselves, should be enough to change people's corrupt behaviors. The problem is that many of these initiatives were never implemented properly to generate the desired outcomes. Without the needed funds, resources, domestic political will, and consistent support, these anti-corruption law and order efforts never took hold to generate long-lasting changes in human behavior.

It is the same with many preventive transparency and accountability mechanisms put in place to reduce corrupt transactions. They may have some limited effect on decreasing corruption, but again, without continuing political will, resources and follow-up actions, the motivation and creativity of corrupt people will produce novel ways of overcoming or bypassing these mechanisms.

Much of the research conducted on these anti-corruption approaches demonstrates that it is not so much the particular approach, but the *context* and other factors that matter. For instance, which initiatives work is usually highly dependent on the consistency of political will by senior government officials to make them work. An official who is intent on changing the way the system operates – for whatever reason – is more likely to ensure that mid- and lower-level managers follow through on anti-corruption reforms to make sure that the necessary regulations, monitoring, and oversight are implemented and maintained for the long term. Political will requires someone in a position of power to use their resources in a clear and targeted way to guarantee that their policy desires are carried out as intended and with effect.

Unfortunately, political will is not always consistent due to situational conditions. Actions taken by political rivals or influential parties, upcoming elections, or economic downturns, and changes in leadership, among other things, can result in major changes to high-level political will to reduce corrupt practices. If this happens, what might be an effective approach to fighting corruption could show disappointing results over the long term. Other contextual factors, such as state fragility and post-conflict situations can also limit the impacts of anti-corruption attempts that might work perfectly well under more stable conditions.

Donors are usually in a big hurry to see results from their anti-corruption investment. After funding a project for three to five years, they often expect to see positive and visible results. But as world history has clearly demonstrated, much more time is required for lasting change to set in when it comes to changing corrupt behaviors. In the United States, for example, it has taken many generations for the corrupt effects of the late 19th-century robber barons to dissipate even after strict legal frameworks, strong law enforcement, and other efforts were established... and the fight is not over. We cannot expect these problems to disappear overnight – fighting corruption is a multigenerational issue.

While some anti-corruption initiatives have shown promise, there is no way to tell if they will have similar impacts on corruption in other countries under different circumstances. It might be wise to rethink our approaches in response to corruption from a new and different platform.

What is needed are focused anti-corruption approaches that target the real motivating factors that promote corrupt behaviors *at a personal and group level*. They need to address the traditions, customary behaviors, and plain human inclination to act in one's self-interest, without thinking of the implications of those actions for others. This is what the rest of this book is about.

Examining extrinsic and intrinsic motivation

Basic obedience to the rule of law, including its anti-corruption provisions, is likely to produce a launching pad for reducing or eliminating corruption. But persons need a mix of both extrinsically and intrinsically motivated values by which to assess society's laws, rules, and authorities, and judge the best path to act in an uncorrupted way. Research has focused on a number of important motivating factors.

A central factor to keep in mind is whether the incentives to act or not are externally or internally motivated. Extrinsic motivators offer explicit costs or benefits for acting in a certain way. The incentives for behavior come from external sources. Obedience to the law and authority, for example, can be compelled by fear, threat, force, or punishment, or by promises of rewards, monetary or otherwise. Intrinsic motivators, on the other hand, are based on internalized principles and values of doing what is right, fair, and just. Reducing corrupt activities requires a mixture of both types of motivating factors to produce a lasting change in behavior. How to incorporate these essential incentives into practical anti-corruption approaches remains the critical challenge.

Punishment and threat of punishment

At the core of most legal systems is the threat of punishment if you don't follow the rules. The threat has been found to be a fairly effective method of achieving compliance with authority under certain conditions. It is useful if the punishment stimulus is of high intensity, if personalized prior relationships have been formed between the punishment agent and the recipient, if verbal reasoning is used in conjunction with physical punishment, and if the stimulus occurs quickly upon the occurrence of the deviant behavior.[2]

The threat of punishment is typically based on the predictability of getting caught while not following the rules. Thus, the likelihood of getting caught must be satisfied first before the punishment threat comes to play in changing behavior. Are there ways to divert attention away from oneself while committing a disallowed action, thus avoiding detection and ultimate punishment? If a person believes they can outsmart the system and not be detected, the threat of punishment will not be very effective.

Punishment cannot be relied on to ensure absolute obedient behavior all of the time. A relevant case study found that fear-controlled behavior tends to aggravate the occurrence of desirable results.[3] It found that a relations-oriented approach to discipline yielded more favorable performance. Similarly, surveys of the legal profession conclude that fear of formal disciplinary proceedings has only moderate impacts on inhibiting unethical values and conduct.[4]

Interestingly, US Supreme Court Justice Oliver Wendell Holmes wrote more than a century ago about the human motivation to obey or disobey law – distinguishing between good persons and bad persons.[5] He wrote "that a bad man has as much reason as a good one for wishing to avoid an encounter with the public force." He defines a bad person as one who "cares nothing for an ethical rule which is believed and practiced by his neighbors," yet he "is likely nonetheless to care a good deal to avoid being made to pay money" or get caught and punished. "Thus, if you want to know the law and nothing else," Holmes says that "you must look at it as a bad man, who cares only for the material consequences which such knowledge enables him to predict."

Holmes' bad person seems to be motivated clearly by economic cost-benefit analysis. Such persons are interested solely in maximizing their own interests and not concerned with others nor how their behavior affects others. They act with no notion of moral obligation. The bad person is always ready to disobey law if such action plays to their advantage and if they feel they can get away with it.

Those who promote corrupt practices are clearly sociopathic. They use antisocial behaviors and attitudes, they cheat, manipulate, are dishonest, lack empathy for others, and act as they do with a clear intention to enhance self-interest at the expense of others. They exploit and manipulate others, violating the public trust that has been given them by holding public office or a position of power.

Those who respond and facilitate the active corruptors – who agree to take the bait – usually do so, not because they believe in corruption themselves, but because they are operating from a position of weakness. They need what the corruptors are offering – even if at a higher price or inferior quality.

The good person, on the other hand, is motivated intrinsically: by their conscience, according to Holmes. Their conduct is motivated by what is right and law-abiding, rather than from fear of punishment. Even if government authorities and courts stopped punishment for violating the law, Holmes' good person would not violate a just or morally binding law. To Holmes, the law provides a moral norm that persons should obey, regardless of threatened punishment for disobedience. The good person "finds his reasons for conduct, whether inside the law or outside of it, in the vaguer sanctions of conscience."

Case study: successful prosecutions by Indonesia's Corruption Eradication Commission

Between 2011 and 2016, the USAID Support to Indonesian Anticorruption Institutions (SIAP-1) project helped to strengthen the capacity of the Corruption Eradication Commission (KPK) to investigate corruption cases and the Supreme Audit Body (BPK) to detect financial fraud and corruption.[6] At the beginning of this project, KPK had been fearlessly pursuing corrupt officials at the highest levels of government with a prosecution rate of nearly 100%. Most of the Commission's top investigators at the time were loaned to it by the National Police Force (NPF). But when KPK detained a high-level police official in 2012, NPF pulled out its investigators, leaving KPK with only a few remaining skilled investigators. As a result, KPK faced a huge challenge of rebuilding its investigation capacity immediately to be able to carry out its mission uninterrupted. SIAP-1 assisted the agency to resuscitate its investigative capacity by delivering 44 professional training sessions conducted for 739 KPK staff.

Utilizing court data and new prosecutorial strategies, KPK enforcement efforts have also shown marked improvement throughout the SIAP-1 timeframe, despite these external challenges. KPK increased the number of cases it handled between 2011 and 2016 by 31%. Using new prosecutorial strategies during that period, KPK arrested 181 government officials, seized stolen assets amounting to more than IDR 1.7 trillion (approximately USD $139.5 million) and returned it to the government budget, and convicted 241 corruptors for a total of 1,482 years in prison. It also opened more investigations into high profile individuals, including as many as 25 governors, ministers or chairs of government agencies.

As a result of these efforts to strengthen legal enforcement, punishment of a large number of corrupt officials was carried out rather rapidly. Did these actions and the threat of continued tough enforcement have any effect on reducing or terminating ongoing or future corruption schemes? This is difficult to determine in the short term.

Rewards

Are rewards for good behavior more powerful than punishments for bad behavior? While there is some evidence that providing poverty-level salaries to civil servants will result in their corrupt behavior, there are inconclusive results on the effects of raising their salaries. In some cases, when wages are increased, there are only modest or minimal effects on corrupt behavior practiced by civil servants.[7] Some microlevel cases have indicated more positive findings on the effects of raising salaries, including the salary supplements provided in Georgia after the Rose Revolution.[8]

Starting in 2004, one of many reforms implemented by the new progressive administration in Georgia was to increase civil servant salaries – for traffic police, the salary increase was tenfold over their previous wages – turning around the previous policy of providing tiny salaries to these government workers with the expectation that they would earn their living primarily through bribes and kickbacks using their positions of power. The United Nations Development Program and the Open Society Institute augmented the government's salary fund over the short-term. This major uplift in civil servant salaries has been credited with a visible decrease in government bribe-taking. But it is difficult to separate the impacts of the salary increase from other anti-corruption reforms that were occurring simultaneously. Other reward approaches, such as crowdsourced recognition of honest civil servants – via tools like IPaidABribe.com – may be helpful in changing behavior, but again, results are inconclusive.

Modes of socialization

Whether a person is motivated primarily by extrinsic or intrinsic factors is largely a function of how they have been socialized – how they have experienced or learned what is acceptable behavior in their society. Socialization largely affects a person's reactions to the threat of punishment or the prospect of reward, and whether one is motivated by external sources or internal beliefs. Several key development paths for socialization are discussed next – what one learns as a child and student, in one's occupational role, and as a member of a society or specialized social grouping.

Early socialization

Socio-economic status (SES), sex roles, family, and education have been hypothesized as likely socializing factors that affect the development of obedience to law and authority. Middle class parents tend to induce an internal governor of conduct into their children, while working class parents socialize the external, punitive consequences of behaviors if you go against the law.[9] Thus, high SES children internalize a sense of power to determine their own actions, while lower SES children are socialized into a subordinate and inhibited role. Similarly, girls traditionally have been socialized to obey external authority and conform to parental rules, while boys generally have been encouraged to be more independent.

Internalization of obedience to law and authority structures is also fostered by the family unit, in which adults dominate and children may be punished for disobedient behavior. The school is another institutional setting in which children are placed in subordinate roles for the first 15–20 years of life and taught the meaning of obedient behavior.[10] The level of education attained has been identified as an important indicator of obedience.[11] Persons with a high school diploma have been found to be more reliable and obedient than those without a diploma.

Some cognitive developmental theorists postulate a growth pattern in values and judgment from extrinsically motivated at early ages to intrinsically motivated in adulthood.[12] At the early end of the developmental continuum, judgments are based on strict obedience to rules and authority figures. At the later end, judgments are based on internalized principles and conscience. Cognitive restructuring and perceptual differentiation that evolve from greater social experience, participation and role-taking activates internalization of system values and goals, and replace the need for external sanctions to ensure acceptable, disciplined behavior.

Ego development theorists address the impact of identity development and obedience.[13] Two ego developmental patterns have been specified that relate to two different styles of adolescent coping and obedience. The first type is called "censors." There, awareness is dependent on a strong reliance on parents and other nurturant authority figures. They are highly obedient and concerned with maintaining the traditional "rules of the game." The second type is call "sensers." These persons are more reliant on their own perceptions, their internal values, and the opinions of peers, rather than on laws or authorities. Obedience among this latter group would probably fall within the intrinsically motivated type.

In terms of the impact of personality, the profile of an obedient person[14] would have high needs for submissiveness, deference, social approval, blame avoidance, and survival. However, obedience is *not* a trait of highly aggressive or autonomous persons.

Case studies: engaging with youth in Ukraine

Over the course of two long-term USAID-sponsored anti-corruption projects in Ukraine there have been many attempts to engage with youth with the goal of providing them with a new way of thinking about corruption. Given the strongly embedded culture of corruption in the country, these initiatives were aimed at demonstrating the negative aspects of these behaviors, that it is reasonable to say 'no' to corruption, and that they have it within their control to make serious changes in society's response.

Youth Awareness in Schools. Public opinion surveys conducted by the USAID ACTION Project (2006–2009) indicate that Ukrainian youth are among the primary groups victimized by corruption and is a group that voluntarily participates in corrupt activities.[15] In view of this, the Lviv-based NGO, For a Common Future, developed an interactive simulation exercise and curriculum for students to make them more aware of the negative costs of corruption and what to do about it. They worked with the Lviv State Administration, which ordered that anti-corruption classes would be included in the school curriculum for grades 9–11 starting in the academic year 2008–2009. Teachers were trained and the course was launched in 1,000 out of 1,450 schools. Next, the NGO developed a manual for the course, with the involvement of specialists from the Ukraine Ministry of Education and Science. In August 2009, the Commission on Educational Work of the Research and Methodological Council of the Ministry approved the manual and recommended it for use in secondary, vocational, professional, and higher education institutions.

Launch anti-corruption master's program. The USAID Support to Anti-Corruption Champion Institutions (SACCI) Program (2017–2022) provided technical assistance to establish a master's degree program in anti-corruption studies at the National University of Kyiv-Mohyla Academy.[16] The program's objective is to create a pool of highly qualified professionals to work in the many newly established anti-corruption institutions. In April–June 2020, two courses were developed: Academic Integrity and Asset Recovery. Five more courses are in development: Investigative Journalism, Anti-Corruption Strategic Communications, Behavioral Economics, Preventing Corruption in Public Procurements, and Writing Policy Papers. The initial assessment results showed that the pilot program remains in high demand among students.

Student simulations. With the help of the SACCI project, a Ukrainian NGO developed a game for students – Web of Corruption Schemes – which was adapted for use in schools to support ethical training among students. In addition, the NGO finalized the webpage, Education without Corruption, which houses all SACCI-developed anti-corruption activities and tools. This NGO also implemented an online conference, with 5,000 participants registered, which featured dialogues about transparency and accountability in education in an online learning environment through multiple webinars. SACCI-supported teacher ambassadors presented anti-corruption tools and shared their findings during one of the webinars. Finally, the NGO is completing a Corruption in Schools guide for teachers that is likely to be approved by the Ministry of Education of Ukraine. Through another grant, SACCI supported the development of a House of Integrity online simulator that will be used at schools and colleges to demonstrate to students the positive outcomes of transparent decision-making.

Innovative ideas that target youth. To provide youth with knowledge, practical skills, and leadership experience, and help build their careers based on principles of integrity and zero tolerance of corruption, SACCI organized an online Integrity Leadership Summer School for selected participants from around Ukraine. For three months, the participants built a community of emerging leaders with new and applicable skills, reinforcing anti-corruption and transparency values. Through skill building and human-centered design sessions, cross-cultural discussions, and chats with local community leaders, the program covered leadership ethics, academic integrity, e-services, and other topics. Participants engaged in sessions on relationship building, negotiation and mediation, and leadership ethics and public speaking, and developed their individual action plans.

Occupational socialization

An adult's socialization into an occupation is often an experience of being put into a submissive role.[17] Traditional authority patterns maintain these values and create a context of domination in which the individual can divest themselves of responsibility to a superior.[18] Once this divestiture occurs, the individual is reduced to an obedient agent. One's actions can be entirely obedient and free of the inhibitions of self-image and moral values since responsibility has been relegated to a corporate authority figure. In this agentic state, a person is only concerned with doing the job properly, following instructions, pleasing the authority, and fulfilling one's obligations. Researchers also describe an alternative pattern in which strict domination defers to a more participant- and relations-oriented managerial style.[19] They hypothesize that this style increases the likelihood of individual initiative based on internal values and principles.

Case study: investigator and auditor professional training in Indonesia

Between 2011 and 2016, the USAID Support to Indonesian Anticorruption Institutions project (SIAP-1) provided extensive professional training for KPK's enforcement staff, including training on ethics.[20] SIAP-1 support included the development of a comprehensive training curriculum for KPK investigative personnel, the development of e-learning options for professional skills building, a blueprint for an investigation training center, and a successful initiative to increase oversight and accountability of cases tried before the specialized corruption court system (TIPIKOR).

Despite the impressive track record of the KPK's limited investigative staff, a training needs assessment conducted by SIAP-1 in 2013 revealed areas for further improvements. The project provided basic, intermediate, and advanced trainings to new recruits and existing investigators and staff whose duties include investigative and pre-investigative functions. Thanks in part to these technical trainings, KPK was able to actually increase both the number of its inquiries and investigations in 2013. SIAP-1 delivered 44 training modules – ranging in topics from asset recovery and digital forensics software to sectoral investigations in construction, forestry, oil and gas, and offshore banking – to a total of 739 participants, 78% of whom execute either investigative or quasi-investigative functions. In support of long-term sustainability, SIAP-1 successfully developed three e-learning modules for KPK investigative staff. The modules – Search Warrant Execution, Investigative Interviews, and Asset Tracing – enhance ongoing staff development initiatives by allowing users to study without limitations of time and place.

Working with the Supreme Audit Body (BPK), the SIAP-1 project strengthened BPK expertise when their auditors are called upon to testify in court during crucial corruption cases. SIAP-1's extensive training program led to 109 officials graduating with professional certificates ranging from Certified Fraud Examiner (CFE) to Certified Information System Auditor (CISA) and Certified in Financial Accounting Standards (CPSAK). The strategic shift toward performance audits was highlighted through two high profile international exchanges, and followed up through the review of performance audit guidelines and the development and delivery of ten custom-made training programs. More than 280 BPK officials personally participated in the performance audit trainings, and special online courses have been prepared to extend in-person trainings. BPK now operates with an expanded understanding of best practices in performance audits, thanks to numerous exchange visits to the United States, including meetings between the BPK Chairman and the US General Accounting Office (GAO) Comptroller General, and a reengagement with the GAO's International Fellows Program.

In addition, under an earlier USAID project in Indonesia conducted between 2007 and 2009, government ethics codes at all levels were developed, followed by large-scale training, to establish a higher level of mutual commitment among officials to uphold ethics.[21] Although it is difficult to quantify concrete changes, it is nonetheless heartening to learn that in Indonesia 83% of the 2,251 judges trained on the new code of conduct said they had changed their attitudes or behaviors since the training.

Societal socialization

When corruption is an everyday occurrence, the population typically does not trust its government nor does it believe that government officials have society's best interests in mind.[22] Citizens suffer or, if they have the means, participate in corrupt transactions themselves to get the services they need. Targeted anti-corruption efforts can turn such transactions around by providing citizens with a new way of looking at their situation. Such anti-corruption mechanisms can motivate intrinsic values of self-worth among the population by convincing citizens that they have rights under the law and demonstrating to them that they can stand up to government to assert those rights. These approaches need to refocus and retrain how the public views its efficacy in fighting corruption, overturning what might be generations of culturally engrained beliefs that corrupt transactions are the cornerstone that make society operate. If citizens across the board can be resocialized to believe that they have a say in their futures, that they can stand up for their rights, and say "no" to corrupt transactions and succeed, then there is hope that age-old traditions can be tossed aside and new approaches to transparency and accountability can be nurtured.

Case study: Citizen advocate offices

Citizens and businesses continually transact with governmental agencies to obtain services (such as education, health care, housing and municipal services, permits, licenses, registrations, and information), fulfill their public obligations (such as paying taxes and other obligatory fees, satisfying requirements imposed by law, and reporting to governmental agencies), and seek justice and resolve disputes (for example, through law enforcement agencies and the court system). All of these interactions are vulnerable to corruption or abuse of public office. Sometimes, citizens are victims of extortion practiced by government officials. Other times, citizens initiate offers of bribes to officials to obtain services or speed up the process.

As victims of corruption or excessive bureaucracy, citizens and businesses may require legal consultation or assistance to help them deal with their problems and stand up for their rights. However, in many countries, there is a prevalent lack of trust in law enforcement agencies or other government departments to respond adequately to citizen complaints. Moreover, the public often fears retribution if grievances are registered directly with governmental agencies. Public opinion surveys show that only between 1% and 9% (varying from country to country) of citizens formally register complaints about corruption with governmental agencies. However, a large number of citizens express their willingness to accept legal help for alleged government abuses from independent nongovernmental legal services if they are made available.

Between 1998 and 2000, Management Systems International (MSI) implemented an anti-corruption program, *Partnership for Integrity*, in three regions of Ukraine. The program was sponsored by USAID. Its overall objectives were to promote and build integrity, accountability, and transparency into government and business activities in Ukraine. The program went about doing this by mobilizing all sectors of society to fight corruption, establishing public-private partnerships for integrity, implementing a set of preventive reforms, increasing public awareness about corruption and citizen rights, and developing public intolerance toward corruption. In large part, the program sought to change the rampant sense of helplessness that citizens felt about not being able to exercise their legal rights and upend everyday corruption.

To address the growing number of citizens and business people frustrated by corruption, the project established *Citizen Advocate Offices* (CAO) in one city, and then rolled them out to several more.[23] These anti-corruption legal service offices offer legal support, seek redress from the government on behalf of citizens, take cases to court, and conduct legal literacy education and awareness for businesses and citizens on corruption issues. Perhaps the CAO's most effective tactic – administrative resolution – is to group together common corruption complaints about particular government agencies and have CAO lawyers approach the agencies' managers, demanding administrative and procedural changes that would eliminate the corruption. If the problems are not rectified quickly, formal cases will be brought to court. With the law on their side, the CAOs have seen a very high percentage of cases resolved and government-citizen transactions reformed quickly and visibly after their administrative visits. Most importantly, based on these positive results, both the lawyers and citizens have been given a new sense of hope that if they exercise their rights, they can reduce corruption in their midst.

This approach is powerful because there are fundamental behavioral incentives at work: corrupt officials realize that the CAO is watching them and has the capacity to "out" them, and they don't want to be embarrassed publicly. To date, MSI has implemented more than 30 CAOs in Ukraine, Russia, Albania, Indonesia, Mali, and Afghanistan.

By seeking administrative solutions, rather than bringing cases through a lengthy judicial process, the CAOs achieve rapid results. During its first four months, for example, the pilot CAO in Ukraine provided assistance to over 700 citizens. In Albania, the CAO handled 580 cases in its first ten months and of those, many cases were resolved quickly and some cases were forwarded to the General Prosecutor's office. In seven regions of Russia, CAOs provided legal services to thousands of corruption victims either through administrative redress of grievances or through the judicial system. In the short run, they have seen more than a 60% success rate for corruption cases handled by CAOs – mostly through administrative resolution and sometimes in court.

In Indonesia, under SIAP-1, Citizen Advocate Offices were established in two provinces. These offices uncovered instances of systemic corruption at the local level, offering the public real power against those in positions of authority. Over the course of a year, these two offices received 568 complaints from victims of corruption and successfully resolved 97% of them. In one case, a class action lawsuit filed by the CAO in Bangka-Belitung reverberated all the way to the national level, resulting in new guidelines on energy conservation.

These CAOs have provided visible evidence to the general public that an effective outlet to fight back at corruption does exist and that victims can get results. The CAOs typically coordinate their activities with Ombudsmen offices, law enforcement agencies, prosecutors, and other governmental agencies. CAO activities have resulted in the restoration of citizen rights, financial restitution, administrative and procedural changes in the delivery of public services, and disciplinary measures and criminal charges brought against corrupt officials.

Using the administrative resolution approach, the majority of cases are resolved without going to court. Sometimes, disciplinary actions are taken against civil servants, and in other cases, abusive bureaucratic procedures are changed to conform with the law. CAO lawyers make government managers aware of the corruption complaints and their liabilities if the problems are not rectified quickly. Some examples of CAO administrative resolutions include the following:

- Privatization – A regional government was planning to sell a factory to a questionable buyer for an unreasonably cheap price without an auction. The CAO intervened and stopped the sale. The factory was sold through auction.
- Traffic Police Bribery – A traffic policeman returned money he had extorted from a pensioner after a call from the CAO to the police department chief.
- Tax Inspection – A tax inspector demanding that businesses pay inspection bribes through his wife's firm was fired upon CAO reports to the prosecutor's office and tax agency.
- Public Services – Employees of the government passport agency were administratively reprimanded for delaying passport issuance as an act of "suggestive extortion."
- Public Procurement – A fraudulent procurement was canceled and a revised one issued as a result of a CAO intervention after complaints by one of the bidders.

By keeping statistics on complaints registered with them, CAOs often find that certain government offices are cited repeatedly with excessive bureaucracy or corruption. When such systemic corruption is identified, CAO lawyers can mobilize even greater evidence and pressure to resolve grievances administratively. Using their outreach efforts, CAOs provide legal education to the public at large, business people, and governmental institutions and law schools. One of the most popular features is the "CAO bus," a mobile legal office that periodically visits neighborhoods and towns, making it easier for victims to register their corruption complaints and get assistance.

After participating in a networking conference of CAOs in 2002, Transparency International established very similar Advocacy and Legal Advice Centres (ALAC), now operating in over 100 countries. These CAOs and ALACs are popular and sustainable because they provide visible, quick and lasting successes for citizens and businesses, yielding greater public trust in government and citizen confidence in standing up for their rights.

The consequences of intrinsic versus extrinsic motives

While reliable compliance with anti-corruption laws and regulations may be obtained from persons motivated by extrinsic factors, research finds that such behavior will be of the lowest acceptable quality and will lack the innovation, spontaneity, and flexibility that leads to creative solutions, greater productivity and critical corrective contingency planning.[24] In essence, under extrinsic controls, individuals have little motivation to do more than what the rules prescribe, and the effort and costs expended to make external sanctions credible may produce suboptimal performance.

The consequences of intrinsic motives, on the other hand, include the likelihood of higher quality and innovative performance while achieving the objectives of law and good governance.[25] Research has found that intrinsically motivated law students attach a high value to legal ethical standards.[26] They are not compelled to abide by these norms by the threat of punishment, but their internalization of system goals has led them to disciplined values in any case (for more, see Chapter 8). Associated research[27] hypothesizes that intrinsically motivated government officials are more likely than extrinsically controlled types to stand up for their convictions and do the right thing in terms of supporting the rule of law.

As demonstrated by many of the case studies presented in this and following chapters, there have been effective pilot tests of attempts to promote intrinsic incentives. Careful implementation of broadly based, long term, and consistent programs across all sectors that focus on energizing intrinsic motivation for anti-corruption behavior are likely to be effective in deconstructing age-old traditions of corruption.

Expanding the motivational lenses

Akin to a global viral pandemic, corruption has existed since the dawn of humankind and continually metastasizes, but a viable potent vaccine has yet to be developed. As we have discussed, while many anti-corruption strategies have been tried, the legal-institutional approaches, by far, have been the most frequently implemented. While these paradigms have shown some efficacy, they are clearly not sufficient. Other frameworks that target the personal and social drivers of corruption deserve to be examined and may offer more productive results if implemented in a substantial and consistent way.

Researchers suggest that to be effective, anti-corruption strategies need to address multifaceted drivers of behavior – at a group and individual level.[28] Five major dimensions of these drivers have been identified, starting with the legal/institutional set of approaches. Then, there are individual and group motivators, including moral beliefs and ethics; social motivators, including social norms and networks, and role models; material incentives, including efforts to reduce poverty and making access to services more readily available; and structural drivers, including existing conflict situations, power structures, and ideology. A comprehensive situational assessment in a particular country that examines all or most of these factors would allow for appropriate anti-corruption action planning that is critically important in targeting the right drivers of corruption and focusing future strategies on those drivers.

For example, policymakers can promote an *ethical frame*, where targeted approaches focus on both the recruitment of ethical officials and the proactive socialization of government staff in ethical conduct to yield major behavioral change. Efforts taken within this frame should also promote a sense of empathy by government officials for the plight of citizens who depend on essential government services. Corruption can divert public funds that will eventually degrade the quality and quantity of these public services. On the other hand, empathy for citizens by officials can serve to quash their impulse toward self-interest and corrupt behaviors.

Other approaches that need to be examined further fall into the *social psychological frame*. Most programs that have been implemented to date are based on rational choice theory – that an economic cost-benefit analysis is at the basis of good decisions. As such, corrupt behaviors are strongly motivated by self-interested goals.[29] But if we reorient our focus to a social psychology frame, we would highlight the factors that influence how humans process information within their social situation, which might bring us closer to understanding why people practice corruption and how it can be curtailed. Within this psychological frame, we would want to examine strategies that address power relationships, self-control, loss aversion and risk acceptance, rationalizations, social norms, and emotion.

Third, we definitely want to follow a *negotiation frame* to limit corrupt behaviors. At its core, a corrupt transaction involves a give-and-take process between two or more parties (each with their own aims, needs, and interests) where each seeks to find a common ground and reach an agreement. When a bribe is solicited by a government official, the citizen/business is usually in a position of weakness and easily intimidated to pay. The citizen/business is often seeking to obtain a service he/she is entitled to (like health care or schooling), but can only get it via approval from the official. When the bribe is offered by a citizen or business, it is they who are usually in a position of power, and a compliant official agrees to use his/her position to speed the process or give approval, doing so for the illicit payment. There is always a *quid pro quo*, a favor or advantage granted or expected in return for something. If this negotiation transaction can be subverted, the corrupt transaction should be suppressible.

We will assess these three frames and explore potential anti-corruption initiatives that emerge from them in the next three chapters.

Notes

1 Jeremy Pope and Frank Vogl (2000). "Making Anticorruption Agencies More Effective." *Finance & Development* 37, 2 (June). At: https://www.imf.org/external/pubs/ft/fandd/2000/06/pope.htm.

2 Cheyne, J. A. and R. H. Walters (1969). "Intensity of punishment, timing of punishment, and cognitive structure as determinants of response inhibition," *Journal of Experimental Child Psychology* 7: 231–244.

3 J. Huberman (1964). "Discipline without Punishment," *Harvard Business Review* 42: 62–68.

4 J. Carlin (1966). *Lawyer's Ethics: A Survey of the New York City Bar*. New York: Russell Sage Foundation; R. Abel (1977). *The Legal Profession: An Annotated Bibliography*. Los Angeles, CA: University of California at Los Angeles (mimeo).

5 Oliver Wendell Holmes (1897). "The Path of Law," *Harvard Law Review* 10: 457. While Holmes uses the terms "good man" and "bad man" in his argument, in today's language, he is certainly referring to both men and women.

6 Management Systems International (2016). *Strengthening Integrity and Accountability Program 1 (SIAP-1), Final Report*. Washington, DC: United States Agency for International Development.

7 Mariana Borges, et al. (2017). *Combatting Corruption among Civil Servants: Interdisciplinary Perspectives on What Works*. Chicago: Institute of International Education, Northwestern University. At: https://www.usaid.gov/sites/default/files/documents/2496/Combatting_Corruption_Among_Civil_Servants_-_Interdisciplinary_Perspectives_on_What_Works.pdf.

8 World Bank (2012). *Fighting Corruption in Public Services: Chronicling Georgia's Reforms*. Washington, DC: The World Bank.

9 J. Aronfreed (1968). *Conduct and Conscience*. New York: Academic Press.

10 S. Milgram (1974). *Obedience to Authority*. New York: Harper and Row.

11 Association of the United States Army (AUSA) (1977). *Manpower for the Military: Draft or Volunteer?* Washington, DC: AUSA.

12 L. Kohlberg (1969). "Stages and Sequence: The Cognitive-Developmental Approach to Socialization," in D. Goslin, editor, *Handbook of Socialization Theory and Research* (pp. 347–480). Chicago: Rand McNally; L. Kohlberg (1958). "The Development of Modes of Moral Thinking and Choice in Years 10 to 16." Ph.D. Dissertation, University of Chicago.

13 A. Moriarty and P. Toussieng (1976). *Adolescent Coping*. New York: Grune and Stratton.

14 Milgram (1974), op.cit.

15 Management Systems International (2010). *Promoting Citizen Engagement in Combating Corruption in Ukraine (ACTION), Final Report*. Washington, DC: United States Agency for International Development. At: https://pdf.usaid.gov/pdf_docs/PDACR665.pdf.

16 Management Systems International (2020). *Support to Anti-Corruption Champion Institutions (SACCI) Project in Ukraine, Progress Report*. Washington, DC: United States Agency for International Development. At: https://pdf.usaid.gov/pdf_docs/PA00X39S.pdf.

17 M. Janowitz and R. Little (1974). *Sociology and the Military Establishment, Third Edition*. Beverly Hills, CA: Sage Publications.

18 Milgram (1974), op.cit.

19 Janowitz and Little (1974), op.cit.

20 Management Systems International (2016), op.cit.

21 Management Systems International (2014b). *Analysis of USAID Anticorruption Programming Worldwide (2007–2013)*. Washington, DC: United States Agency for International Development.

22 Jon Vrushi and Roberto Martínez B. Kukutschka (2021). *Corruption Perceptions Index 2020: Research Analysis*. Berlin: Transparency International. At: https://www.transparency.org/en/news/cpi-2020-research-analysis-why-fighting-corruption-matters-in-times-of-covid-19.

23 Svetlana Winbourne and Bertram Spector (2019). "A Rapid Results Anti-Corruption Tool – That Builds Citizen Trust and has Lasting Impact... and Now, with Worldwide Reach," *Global Anticorruption Impacts, Technical Note 12.* Arlington, VA: Management Systems International. At: https://msiworldwide.com/sites/default/files/2018-11/GlobalACImpacts_12.pdf.

24 Daniel Katz (1964). "Motivational Basis of Organizational Behavior," *Behavioral Science* 9, 2: 131–146.

25 Ibid.

26 Bertram Spector (1977). *Intrinsic/Extrinsic Motivation, Ethical Values and the Legal Profession.* Arlington, VA: CACI, Inc.

27 Bertram Spector (1973). *The Stages of Moral Development and their Implication for Principled Government Leadership.* New York: Center for International Studies, New York University, Seminar Paper; Edward Weisband and Thomas Franck (1975). *Resignation in Protest.* New York: Grossman Publishers.

28 Cheyanne Scharbatke-Church and Diana Chigas (2019). *Understanding Social Norms: A Reference Guide for Policy and Practice.* The Henry J. Leir Institute of Human Security. Medford, MA: The Fletcher School of Law and Diplomacy, Tufts University. At: https://sites.tufts.edu/ihs/social-norms-reference-guide/.

29 Kendra Dupuy and Siri Neset (2018). *The Cognitive Psychology of Corruption: Micro-level Explanations for Unethical Behaviour.* Bergen, Norway: Chr. Michelsen Institute, U4 issue 2018: 2.

8 The view through an ethical lens

It seems logical that the most fundamental approach to reduce or eliminate corruption would be to anchor policies and procedures in an ethical framework and appeal to the ethical values held by individuals and groups in society. The principles and resulting behavior of ethical persons should produce a social environment where justice and fairness are paramount and the self-interest of a few with the inclination to engage in corruption is minimized. Both officials and citizens ought to be governed and act in line with a set of ethical principles that put honest decision-making and dealings as the highest objective – to benefit the public they serve – and denigrate corrupt and self-interested actions. Most government agencies have written codes of ethics and conduct but the question is whether these are effectively understood, implemented, and monitored. The problem is that too many who are attracted to positions of power have not been socialized with ethical norms nor inclined to learn them on the job. To the contrary, they seek their positions to take advantage of the power that it provides them with to enrich themselves to the detriment of others.

How can ethical approaches to governance best be implemented? Are people who seek out responsible government posts ethical to start with? Obviously, many are, but some are not and hence the continuing high rates of corruption in most countries. Recruitment of more ethical officeholders could be a first step. Training and socialization of government officials and the public on ethical approaches to behave with one another in the public marketplace is also essential. And does there need to be more intrusive oversight and monitoring to detect when ethical principles are breached?

Let's reconsider Oliver Wendell Holmes' discussion of how and why good and bad persons abide by the rule of law.[1] If we look a bit more closely at the distinctions he makes, we may be able to add a new and essential dimension to the framework. Holmes writes that bad persons are inclined to ignore laws and do what is good for themselves except when confronted with the threat of punishment for disobeying the law. But detection of disobedience is a matter of probabilities. The bad person who believes that they will certainly get caught, will follow the law, but not because they believe it is right. At the same, the bad person who believes they can cover their tracks, with a

DOI: 10.4324/9781003241119-10

good chance they can avoid being detected when disobeying the law or committing corrupt acts, will readily proceed to commit the crime. In the end, Holmes' bad persons can be considered egoistical and sociopathic.

Good persons are prepared to obey laws because they believe that it is the right thing to do. There is an obligation to obey the law. They have been taught and socialized to understand and obey the rule of law that keeps the many strands of society together. Deep down, Holmes' good persons are motivated by a similar cost-benefit risk assessment as are bad persons. They are convinced of the righteousness of the law, but also fear punishment for disobeying the law, so they stay in line with the law. The good person is motivated largely by extrinsic factors, but with a tinge of intrinsic beliefs as well.

What seems to be missing from Holmes' presentation are the *ethical persons*. True, these people are motivated by the rule of law, but even beyond that, by their own beliefs of what is fair and just: their intrinsic conscience and morality. Even Holmes suggests that law and morality are two different things. These ethical persons act to do the right thing, whether it is in accordance with existing law or based on rules that ought to govern society. Empathy for the plight of others in society is also part of their directive. Helping and caring for how others in society are treated is important; thus, corrupt self-interested behavior would not be tolerated.

This triad of bad, good and ethical persons can be a more comprehensive way of understanding how and why people obey the law or are corrupt in their actions. We focus now on the ethical frame, how it impacts on suppressing corrupt behavior and how it can be developed into practical policy strategies that can make corruption fail. Let's first look at some data-based research that throws light on this ethical frame.

Ethics in the legal profession

When I was in graduate school at New York University, I supported two professors – Edward Weisband and Thomas Franck – who were conducting research for a book on why only a small minority of high-level government officials in the United States resign in protest, that is, publicly announcing their strong policy differences with the administration when resigning from their positions.[2] These differences often rest on matters of conscience and ethics, but it could be a serious threat to their future careers to "go public" and state their opposition to their administration's policy. Those who stay the course with the administration and those that leave, but in silence, are playing to political loyalty and the unwritten rules of the game. But those that do broadcast their disagreements publicly usually do so because of their deep internalized beliefs and conscience. They feel it is their moral duty to state their opposition with the goal of making changes to what they see as mistaken policy decisions and actions. They are motivated by doing what they feel is right. Written in the shadow of the Watergate scandal, this book largely analyzed the British system where the likelihood of resigning in protest was much greater than in the United States.

My contribution to that research effort was to study the extent to which those in the legal profession – as many in high-level government positions are often lawyers – conduct their work in accordance with ethical beliefs. In the early 1970s, especially after Watergate, a great veil of suspicion was raised on the ethical commitments of the legal profession. Weisband and Franck suggest that the processes of legal selection and socialization may serve to attract and reinforce individuals with tenuous ethical values.[3] This is especially ironic in a profession that is clearly obsessed with normative rules concerning its own ethics, behaviors, and responsibilities.

Is the problem that these norms have been misconstrued or poorly taught? Or are they insufficient on their own to maintain moral behavior given the ever-present enticements to stray? We needed to test the assumption that the latter is true, that the development of extrinsically motivated persons is insufficient to maintain truly high moral values and resultant actions.

Autonomy and heteronomy

My analysis focused on two opposing types of motivation that are hypothesized to have a major impact on the ethical behavior of lawyers. Piaget[4] and Kohlberg[5] distinguish between two very different socialization processes that are found empirically to evolve during early childhood and continue into early adulthood.[6] The result of one process is labeled *heteronomy*, and of the other, *autonomy*.

A heteronomous person lacks a moral attitude and self-determination, and is essentially subject to external controls. Such a person is motivated by a socialized fear of punishment for wrongdoing, hedonistic desire for pleasure and need satisfaction from external stimulation, unquestioning respect for authority and regulation, and social conformity to gain social approval. Obedience to authority and regulation is the response to perceived external pressures urging compliance. Behavior is controlled by conditions in the external world, either avoidance of harmful stimuli or fear of dominant figures, institutions, or norms. However, obedience is the behavioral outcome only so long as the external motive remains present and credible.

In his now famous experiments on obedience to authority figures, Milgram found that obedience among his subjects dropped sharply when the experimenter, posing as an authority figure, left the subjects alone to proceed with the experiment as ordered.[7] Obviously, a sense of obedience had not been internalized by these subjects; the motive for obedience remained entrenched in the presence of the external authority figure. While this external source is present, obedience is probable, but when the source is absent, disobedience is more likely. This motivational type clearly displays an extrinsically motivated pattern.

At the other end of the spectrum, the autonomously motivated person is driven by inner judgment and acts out of respect for justice, the rights of others, and principles of right and wrong. This intrinsically motivated person is more confident in his or her own reasoning and choice, and savors self-control. Action is motivated by internal conscience, rather than external sources of social coercion and domination. Behavior is stimulated by a principled respect for the rights and will of other human beings, one's duty toward others in society, and a sense of justice and conscience to do what is right.[8] Persons at this stage of conscience are likely to obey benevolent commands and authority that will maximize these principled motives. However, they are likely to be disobedient and revolt in the face of malevolent authority that requests acquiescence to behaviors that attack these principles.[9] This intrinsically motivated person will evaluate external rules and commands against internal principles. If they are acceptable to the individual, obedient compliance occurs, but if they are unacceptable, disobedience or defiance is the result.

The extrinsically motivated heteronomy is a tenuous form of morality; without external compulsion, moral behavior may lag. Intrinsically motivated autonomy, on the other hand, is a more vigorous and lasting form of morality; internalization of values enables independent consideration and choice.

Peer relationships, as well as schooling, play a major role in shaping the direction of one's socialized motivation. Students pursuing a legal education are confronted with a peculiarly cross-cutting message with regard to this dichotomy of internal versus external control. There is an inherent conflict in the law between achieving control over people by enforcing external rules and regulations over them and achieving justice by relying on the conscience and sense of right in most people. The law recognizes the need to rely on human judgment, conscience, and sensitivity as manifested by such legal institutions as courts, judges, and juries. However, it also recognizes that reliance on conscience alone is not always reliable, that personal bias sometimes enters to distort one's sense of right and external constraint is often necessary. That explicit laws and regulations exist indicate a bias in society's values in favor of external control. This bias is carried over into the legal education process.

Law students are exposed to this conflict at a sensitive period in their moral development. It is hypothesized that the occupational socialization that they undergo greatly shapes their personal and professional motivation between internal and external control.

> *Hypothesis 1.* Lawyers who are internally controlled are likely to possess ethical values with regard to their practice of law and behave in accordance with them.
> *Hypothesis 2.* Lawyers who are externally controlled are less likely to be oriented toward ethical beliefs and actions in their professional life, except if they fear sanctions from external authority.

Data collection

A questionnaire was distributed to 380 law students at a large New York City law school. In its entirety, the questionnaire tapped aspects of the respondents' legal education, beliefs concerning ethical standards of the legal profession, moral judgments in complex social situations,[10] risk-taking potentials in hypothetical political scenarios, and personality need structure.[11]

Kohlberg's Moral Judgment Interview was included in the questionnaire. It maintains the Piagetian tradition of asking the respondent to judge the morality of conduct in hypothetical social situations. But Kohlberg's moral dilemmas are more complex and mature in comparison to Piaget's stories that reflect an understanding of simple sins and virtues.[12] Kohlberg's stories usually counterpose a legal-social rule with an essential human need. These dilemmas place the respondent in the position of either conforming to rule and authority or reacting in terms of higher personal principles. Thus, the interview measures motivation – from independence of thought and action to dependence on external control, as well as the extent of moral development.

Open-ended written responses to each of three stories were content analyzed to place the respondent in one of six stages in Kohlberg's moral development typology.[13] Each stage shows an increasing ability to differentiate moral values ranging from external, heteronomous control to internal, autonomous control over one's beliefs and actions. Stages 1 through 4 describe a heteronomous orientation, and Stages 5 and 6 an autonomous style. The six stages are listed in Table 8.1.

Stein's Self-Description Questionnaire (SDQ) was chosen as an appropriate instrument to measure personality on the basis of several criteria. It explicitly measures respondents' manifest social and psychological needs (based on Henry Murray's typology of needs).[14] Unlike many personality tests, the Stein SDQ measures the hierarchical structure of needs to construct a profile of the total configuration of personality. The instrument

Table 8.1 Kohlberg's stages of moral development

Stage 1. Obedience and Punishment Orientation	Values arise from fear of punishment and physical external compulsion
Stage 2. Egoistic Orientation	Values are motivated by hedonistic need satisfaction and opportunism
Stage 3. Good-Boy Orientation	Values arise from the need for social approval and conforming behavior
Stage 4. Authority Orientation	Values are based on respect for authority
Stage 5. Social Contract Orientation	Values are motivated by a sense of social contract to respect the rights and wills of others
Stage 6. Conscience and Principled Orientation	Values arise from an inner sense of conscience, justice, free will, and shared universal principles

avoids the single-trait perspective by asking each respondent to rank a list of 20 needs in terms of how well each describes their motivational system. It enables motives to appear in context with relation to the entire organization of personality. Although the respondents' self-awareness, defensiveness, and needs for social desirability may distort the self-ranking process without additional personal data, Stein and Neulinger argue that the SDQ nevertheless provides valuable insights into an individual's personality constellation.[15] Moreover, Stein's SDQ has shown a high degree of reliability and validity over several experimental, cross-cultural, and assessment studies that have tested the relationship among personality needs and behavior potentials, values, and attitudes.[16]

The final scale employed in this analysis measures the degree to which each law student respondent has internalized the traditional ethical standards of the legal profession as set down by the American Bar Association's (ABA) *Canons of Professional Ethics*.[17] Six scenarios, each conveying a different ethical conflict for practicing lawyers, were presented to the respondents for their reaction. The scenarios counterposed the concepts of client confidentiality, colleague loyalty, personal achievement, and principles of formal law. Respondents were scored by the frequency with which their answers reflected ethical values based on the ABA's ethical code.

Ninety-six questionnaires were completed providing a self-selected sample that did not appear particularly biased or skewed. A majority of the questionnaires were distributed to first year law students and they constitute 53.9% of the respondents. In terms of financial status, 79.5% rated themselves as upper-middle or middle class on a subjective scale. For a prestigious urban law school, this percentage is probably an accurate reflection of the entire student population. As for the personality characteristics of the volunteer respondent sample, they are fairly similar to a much larger group of students from the same university, that was surveyed on an involuntary basis.[18]

Findings

The first question asked is whether Kohlberg's instrument, in fact, distinguishes between an internally derived motivation and an orientation motivated by external controls and restraints. In other words, is Kohlberg's instrument a valid measure of the concepts of internal and external control? A difference of means test was performed by dividing the sample into two subgroups: those in Kohlberg's Stages 1 through 4 were hypothesized to be externally controlled types, and respondents in Stages 5 and 6 were assumed to be controlled by internal self-control.

The means for each personality need measured by Stein's SDQ were calculated for these two subgroups to determine if there are relevant personality differences between the internally and externally motivated person. Of the 20 needs measured by the SDQ, three indicate a statistically significant difference between the internally and externally controlled groups. Externally motivated types tend to have higher needs for *abasement* – to submit passively to external forces – and for *rejection* to avoid people who may be threatening to one's position. Internally controlled persons tend to have significantly higher needs for *affiliation* to cooperate, trust, and befriend others.

These results tend to validate the use of Kohlberg's measure as a means of identifying externally from internally motivated orientations. Not only is each orientation related to different personality traits, which suggests deep-seated differences in their socialized roots, the personality needs also distinguish in a reasonable and substantively understandable way between the internal and external control concepts. Externally motivated types tend to be defeatists, resigned to control by external authority, and rejecting of personal relationships that pose a potential external threat. Internally controlled persons are humanistic, enjoy the companionship of others, and respect their rights and free will.

As expected, given the bias in legal education in favor of external control and the importance of peer relationships and schooling as socialization mechanisms,[19] the majority of law students in the sample (73%) fell into the externally motivated category. Only 25 respondents (27%) were internally controlled according to Kohlberg's measure. There were insignificant differences between male and female breakdowns on this variable.

Socialization of internal and external motivation was also found to be related to attitudes of law students concerning legal ethics at a statistically significant level. Sixty-four percent of externally motivated types tend to place low to moderate value on the ethical standards of the legal profession. Sixty percent of internally controlled persons, on the other hand, attach a greater sense of value to legal ethical norms.

This analysis resulted in three major findings:

- Kohlberg's Moral Judgment Interview and typology of moral development stages appear to be a valid means of identifying and distinguishing among internally controlled (autonomous) persons and externally motivated (heteronomous) persons.
- A substantial majority of law students who were sampled appear to be externally motivated persons.
- Those law students who were internally controlled had a significantly higher regard for legal ethics than students who were motivated by external control and restraints. The two hypotheses stated earlier have not been disconfirmed.

What are the implications of these findings for the legal profession? If the law continues either to attract externally motivated persons into its ranks or socialize them through the educational process, the long-term consequences for restoring ethical standards and renewing public trust are not optimistic.

Externally motivated persons are kept in line by fear of punishment, authority, and regulation. Enforcement of legal ethics is relevant to these individuals only if it ensures that negative and harmful consequences will be averted. It is obvious that neither the legal profession nor society can or should provide an external watchdog to monitor each action of every attorney. Developing self-discipline and a sense of internal self-control among lawyers is the only way to ensure a healthy future for the legal profession.

Remedies to this dilemma can take two paths. First, a conscious public relations and face-lifting effort can be pursued to alter the marred image of the legal profession. The objective of such actions would be to weed out the highly unethical types and attempt to attract a new breed of ethically sensitive persons into the profession. This appears to be the path that is currently being taken.[20] Such actions will probably do some good for the legal profession, but will leave much to chance given the vagaries of the selection, self-selection, and recruitment processes for law students.

A second path involves a more fundamental change in the orientation of legal socialization. Greater emphasis must be placed on developing humanistic perspectives and flexibility in the structure of the law. Rather than remaining a bastion of rigid and highly static rules and regulations, the law should become society's *source* of change and innovation. The law should be more adaptable and compassionate than at present to different human circumstances and needs. What is considered just should be relative to the persons, situations, and times. Moreover, this change process should be spontaneous and free of red tape, abstruse procedures, and excessive time lags that are characteristic of the current legal system. Such an organic and humanistic system of law is likely to attract and socialize more autonomous and internally self-disciplined persons through the legal education process. Hopefully, the outcome of this process will be the development of more ethical lawyers and an improved legal system.

What do these findings suggest for stemming corruption in the civil service? First, practical actions can be taken to screen for ethical persons coming to government service through a strengthened recruitment selection process for civil servants. Second, once in government service, improved behavioral training can be provided on ethical behavior and codes of conduct, along with the strengthening of monitoring and oversight. Third, greater emphasis can be exerted to promote situations where civil servants can put themselves in other people's shoes to encourage greater empathy with the citizens that they serve.

Recruitment of ethical persons

It is easier to work with honest persons in government to resist the lure of corruption than to discourage corrupt opportunists in government from abusing their positions.[21] Experimental research conducted in India concludes, unfortunately, that people with a greater propensity to cheat have a stronger interest in getting government jobs.[22] Cheating or not was not related to the recruit's abilities, so it appears to be important to screen candidates on a honesty-dishonesty dimension, as well as for their technical abilities. So, how can you develop mechanisms for detecting persons with unethical beliefs from being appointed or selected for government office? And how can you attract ethical persons to government positions at all levels?

Some screening mechanisms, perhaps similar to the Kohlberg scenarios, can be used along with other tests and interview approaches to weed out those who do not have some basic level of ethical awareness. Over the longer term, as government becomes more trusted by the public as an institution free of corruption, public awareness campaigns can be used to promote public service as an appropriate employer of ethical persons.

Case study: Indonesia

In Indonesia, a USAID-sponsored program called CEGAH ("prevent" in English) embarked on a new area of programming to assist the Ministry of Administrative and Bureaucratic Reform (KemenPAN-RB) and other government agencies in charge of civil service affairs to prevent the growth of radicalization in the civil service.[23] Across several tasks, this program worked to design measures that ensure that prospective civil servant candidates are adequately screened for radical ideologies. The project developed an instrument known as the Tolerance and Pluralism Awareness/Attitude Test (TePAT) for use in the existing civil servant recruitment system. The instrument assesses applicants' attitudes against the obligations found under Law No.5/2014 on Civil Servants, which include nondiscriminatory provisions of public services and support for the national ideology, *Pancasila*.

In its initial implementation, TePAT was adopted into the recruitment processes of six ministries/agencies, and was used to screen more than 33,000 applicants for civil servant positions. USAID CEGAH devised an additional version of the TePAT instrument that utilized a written exam rather than an interview process. This revision allowed the tool to be deployed at the Ministry of Villages, Disadvantaged Regions and Transmigration (Kemendesa) and the Ministry of Manpower (Kemenaker), where it was used to screen a combined total of 759 new civil servants who were still in their probationary period.

While this recruitment test does not target ethical awareness or attitudes, it is a good example of how such an ethical values tool could be designed and used during the application process for civil servant positions as a screening mechanism early in the recruitment process. It can be applied to set a certain threshold for mindfulness of ethical principles, as well as to help develop appropriate ethics training for existing and future government officials that focuses on the areas where stronger socialization is needed. In fact, Indonesia's Corruption Eradication Commission (KPK) has added integrity tests, in addition to competence and psychometric profiles, to its online recruitment system for all candidates. Unlike the other tests, a perfect integrity score is required for candidates to proceed in the recruitment process.[24]

Socialization of ethics

Occupational training in ethical behavior for civil servants – on a recurring basis – should be instituted focused on implementing codes of conduct and ethics in a practical sense. Training of the basic principles, attitudes, and actions of ethical behavior need to be at the core of these sessions, but it is important to make them more than just academic exercises. In addition, monitoring of civil servant behavior and accountability in relation to public complaints needs to be a continuing activity by management to ensure that ethical behavior becomes the norm in government activity.

Case study: Indonesia

Again, referring to the USAID-sponsored Indonesia project mentioned above, training in ethical behavior for civil servants has become a prominent activity. The project supported the State Civil Apparatus Commission (KASN), which has a mandate to supervise civil servants through codes of ethics and conduct, and the application of merit system policies and management.[25] The project implemented an e-learning system to train ethics for mid-level civil servants, local government staff, selection committees, and local staffing agencies. Courses included training on the merit system and senior career staff selection. Through this e-learning platform, training is able to reach the more than 4 million civil servants throughout the country and is more amenable to rapid adjustments as policy and regulations change.

Another USAID-sponsored project continued ethics training support for the Corruption Eradication Commission's (KPK) Anti-Corruption Learning Center, targeting the Ministry of State-Owned Enterprises.[26] It developed in-class training and e-learning modules for Inspection Units on corruption crimes law, corporate criminal liability, conflicts of interest, gift management, and whistleblowing. With the rising number of corruption cases involving state-owned business in Indonesia, increasing the capacity of inspection units to detect and prevent corruption within their organization is crucial to improve the operations of the organization, reduce corruption, and promote overall economic growth and development.

Working with the Indonesian Ministry of Administrative and Bureaucratic Reform, this USAID project also provided technical advice and organized workshops to develop a set of guidelines on "Integrity Strengthening for Civil Servants." The guidelines provide supervisors at every government working unit with recommended actions to build the integrity of civil servants under their supervision. The guidelines were enacted via regulation after being formally endorsed by the Ministry of Law and Human Rights. The integrity guidelines will be used to socialize government staff and build integrity zones and corruption-free work spaces in ministries and agencies.

From the monitoring/accountability perspective, the USAID project developed an approach to monitor civil servant ethics code violations, particularly regarding civil servant neutrality in the 2019 elections.[27] Maintaining neutrality during election periods has historically proven to be a tough challenge for civil servants, in part because the use of government resources for partisan purposes is a clear violation of prevailing regulations, while prohibitions of other behaviors, such as personal endorsements, are less known. The program developed a civil servant neutrality monitoring program, identified discriminatory practices in public service delivery, and promoted online tools for citizens to report such ethics code violations. These efforts encouraged public participation.

A monitoring manual was devised to lay out different types of ethics code violations and tools to submit complaints. Trainings were conducted for both government staff and civil society organizations. Once trained, these participants used what they learned to monitor social media, particularly using Facebook, for potential ethics code violations. The CSOs who attended the training also utilized their networks of student volunteers to monitor lecturers from public universities and urged teachers to remain neutral in the elections. Press conferences and the news media were used to publicize monitoring results and ensure that violations were not brushed under the rug. During the preelection period, 89 reports of suspected violations were filed.

Another activity of this project developed a self-assessment method to monitor the implementation of a merit system in civil service management within government agencies.[28] It allows managers to determine which institutions have done well and those that are struggling in the implementation of the merit system.

Promoting empathy

It is clearly problematic to expect ethical behavior from persons who are born into a traditionally corrupt society and socialized throughout their lives that to get things done you have to activate corrupt transactions. A first step to resocialize civil servants in such straits is to promote in them a sense of empathy for those who are victims of corruption. Practical efforts can attempt to put civil servants into the shoes of ordinary citizens who are victimized using simulations, getting them to empathize with the victims and asking them to imagine how they would feel if they were on the other side of a corrupt transaction.

One approach that is becoming popular for instilling empathy is community-oriented policing, where officers focus on developing relationships with community members, to understand their issues, problems, and desires. Applying this type of policing, officers are assigned to patrol a particular area for a prolonged period of time, allowing them to feel a partnership with citizens. They use strategies that tackle the root causes of neighborhood crime in a manner that builds trust in law enforcement. Through shared problem solving, the police and community members work together to devise ways to prevent crime. Another approach to instill empathy in some societies might be to appeal to cultural/religious ethical beliefs that denigrate corruption.

Case studies: Indonesia and Afghanistan

A USAID-sponsored project in Indonesia reached out to Islamic boarding schools in the Greater Jakarta area to train teachers, administrators, and students on practical anti-corruption issues, especially from an Islamic perspective.[29] The training evolved into an introspective exercise to assess how corrupt practices affect the schools directly. In another USAID program, the Indonesian government reached out to influential faith-based organizations to build their engagement in anti-corruption efforts.[30] The Corruption Eradication Commission (KPK), with support from the program, worked with Indonesia's largest Muslim organization, Nahdlatul Ulama (NU), whose broad base of support and progressive political outlook make it an attractive partner in the struggle against corruption. Targeted anti-corruption training modules were developed and presented to NU's leadership, clerics, and school administrators on transparency and accountability within their own organization, as well as on how to incorporate anti-graft messages into religious sermons.

In Afghanistan, another USAID-sponsored project reached out to the ulema, a body of Muslim scholars recognized as having specialist knowledge of Islamic sacred law and theology, who regularly vocalize their concerns about how corruption is eating away at the moral and ethical values of the Afghan society.[31] They appeared ready and willing to join others to proactively speak out against pervasive corruption in Afghanistan. Plans were developed to solicit help from the ulema in spreading the anti-corruption message through their sermons. They agreed that such sermons from such a powerful force in society would carry special significance.

Expected results

The outcomes and impacts of such ethical strategies can be measured and reported in a fairly straightforward way. For example,

- The recruitment of more ethical persons to government positions can be monitored by conducting periodic testing of civil servants to determine the ethical (or unethical) drivers of their decisions and actions.

- More focused efforts to socialize ethics among civil servants – and the society as a whole – can be monitored over time through the same testing of government staff, as well as in schools to assess progress made in socializing the next generation.
- Progress in efforts to promote empathy for those potentially victimized citizens can be monitored by testing civil servants and sampling citizens on a regular basis using scenarios of how they would react to victimized citizens seeking public services.

Notes

1 Oliver Wendell Holmes (1897). "The Path of Law," *Harvard Law Review* 10: 457.
2 Edward Weisband and Thomas Franck (1975). *Resignation in Protest: Political and Ethical Choices between Loyalty to Team and Loyalty to Conscience in American Public Life.* New York: Grossman Publishers.
3 Ibid.
4 J. Piaget (1965). *The Moral Judgment of the Child.* New York: Free Press.
5 L. Kohlberg (1964). "Development of Moral Character and Moral Ideology," in M.L. Hoffman and L.W. Hoffman (eds.) *Review of Child Development Research* (Vol. 1, pp. 381–431). New York: Russell Sage Foundation; L. Kohlberg (1969). "Stages and Sequence: The Cognitive-Developmental Approach to Socialization," in D. Goslin (ed.) *Handbook of Socialization Theory and Research* (pp. 347–480). Chicago: Rand McNally.
6 L. Kohlberg and R. Kramer (1969). "Continuities and Discontinuities in Childhood and Adult Moral Development," *Human Development* 12, 2: 93–120.
7 S. Milgram (1974). *Obedience to Authority.* New York: Harper and Row.
8 Kohlberg (1964), op.cit.
9 L. Kohlberg and P. Scharf (1972). "Bureaucratic Violence and Conventional Moral Thinking," *American Journal of Orthopsychiatry* 42: 294–295; Milgram (1974), op.cit.
10 See the Moral Judgment Interview in Kohlberg (1964), op.cit.
11 See the Self-Description Questionnaire in Morris Stein (1963) "Explorations in Typology," in R. White, editor, *The Study of Lives* (pp. 280–303). New York: Atherton Press.
12 Piaget (1965), op.cit.
13 Kohlberg (1969), op.cit.
14 Henry Murray (1938). *Explorations in Personality.* New York: John Wiley and Sons.
15 Morris Stein and J. Neulinger (1968). "A Typology of Self-Descriptions," in M. Katz, et al., editors, *The Role and Methodology of Classification in Psychiatry and Psychopathology* (pp. 390–403). Washington, DC: GPO, No. 1584.
16 Stein and Neulinger (1968), op.cit.; Morris Stein (1971). "Ecology of Typology," Paper presented at the Association of American Medical Colleges Conference on Personality Measurement in Medical Education, Des Plaines, IL.
17 This scale was developed by Joseph H. Moskowitz.
18 Stein and Neulinger (1968), op.cit.
19 Kohlberg, L. (1958). "The Development of Modes of Moral Thinking and Choice in Years 10 to 16." Ph.D. dissertation. University of Chicago.
20 *U.S. News and World Report* (1977). "Lawyers – Can They Police Themselves?" (June 6).

21 Matthew Stephenson (2014). "The Importance of Personnel Selection in Promoting Government Integrity: Some Evidence from India." *The Global Anti-Corruption Blog* (June 26). At: https://globalanticorruptionblog.com/2014/06/26/the-importance-of-personnel-selection-in-promoting-government-integrity-some-evidence-from-india/.

22 Rema Hanna and Shing-Yi Wang (2013). Dishonesty and Selection into Public Service, Working Paper 19649. Washington, DC: National Bureau of Economic Research. At: https://www.nber.org/papers/w19649.

23 Management Systems International (2019). *USAID CEGAH Project, Annual Report FY 2019*. Washington, DC: USAID.

24 Gabriel Kuris (2012). *Inviting a Tiger into Your Home: Indonesia Creates an Anticorruption Commission with Teeth, 2002–2007*. Princeton, NJ: Innovations for Successful Societies. At: https://successfulsocieties.princeton.edu/sites/successfulsocieties/files/Policy_Note_ID211.pdf.

25 MSI (2019), op.cit.

26 Management Systems International (2020). *USAID CEGAH Project, Annual Report FY 2020*. Washington, DC: USAID.

27 MSI (2019), op.cit.

28 MSI (2020), op.cit.

29 Ibid.

30 Management Systems International (2016). *Strengthening Integrity and Accountability Program I (SIAP-1), Final Report*. Washington, DC: USAID.

31 Management Systems International (2013). *Assistance for Afghanistan's Anti-Corruption Authority (4A) Project, Final Report*. Washington, DC: USAID.

9 The social psychological lens

Looking at corruption through a rational choice, economic cost-benefit lens provides a simple, straightforward explanation of this kind of behavior. People are motivated to behave in a way that accrues to their own advantage or that of their friends and family. They make their decisions and act upon them based on calculations that maximize rewards, while minimizing risks.

Another explanation has us look at psychological factors that motivate or demotivate corrupt actions. Researchers focus on three critical areas: how we *rationalize* corrupt behaviors in a way to avoid true explanations, the effects of *social norms and group conformity* that keep corruption sustainable, and *risk aversion* by obedience to managerial oversight. A range of practical behavioral change initiatives that emerge from these social psychological categories are discussed below. They include conducting oversight, with the fear of naming and shaming; reminding people of their engrained moral standards; using investigative reporting by the media to expose senior officials and societal leaders, thus diminishing their position as respected role models; and constant supervision and external monitoring by citizens and government.

Rationalization

Corrupt officials often explain and justify their dishonest behaviors by rationalizing their actions and making excuses for those behaviors to defend themselves. In most surveys in countries across the world, the public says that they disapprove of corruption, but they accept it as a norm of life. They justify acting corruptly by citing several explanations.[1] One such rationalization is that corruption is such a common occurrence in everyday life that they do not view it as bad or special, but just commonplace – the way things are typically done. Everybody else does it, so it must be OK.

Another rationalization for corrupt actions is that you do not view these behaviors as causing harm to others; from your perspective, corruption has no harmful consequences or they are significantly remote or abstract. If this is the case, then what could be wrong with acting corruptly? You can do it because you believe that there is nothing bad that comes of it. The larger

DOI: 10.4324/9781003241119-11

public does not consider corruption corrupt if it does them good. For example, a recent survey in Ukraine indicates that a majority of citizens identify grand corruption as harmful, but considers petty corruption as offering a reasonable way to secure needed public services with a high degree of certainty and ease in a context of red tape and inefficiencies.[2]

Another rationalized excuse is that corruption happens only because of a few rogue actors, not because of widespread contagious acceptance. Just the few who are "infected" are responsible for the misdeeds, not the larger population.[3] An additional reason for committing corruption is that most people are "intermittent moral actors." They act in an ethical way much of the time, but are easily driven by instinctive thinking at the moment if there is an immediate problem that needs to be resolved. This immediate issue might require dishonesty, but that is OK because it is just a small disclaimer.[4]

The rationalization lens has another more complex dimension: our motivation to view ourselves as being honest, even as we act corruptly. Ariely's book on the origins of honesty and dishonesty examines engrained human behaviors of cheating and deceit through a review of the literature and a series of laboratory experiments, and finds that there are several psychological reasons that can activate or deter us from corrupt behaviors.[5]

Ariely finds that we constrain our natural urges to cheat and be dishonest if we are confronted with the probability of getting caught or being punished for our acts, thereby being publicly shamed for our bad behavior. The experiments show that we want to retain our self-image of being honest and upright, but if there is a strong possibility that "the cat will be let out of the bag" and it becomes publicly known that we have cheated or lied, we will constrain ourselves, because we view ourselves – and we want others to view us – as being honest. Interestingly, the data show that persons are willing to cheat to a certain level and then will stop, like the intermittent moral actor described above, just before they believe others will find out or they consider themselves going over the line. The human instinct is to achieve the benefits of dishonesty as much as we can, while still rationalizing that we are honest beings.

What is important in reducing cheating and corruption is understanding how we rationalize our behavior, and what makes us uncomfortable about cheating or lying. Certainly, we can develop or strengthen some practical solutions that include control mechanisms, such as the laws and rules we live by and institutions that are supposed to guide our actions. While such controls will structure our environment and how we behave in part, there is little evidence that strict enforcement of laws, extensive oversight, and zero tolerance policies, along with more transparency, will work well to reduce cheating or corrupt acts. This is what Ariely found in his experiments and this is what has been demonstrated by the real-world anti-corruption examples described in earlier chapters. People sometimes seek out the rational, economic benefits versus costs, but their actions are more influenced by how they view themselves and how they rationalize their actions.

What seems to be effective in preventing dishonesty, based on Ariely's experiments, is if persons refer back to a set of moral standards, like ethical codes and what is considered to be right and wrong behavior. Similarly, in other experiments, corrupt behavior drops significantly when participants receive short anti-corruption pitches prior to engaging in the experiment's simulation.[6]

In the end, Ariely concludes that people want to be honest because that is how they view themselves.[7] But they are tempted by many things to be dishonest. Experimental results suggest that what may work are reminders about moral behavior at the moment of temptation, combating the social contagion of cheating, and avoiding conflicts of interest.

Case studies: Indonesia and Afghanistan

In Chapter 7, the Citizen Advocate Office (CAO) was described, variants of which have now been implemented in over 100 countries, thanks to Transparency International. These are legal offices that seek quick administrative resolution of citizen complaints about corruption, rather than legal court hearings. One of the incentives for corrupt officials to comply with the CAO is to avoid the public "naming and shaming" that typically accompanies a public court case, especially when the incident occurred within a local community where everyone knows everyone else. The corrupt officials' rationalization that they are only doing their jobs and are honest at heart can be maintained if they agree to the CAO's demands to stop past abusive behaviors.

In Indonesia, based on complaints from teachers, the CAO helped to investigate and document extortion schemes involving the operational fees for early childhood education in one district and teachers' allowances at the Religious Affairs Office in another district.[8] The CAO team's investigation found that the case of kindergarten extortion affected 299 kindergartens, with government officials seeking kickbacks of 10% on operational budgets. The CAO's demands succeeded in the return of approximately US$ 14,000 to the originally intended recipients, allowing 7,475 students and 879 teachers to resume their regular classroom activities. Results in the case at the Religious Affairs Office were even more impressive, with approximately US$ 140,000 being returned to 3,700 contract-based teachers.

In Afghanistan, when a small business taxpayer went to pay his annual tax of about US$ 100, the tax officer in the Tax Department demanded an extra US$ 65.[9] When the taxpayer refused to pay, the officer told him that he would not receive an official receipt. The taxpayer believed that complaining himself to a government office would be a waste of time. As a result, the taxpayer just paid the tax plus extorted fee and obtained the tax receipt. However, the receipt only showed a payment of US$ 65. He felt cheated. Then he saw a CAO poster and visited the office immediately, conveying his story to a lawyer. The lawyer accompanied the taxpayer to the tax office and demanded the extorted money back. The tax officer claimed that he did not take any bribe. But the CAO lawyer explained that unless he returned the money, he would refer the case to the Attorney General's Office and, if convicted, the officer would not only have to return the money but would likely go to prison, lose his job, and bring shame on himself. The tax officer immediately recanted, returned the bribe, and promised not to take bribes in the future.

Naming, with the potential for shaming, has been shown to be an effective approach for resolving and reforming corrupt transactions. It blows up the rationalization excuse that demanding bribes for public services is acceptable behavior. By confronting the corrupt officials directly, and sometimes their supervisors as well, with the reality of how corrupt actions victimize citizens, the rationalization of their actions is struck down, the bribe payments are returned to the victims, and, in many cases, bureaucratic processes are reformed to prevent such behaviors in the future. The CAO model has demonstrated that across many countries it can resolve the majority of its cases successfully and rapidly using this naming and shaming mechanism.

Social norms and group conformity

There is an infectious nature to cheating and corruption. If we see other people doing it, it can become socially acceptable in our own eyes. We can rationalize dishonesty if we believe that everybody else does it and therefore if we imitate that same behavior, it is not our fault.[10] People in many countries have lived their lives seeing corruption and abuse of power as the norm and their role models have reinforced this belief. It's hard for them to see alternative ways of behaving. With this mindset, citizens become complicit with officials' use of corrupt practices. It seems acceptable to use corruption to benefit themselves, friends, and family – even to the detriment of others. And officials will continue to use corrupt ways for self-benefit because they've seen many of their managers and colleagues do it with impunity, fearing no detection or punishment.

This social contagion of corruption can be easily spread throughout communities by traditional and social media, through membership organizations, from family behavior, and simply by just observing how most others act in society. It becomes a part of one's social identity. As a member of a corrupt government or a corrupt society, we need to be complicit with how others behave because we need to conform to the predominant identity of the group.

Such group conformity is spurred on by social norms that represent mutual expectations held by members of a group about the right way to behave in particular situations.[11] The pull of these norms is that people want to fit in, belong and get the respect of the group. When you are a member of the group, there is collective social pressure to sustain the values and actions.

When conforming to social norms that enable and drive corrupt behaviors, they can become a normalized way of life – with impacts on both the supply and demand sides of corruption. And these norms can trump all other aspects of robust integrity systems or attempts for positive behavior change.

Closely intertwined with social norms and values are the social networks you engage with that embrace these shared norms and values.[12] If these norms and networks are linked to corrupt values and behaviors, they generate a sense of obligation and reciprocity that legitimizes corruption. Typically, you are expected to help close family and friends. If you are in a position of power, you are especially expected to benefit your network more broadly. This normalizes bribery, gift giving, nepotism, and favoritism. You are also expected to coverup and/or rationalize the corrupt activity for the sake of your social network. Even in response to anti-corruption initiatives, these corrupt social networks appear to evolve and adjust over time to preserve their power, wealth, benefits, and control over their membership.

Researchers view group conformity as a type of loyalty and commitment to the larger group.[13] If someone else in one's close circle, especially if they are in management, is acting in a corrupt manner, then it is acceptable – even incumbent upon others – to follow suit. People often act like lemmings – blind followers – when it comes to loyal group behavior, even when it is clearly unethical.

Within business organizations, corporate cultural factors can promote group conformity to corrupt behavior. Leaders of corrupt organizations often see themselves as fighting a war, where "the end justifies the means," and where corruption is seen as reasonable if it gets you what you want.[14] Researchers identify additional ways that corrupt behavior can infect corporations and produce widespread conformity with these practices.[15] If management decides and acts in a corrupt way, members of the organization typically become complicit with the organizational trend by denying or rationalizing those corrupt behaviors. They use language and processes that normalize or legitimize unethical behavior. And within complex organizations, like government, it is easier to diffuse individual accountability for such actions.

Case study: Ukraine

Investigative journalism is a primary tool for detecting and exposing corruption, but it can also be an effective vehicle for influencing and adjusting long-held social beliefs and norms about corrupt behaviors. In 2006, investigative reporting by major media outlets about corruption issues was relatively rare in Ukraine. The USAID-sponsored ACTION project (2006–09) implemented targeted support for investigative journalism to bolster the media's role as public watchdog.[16] More than 700 journalists, editors, and media owners received capacity building training and participated in workshops concerning the value of investigative journalism about corruption issues. During the ACTION project, investigative journalists produced many corruption-related reports. 63.9% of these reports went on to be further investigated by the authorities and 27.2% of those investigations were brought to court. Of the media's reports on corruption, 10.8% resulted in judicial decisions for conviction and 46.8% yielded administrative sanctions against corrupt officials.

Investigative reporting can serve to counter the contagion effect of corrupt behavior that we see throughout society. By digging down to the hard and indisputable evidence, this type of journalistic endeavor seeks to show that these abusive practices are wrong, against the law, against ethical norms, and do real harm to the victims, who are typically just ordinary citizens. These reports can show that following and copying the behavior of corrupt role models and networks is not a positive act. While corruption may be deeply embedded in social norms and interactions, it is deleterious to ethical behavior and economic progress. The public nature of investigative journalism, which uses traditional print and broadcast media, but also newer social media to spread the investigative findings, can have an important impact on changing negative social norms and the networks that promote them.

Here are a few examples of investigative reporting that were accomplished under this project. One journalistic investigation resulted in allegations about extortion for school contributions and presents for teachers faced by parents and students. The journalists questioned several dozen sources – students, teachers, parents, members of parent boards, school principals, and teachers. They also surveyed 300 parents of school children in the affected district. Based on their findings, professional sociologists were engaged by the city Department of Education to conduct training for school heads on "character building" to change these corrupt social norms. In addition, an order was issued that prevents the collection of funds by school staff and their use without proper reporting.

Another investigative reporting effort inquired into who received land plots allocated by the city council free-of-charge between 2006 and 2009. In a series of articles entitled "Two Hectares of Impudence," the journalist described the stories of ordinary citizens who attempted to receive their land plots of 10,000 square meters, pursuant to the law, but were unable to do so. At the same time, members of the city council and their families had no difficulty registering for the land titles. The investigation examined schemes used by the officials and town council members for land privatization. In particular, the case of the Deputy Mayor drew the attention of the oblast Prosecutor's Office. The prosecutor filed a protest against the allocation of land to the official. During the nearly year-long investigation, the local Department of Land Resources refused to provide any information to the newspaper's editorial office about applicants for land plots and it denied the existence of a land plots database. The most difficult task was to find a connection between the false names used in city council resolutions and specific officials and city council members. However, despite all these difficulties, the perpetrators were exposed. The investigative report was very popular with readers and the newspaper has not encountered any legal repercussions from officials.

As demonstrated here, the strategic use of investigative reporting can have a critical impact on the viability of social norms by outing mid- and high-level officials and their networks, showing up the negative aspects of their behaviors, and destroying their position as role models for others. Over time, when such examples are widely publicized, they can have an important effect on refuting even long-held social norms and behaviors.

Risk aversion

Some researchers have found that even if the risks of committing bribery are perceived to be high – including punishment – it is an "after the fact" risk.[17] The rewards of committing corruption can be achieved and who knows if you will be caught? As a result, the mere probability of detection is not always a good way to stop corruption from happening in the future.

At the same time, there are some risks that are more certain when behaving corruptly that you may want to avert. The knowledge that every action you perform within your organization is being watched carefully by management or auditors can inhibit bad behavior. In fact, actual oversight may not be necessary, just a warning that you may be watched and your behavior evaluated could be enough to increase honesty.[18] Experiments have shown that being closely observed and supervised eliminates cheating. When the supervisor is physically present, cheating stops. However, when the supervisor leaves and you are just in the presence of coworkers, the cheating will continue. These findings by Ariely are corroborated by other experiments.[19] But overall, just the presence of another person – whether or not they are a supervisor – can be a potent remedy to curb corruption and cheating levels.

External oversight is also an option. The actions of whistleblowers and social auditors, and the publicity accompanying their charges that may expose dishonesty and corrupt behaviors, can turn things around. Averting the risk of being outed publicly within your community is a powerful incentive to curb your corruption. Whistleblowers and social auditors can have a positive effect on social morality, and stave off cheating and lying, by demonstrating and publicizing evidence of corruption and showing it off to be bad from a moral perspective.

Citizens and government need to initiate proactive and sustainable supervisory and oversight tactics. At the heart of these approaches is making it clear that public servants are being watched and any corrupt or abusive practices will be detected, addressed, and punished. They will be made to account to the public. Oversight can be conducted by government bodies through internal control units within departments or ministries, by supreme audit bodies or by inspector general offices. External watchdogs can also be established by citizen groups using social audit and accountability techniques. Transparency and open data approaches can provide citizens with a clear idea of how government decisions are being made and how public funds are being spent.

What should be done with the information collected by oversight groups? It needs to be put to use in very transparent ways to reduce corruption and/or punish abusers. The media can be mobilized to publish investigative reports. Citizen review boards can be set up within agencies to examine and act upon the resulting information. Citizen complaint systems can be used to rectify uncovered problems with assured follow-up and feedback. In some cases, negative incentives – such as naming and shaming – can produce quick and effective results, but positive incentives like bonuses and awards are preferable when honest behavior is observed. Ultimately, formal investigations leading to legal proceedings can be initiated to indict and convict corrupt officials. Sometimes, just the threat of predictable punishment can have an immediate effect on putting a halt to corruption abuses.

Case study: Indonesia

The USAID-sponsored Strengthening Integrity and Accountability Program (SIAP-1) in Indonesia (2011–16) targeted many of its initiatives at strengthening monitoring and oversight of government officials, both internally and externally, to ensure accountability to the public.[20] With a higher probability of being detected, exposed, and punished for corrupt acts as a result of improved oversight, it was felt that officials would be more likely to engage in risk averse decisions and behaviors.

Performance Audits. One important area of attention was to strengthen performance audits conducted by government auditors and offer a way to measure government accountability. These audits serve as a key monitoring element in any effort to tackle corruption. Unlike financial audits, which focus on the verification of financial statements from government institutions, performance audits assess the effectiveness and efficiency of government programs and uncover any potential fraud, abuse, and corruption.

While the Indonesian Supreme Audit Board (BPK) – the nation's independent audit institution – has the authority to conduct performance audits, the relative novelty and underutilization of the performance audit approach had left staff unprepared to bring this important measure of oversight and accountability to bear. By upgrading and promoting this official form of oversight, the corruptors may decide to avert the risks and costs they will face for being uncovered when conducting dishonest behavior.

A comprehensive training curriculum in performance auditing was developed and conducted for over 175 BPK auditors, enabling them to investigate the root causes of corrupt behaviors that can impede government programs from achieving their ultimate objectives. Within three years after the project's support for performance audits began, impressive results were achieved. The BPK conducted 168 performance audits in 2012, but by the end of 2015, that figure rose to 282 performance audits, an increase of 68%. In the subsequent USAID program, capacity building in performance audit techniques was expanded to include Indonesia's Inspectorate General units.

Citizen Watchdogs. In another set of activities, the SIAP-1 project turned to enhancing the capacity of citizen watchdog groups as external sources of monitoring and oversight – in this case, concerning money in politics. Like many developing countries, political parties in Indonesia are characterized by a lack of ideological consistency, the dominance of personalistic leadership, and a lack of financial transparency. As one of the few institutions to avoid deep and meaningful reforms in the post-Suharto democratic transition, political parties' lack of openness and frequent involvement in corruption scandals has led to abysmally low levels of public trust. Political parties often rely on the financial resources of small groups of influential business players in a transactional form of politics that provides them with an undue amount of influence over policy decisions, largely outside of the public view.

The SIAP-1 project, along with several local partners, launched a campaign to strengthen public access to information and to provide greater oversight of political parties. Requests for financial reports from many political parties in several regions of the country were made by citizen watchdog groups to assess the parties' use of public subsidies they received from the central and provincial governments. When parties failed to respond, the watchdogs resorted to mediation performed by local Information Commissions to seek resolution to these citizen information requests. The majority of political parties released their financial reports as a result of this pressure.

While legal loopholes and loose enforcement of existing legislation remain important challenges, acclimating political parties to the need for financial openness was a relatively new activity in the country at the time. These citizen watchdogs were able to increase political party transparency by bringing this financial information to the public and they then acted to verify this information to hold political parties accountable. The result was a heightened sense of oversight and risk aversion by political parties, focusing their attention on building public trust rather than on pursuing fraudulent activities.

Mystery Shopper. Yet another risk aversion activity pursued by the SIAP-1 project was adapting and implementing the "mystery shopper tool" that has been borrowed from the private sector. This tool is used to monitor and analyze the integrity of employees. Mystery shoppers typically pose as employees or customers to collect data on attempts by other employees to commit theft or other activities that could harm the organization. Working with the Indonesian Ombudsman's Office and the Ministry of Administrative and Bureaucratic Reform, SIAP-1 adapted the mystery shopper tool to monitor the quality of service delivery implementation by government agencies. It was used as an investigative mechanism to detect corrupt activities related to port dwelling times, new student enrollment fees, subsidized diesel fuel distribution for fishermen, haj management, business licensing services, standard operating procedures for police interrogations, civil servant salaries, teacher transfers, unofficial processing fees for civil registry documents, and labor disputes, among others.

Using this monitoring mechanism allows government officials to observe civil servants under natural circumstances, compared to more formal procedural audits and reviews, thus offering an important new perspective on the quality of services being delivered to the public. Because of the rigorous methodology and the strong evidence collected, including audiovisual recordings, the heads of government units readily accepted the findings and the recommendations derived from the mystery shopper approach.

Using mystery shopper oversight, government teams identified the use of middlemen that were used to "expedite" regulatory processes through extortion. Agencies confronted with this evidence admitted that this is a challenge and are taking steps to address it. There are lots of other findings from the field, including a number of less-than-ethical behaviors that need to be reviewed and reformed. This tool is not so much about criminal investigations, but is about on-the-spot monitoring of how public services are provided to citizens and how corruption is sometimes part of that process. With these inputs, government has the information needed to improve policy and implement change to eliminate the opportunities for corruption. And when government officials know they may be monitored for their actions, they are more likely to avert the risk of being detected and will operate honestly.

Expected results

The outcomes and impacts of these social psychological strategies can be measured and reported. For example, testing of civil servants and school students can be conducted on a periodic basis using focused scenarios that assess how and if they agree with rationalizing dishonesty or are willing to copy the bad behavior of others to abide by traditional social norms and conform to group ways. In addition, the willingness to avert corruption risks can be monitored by analyzing the results of social audits, investigative reporting, citizen complaints, and government audits.

Notes

1 Anusha Pamula (2015). "The Social Psychology of Corruption," *The Global Anti-Corruption Blog* (August 28). At: https://globalanticorruptionblog.com/2015/08/28/the-social-psychology-of-corruption-lack-thereof/.

2 USAID(2018). "NationalAnti-CorruptionSurvey,December5." At:https://dif.org.ua/article/kozhna-tretya-ukrainkaets-gotovi-doluchitisya-do-organizovanoi-protidii-koruptsii.

3 John M. Darley (2005). "The Cognitive and Social Psychology of the Contagious Organizational Corruption," *Brooklyn Law Review* 70. At: https://brooklynworks.brooklaw.edu/blr/vol70/iss4/2.

4 Ibid.

5 Dan Ariely (2012). *The (Honest) Truth about Dishonesty.* New York: Harper Collins.
6 Nils Kobis (2018). *The Social Psychology of Corruption.* Ph.D. dissertation, Free University of Amsterdam. At: https://www.researchgate.net/publication/322476552_The_Social_Psychology_of_Corruption.
7 Ariely (2012), op.cit.
8 Management Systems International (2016). *Strengthening Integrity and Accountability Program 1 (SIAP-1), Final Report.* Washington, DC: United States Agency for International Development.
9 Management Systems International (2013). *Assistance for Afghanistan's Anti-Corruption Authority (4A) Project, Final Report.* Washington, DC: USAID.
10 Pamula (2015), op.cit.
11 Cheyanne Scharbatke-Church and Diana Chigas (2019). *Understanding Social Norms: A Reference Guide for Policy and Practice.* The Henry J. Leir Institute of Human Security. Medford, MA: The Fletcher School of Law and Diplomacy, Tufts University. At: https://sites.tufts.edu/ihs/social-norms-reference-guide/.
12 Claudia Baez Camargo and Lucy Koechlin (2018). "Informal Governance: Comparative Perspectives on Co-optation, Control and Camouflage in Rwanda, Tanzania and Uganda," *International Development Policy | Revue internationale de politique de développement* 10: 78–100. At: http://journals.openedition.org/poldev/2646.
13 Darley (2005), op.cit.
14 J.L. Campbell and A.S. Göritz (2014). "Culture Corrupts! A Qualitative Study of Organizational Culture in Corrupt Organizations," *Journal of Business Ethics* 120: 291–311.
15 Alison Taylor (2015). "The Characteristics of Corrupt Corporate Cultures," *The Global Anti-Corruption Blog* (July 2). At: https://globalanticorruptionblog.com/2015/07/02/guest-post-the-characteristics-of-corrupt-corporate-cultures/.
16 Management Systems International (2010). *Promoting Citizen Engagement in Combating Corruption in Ukraine (ACTION), Final Report.* Washington, DC: USAID.
17 Lauren Kirchner (2014). "The Psychology of Bribery and Corruption." *The Week* (November 20). At: https://theweek.com/articles/442692/psychology-bribery-corruption.
18 Ariely (2012), op.cit.
19 Kobis (2018), op.cit.
20 Management Systems International (2016), op.cit.

10 Deconstructing negotiations to make bribery fail

Many countries in transition suffer from chronic and systemic corruption that compromises governance and slows economic growth.[1] As a primary manifestation of corruption, bribery is conceived as a classic negotiation transaction between public officials and citizens, but one that exists in an illegal context. The satisfaction of interests through bribery negotiations may serve personal goals, but subvert the larger system of governance. While governments and international donor organizations have been seeking effective approaches to reduce or eliminate bribery and corruption through stricter law enforcement, administrative and institutional reforms, and public education strategies, one novel approach may be to deconstruct the bribery negotiation process to eliminate the opportunity for such transactions. This chapter analyzes this particular negotiation context in relation to Zartman's ripeness theory to identify ways to change the process and alter incentives, making negotiations concerning bribery a rare and high-risk activity.[2]

As one of the most common modes of human interaction, the negotiation process constitutes the core dynamic of many problem-solving transactions, whether it be familial, business, governmental or international. In all of these domains, negotiation also serves as the vehicle for one of the oldest of human activities, corruption. Most acts of petty, low level corruption can be characterized in negotiation terms: they include actors with clear interests who use power and persuasion to obtain beneficial outcomes. Taking a broader societal perspective, most analysts view corruption as negative to economic growth, public confidence, and good governance[3]; the fact that corruption operates as a negotiation process appears to be inconsequential. However, this linkage to negotiation processes may be the key to developing an ameliorative strategy for fighting corruption.

Over the past few decades, the international community, many governments and civil society organizations have focused attention on the persistent problem of corruption in transitional economies, as well as in developing and industrialized states, blaming it for slowed economic growth and deterioration in the quality of public service delivery. They have struggled to design and implement anti-corruption strategies that can effectively reverse or control these negative trends, in close coordination with host

DOI: 10.4324/9781003241119-12

governments.[4] While traditional anti-corruption approaches have sought to build effective rule of law procedures and institutions, and strengthen law enforcement activities, international experience has shown that, by themselves, these initiatives have only a transient impact. Other approaches need to be stimulated – including preventive reforms and public education – and other stakeholders need to be mobilized – including civil society, the private sector, and the mass media – to develop sustained and comprehensive pressure on state officials and institutions to keep them accountable for their actions.[5] These demand-side strategies seek to reduce the opportunities for corrupt encounters by generating a system of checks and balances, creating citizen awareness of legal rights to shield them from threats of abuse and harassment by corrupt officials, and developing independent watchdog groups that monitor government and increase transparency of government operations. But is there more to be done?

Public sector corruption is typically defined by researchers as the misuse of entrusted authority for private gain.[6] But when ordinary people are asked to define the corruption phenomenon, they overwhelmingly focus on the act of bribery, just one of corruption's many manifestations. Bribery is the quid pro quo transaction between a citizen and a government official in which cash, gifts or favors are provided by the former to obtain illicit access or services or faster access or services from the latter.[7] Inherent in this bribery transaction is a negotiation between two actors – one who wants something and the other who can provide it, either as part of his/her official state functions or in return for unofficial personal payments or favors. The transaction is a basic tit-for-tat negotiation encounter. From this simple conception of the bribery scenario as a reciprocal negotiation relationship, we propose an unorthodox approach to reduce bribery by eliminating its embedded negotiation elements. If the negotiation can be removed from the bribery transaction, perhaps the corruption can be averted entirely.

Our goal here is to evaluate the role that negotiation plays in the typical bribery transaction and how those negotiation elements might be *deconstructed* to prevent the negotiation and hence the bribery from occurring. Most negotiation literature seeks to uncover the factors and conditions that are favorable to initiating effective bargaining: what situations prompt the onset of negotiation, promote negotiation, or make the situation ripe for negotiation.[8] In an unusual twist to this plot, we seek to understand what is required to *stop* negotiation in particular cases where the vulnerability to bribery activity is high. If the relevant criteria can be identified, the elimination of certain types of negotiation can become the central theme in national and international anti-corruption strategies. In particular, we want to examine the implications of Zartman's concept of negotiation ripeness for this bribery negotiation deconstruction.[9]

Bribery and negotiation

Self-interest is the major motivating feature behind bribery transactions; either the official is actively seeking to benefit at the expense of the public or a citizen is offering illicit rewards to an official to extract special access or waivers from regulations. Corruption can take on many forms other than bribery: extortion, influence buying, favoritism, nepotism, kickbacks, fraud, and embezzlement, among others. Some of these corrupt actions take advantage of the special access to public funds and public decision-making that government officials have as a natural result of their positions. These actions may not require another party to accomplish their objectives; the corrupt official may just take what he/she wants. But bribery transactions necessarily involve demands and offers, a giver and taker, and bribery involves negotiation. Negotiation as a process is value-free, but when performed in the service of an illegal transaction, such as bribery, must be viewed as perverse.

The bribery transaction is a cost-benefit exchange, operating as a distributive negotiation. It usually involves parties that are unequal in their power position.[10] Corrupt transactions – such as giving or taking a bribe in exchange for preferential treatment, or better or faster services – can be viewed as negotiation encounters between citizens/businesses and government officials. These transactions involve a give-and-take process between two or more parties, each with their own aims, needs, and interests, where each seeks to find a common ground and reach an agreement.

When a bribe is solicited by a government official, the citizen/business is usually in a position of weakness and easily intimidated to pay. The citizen/business is often seeking to obtain a service he/she is entitled to (like health care or schooling), but can only get via access from the official. When the bribe is offered by a citizen or business, it is they who are usually in a position of power, and a compliant official agrees to use his/her position to speed the process, doing so for the illicit payment.

In either case, whether it is the official or the citizen/business that is initiating the corrupt negotiation, the negotiation interaction consists of back-and-forth bargaining – offers, demands and counteroffers – designed to reach an agreement based on their interests. The citizen/business that needs access to public services may be inclined to pay a bribe to get the service. The official who is in a controlling position may demand the bribe or be willing to accept one just because he/she can do it.

At its core, corruption operates as a negotiation transaction with power asymmetry. There are two predominant forms of corruption negotiations. Either the unchecked and powerful government official makes demands of the weak and needy citizen for extra payments or gifts in exchange for the public services that are supposed to be provided for free. Or a rich and powerful citizen offers bribes or kickbacks to poor government officials, while demanding something valuable – government contracts or special services – if the official turns a blind eye to the illicit activity. In this way, one party can impose a cost or benefit on the other party to extract a desired behavior. Goods are distributed in the transaction to both sides – often money or a favor to obtain an illegally obligated service or some special government dispensation or service. The asymmetry between the parties is an essential feature, without which the corrupt negotiation would not proceed.

Negotiation requires mixed motives – a desire for cooperation at the same time that there are conflicting interests among the parties. However, some may say that the bribery transaction is entirely a coordination situation among consenting partners; all sides want to achieve something illicit through their transaction – it is not a negotiation of mixed motives. While this might be the case in a few situations, survey research has indicated that a large number of citizens and business people believe they are victimized by the transaction and frustrated by being forced into it; they may consent to the transaction but they are by no means pleased about it.[11] Under these circumstances, conflictual and cooperative interests do exist side-by-side in a bribery negotiation setting; there is competition among the parties, for example, to get expected services or approvals but not to pay extra for them.

A bribery scandal in Peru during the 1990s serves as a stark and vivid example of how negotiation processes permeate this form of corruption and how it can be manifested,[12] not only as low-level administrative corruption but as a potent form of high-level *state capture*,[13] in this case by the intelligence service. For ten years, Vladimiro Montesinos, the National Intelligence Service chief, systematically conducted "secret" bribery negotiations with politicians, judges, and media owners. He offered them large cash bribes, promotions, judicial influence, and legislative votes, in return for their political support, compliance, or silence. We know of his explicit negotiations because Montesinos videotaped them all (there are estimates that 1600 Peruvians were bribed), kept meticulous records of bribes given, and extracted signed agreements (pledges) from the bribed individuals, documenting the transaction and the quid pro quo! He apparently kept these records to prove the others' complicity, enforce the pledges, and threaten blackmail if necessary. In an unusual turn of events, some of these secret tapes were leaked to the press and broadcast on Peruvian television by one of the few stations that had not been bought off, leading to Montesinos' arrest and prosecution and the rapid fall of the Fujimori government in 2000.

These negotiations were simple transactions. Offers of cash payments, favors or influence were made to officials and the media to facilitate the regime's evasion of typical democratic constraints. The offer, coming directly from the head of the National Intelligence Service, was hard to resist or reject; Montesinos had the muscle to retaliate harshly for noncompliance. To reduce the possibility of defection, he usually paid the bribes in installments over time and created a strong sense of camaraderie among his bribe recipients where commitments could not be forgotten.

In Russia, a public opinion survey asked citizens who had transacted with government officials recently to obtain basic services if bribes had been demanded or offered as a condition for receiving the service.[14] Interestingly, for most business-related services where government provides permissions (customs, privatization, utilities), bribes were demanded by officials more frequently than offered by citizens. However, for personal services (getting drivers licenses, obtaining health care, and dealing with Army draft boards, schools, and universities), bribes were more typically offered by citizens. The marketplace for government-provided public services is clearly a negotiation involving demands and offers, where power asymmetry predicts likely strategies.

Ripeness and reversing bribery negotiations

Ripeness theory, introduced by Zartman in the early 1980s, has become a central conceptual framework employed by researchers to explain the onset of negotiation processes and by policymakers to decide on those conflicts amenable to resolution and positive interventions.[15] The ripeness metaphor is easily understood and intuitive which is why it has been embraced by both researcher, as well as practitioner, communities. It posits that there are ripe moments in the life cycle of conflicts, which, if seized, will result in successful resolution of those conflicts. What makes a conflict ripe for resolution, in part, are "mutually hurting stalemates" – perceptions of increasingly painful conditions which will yield only further pain and ultimate catastrophe for the conflicting parties if they are left to fester. Under these circumstances, the interests of the parties will not be achieved or even approximated; an alternative approach to relieve the stalemate needs to be found. Thus, ripeness theory also proposes that in addition to these painful stalemates, the parties must be able to see a way out of the conflict; they must have a vision of a feasible and peaceful outcome which can be achieved through negotiation or mediation.

When the conflicting parties perceive a mutually hurting stalemate and a way out of their predicament, the moment is ripe for resolution. Zartman's theoretical construct offers an explanation of conflict resolution that focuses on perceptions (how aware the parties are of their conflict status), incentives (how motivated they are by the increasing pain imposed by the conflict), and timing (how they seize upon the fleeting opportunity). Ripeness is a necessary initiating catalyst to transform conflicts and Zartman's framework can also be a key to understanding bribery negotiations.

In his 2000 chapter revisiting ripeness theory, Zartman addressed an important but troubling aspect of the theory: are conflicts amenable to resolution only when the pain of stalemate and catastrophe become too great to bear? Do international conflicts have to reach a crescendo or threat of violence, possibly endangering the order of neighboring states and regions, to produce the conditions for resolution? Clearly, this is the situation by which many conflicts are transformed. But it is not the only possible path. Zartman posits an extension to ripeness theory: "mutually enticing opportunities." Positive incentives, not only negative incentives, can motivate conflict transformation. The vision or promise of overwhelming reward or benefit can be "the straw that breaks the camel's back," pushing decision makers to commence negotiation and search for mutually acceptable solutions. Moreover, such positive incentives have the potential to produce more attractive and therefore stable outcomes over time than negatively induced solutions. The psychological literature on incentives backs up this assumption.

If ripeness is determined not only by how bad it can get but how good it can become, new approaches and strategies that promote negotiation are feasible. Diplomats and policymakers can push conflict situations into ripeness by introducing new "carrots" – future trade agreements or promises of foreign assistance and investment, for example. Conflicts may become ripe for resolution at an earlier stage in their development, thereby reducing suffering and loss of life and property. In Zartman's new extension of ripeness theory, he opens the door to creative and flexible strategies to transform conflicts, not only by the immediate parties to the conflict but by interested third parties as well. By offering and manipulating positive incentives, ripeness can be positioned and engineered to catalyze the conflict transformation process and engage the parties in a more attractive negotiated or mediated search for solutions.

Ripeness theory and its extension present novel ways for understanding how conflicts are transformed and how the negotiation process gets started. Zartman's original ripeness construct motivated many researchers to examine and test the concepts. Policymakers can be energized by the additional concept of mutually enticing opportunity, because it suggests an activist path to generate perceptions of ripeness. Visions of future mutually beneficial solutions, promises of financial and material assistance, and possibilities of winning quickly or developing new international relationships may be able to bring the conflicting parties to quicker realization of their interests through negotiation. Proactive interventions can be introduced by potential mediators or international organizations to ripen conflicts more rapidly. As such, manipulating ripeness can be seen as a new form of preventive diplomacy.

In the case of bribery negotiations, the incentives of cash payments, gifts or favors can bring on ripeness. When offered, they are usually sufficiently attractive to the government official to result in his/her acceding to the demand for services or turning a blind eye. When the bribe is extorted from a citizen by an official, payment can be viewed as generating ripeness, because obtaining the desired service is sufficiently enticing in itself. The concept of mutually enticing opportunities seems to be the major motivator of bribery negotiations. Certainly, from the perspective of the victim of the corruption transaction, not being able to get the public services requested without the bribe can be viewed as hurting – health care might be delayed and school enrollment for children may not be possible, for example. But rarely would you describe the bribery situation as a *mutually* hurting stalemate; the government official would not generally feel the pain.

If ripeness ensures bribery negotiations, could ripeness *turned in reverse* avert negotiations? If ripeness can be manipulated to promote negotiation, it should be possible to engineer situations of "under-ripeness," that is, where the incentives – positive or negative – are insufficient to stimulate the bribery encounter. This was one of the intentions of raising civil servant salaries in Georgia after the Rose Revolution. By increasing wages from poverty level to a good livable salary, the concept was that government workers would not have to ask for bribes or kickbacks to put food on their family's table; that is what happened.[16]

Perhaps the prescription for reducing bribery is to create an environment in which the benefits and incentives of bribery are minimized, thereby being under-ripe for negotiation. This suggests that the perceived benefits of bribery need to be tempered by the risks of discovery and certain punishment. Adding this ambiguity to the motives of bribery negotiators can yield a deterrent to the deal and turn a potentially ripe moment into an unripe one. While this manipulation of incentives may not represent a novel revelation about bribery dynamics, viewing bribery as essentially a negotiation process is. This different perspective on the bribery problem may open up new opportunities to sabotage it.

The building blocks of bribery negotiations

We can examine how ripeness can be turned in reverse by analyzing and deconstructing the fundamental elements that facilitate bribery negotiations. The following analytical review of the essential building blocks of negotiations points to vulnerabilities in the bribery process.[17]

Actors and structure

The actors in most corruption negotiations are government officials and citizens. They can be depicted in a principal-agent-client structure to explain the governance relationship that can turn corrupt.[18] The principal might be the chief of a government department who is responsible for various functions and services. The agent might be a bureaucrat who is charged with actually carrying out specific functions and services and interacts directly with the public. The client might be a citizen or business person who seeks a service or permission from government, in particular, from an agent. With the proper controls, accountability mechanisms, and transparent processes, these three actors can interact relatively smoothly, passing requests, information, and feedback among themselves, and carrying out functions in a predictable fashion in accordance with laws and regulations. However, in systems with wide discretion, limited accountability, and low transparency, there can be many opportunities for negotiation leading to bribery among these stakeholders. Principals can select agents based on favoritism and nepotism so their loyalty is not pledged to the public at large and they fail to see themselves as "public servants." Agents can negotiate for extra unofficial payments from clients (for example, extortion) to deliver services or permissions and then pass part of these payments up the ladder to the principals as kickbacks. Agents can also threaten to harass clients if payments are not made. Clients, too, can negotiate with agents, offering bribes to get special treatment or causing agents to turn a blind eye to illegal activity.

In a survey of public officials in four countries of Eastern Europe, researchers found that officials believed it proper to expect and/or demand bribes from clients.[19] Sixty percent of officials thought it right to accept bribes if offered in return for extra work to solve client problems. Fifty-three percent thought it right to accept bribes to solve problems faster than normal. Fifteen percent thought it right to ask for a bribe.

The question often asked in a corruption negotiation is "who is the corrupter?" The question revolves around who holds the stronger power position and who initiates the corrupt promise or threat. Is the government official who withholds a legal service or permission if a bribe is not provided thereby victimizing the citizen? Or is the citizen the corrupting agent, offering bribes and favors to low paid government officials who desperately need to increase their family income? Or are both actors willing accomplices, each understanding the system and how things are accomplished? Miller, et al. conducted public surveys in Ukraine, Bulgaria, Slovakia, and the Czech Republic in 1997 and 1998 to understand these negotiation relationships.[20] Their results do not always support the popular allegation that citizens and business people are the source of corruption, tantalizing government officials with bribes and favors. In the Czech and Slovak Republics, their findings suggest that citizens were not simple victims of official corruption, but accomplices – the public and officials were working in collusion to perpetuate the pervasive system of corruption. On the other hand, in Bulgaria and Ukraine, citizens clearly believe that they are the victims of greedy officials. In all cases, it was a combination of official greed and citizen submissiveness and tolerance that perpetuated high levels of bribery.

The corruption culture – and the resulting corruption negotiation – among domestic actors is often different from transactions between domestic and foreign parties. The expectations of the transaction are not likely to coincide. Domestic government officials may perceive foreign investors as likely prey who can pay much higher bribes than domestic business people. Foreign investors may not anticipate the domestic corruption culture. The result may be a highly contentious negotiation process.

The dynamics motivating corruption negotiations between principal, agent, and client hinge on self-interest. Where the rule of law is strong, respected, and enforced, self-interest is naturally bounded by law and the firm expectation that wrongdoers will be caught and punished. But where the rule of law is weak, the controls that circumscribe self-interest may not be present. Self-gratification and power prevail. By initiating a corruption negotiation, the official or the citizen can seek certain benefits that would be denied or delayed otherwise.

What happens if the key actors in corruption negotiations do not ever interact with one another? Technology offers the opportunity for citizens to get the public services they are entitled to without ever discussing the transaction face-to-face with a government official who might be a corrupt predator. One example of such technology is the e-governance system. Let's look at one such system in use in Ukraine – ProZorro.[21] This electronic procurement system was initially implemented across the country – at all levels of government – in 2016. It contributed to reducing corruption in public procurement by increasing transparency in the procurement process and by replacing direct human interaction, with proposals and bidding that are submitted online, and with no face-to-face transaction. Also, by implementing Business Intelligence modules, ProZorro allowed the public to closely monitor the progress of public procurements in real time and analyze the procurement decisions upon their completion. This objective analysis raises red flags if there is detection of possible malpractices, corruption or fraud.

The success of the ProZorro system is evidenced by a rapid reduction of corruption instances in public procurement cases. A survey conducted in late 2016 showed that corruption was reduced from 54% under the old "paper-based" system to 29% under ProZorro. Also, private sector trust that the system reduced corruption was on the rise; the majority of entrepreneurs believed that ProZorro significantly (27%) or partially (53%) reduced corruption in public procurement.

Process

Corruption is an implicit, and sometimes explicit, negotiated contract specifying what each party has committed itself to accomplishing, that is, the quid pro quo. It is usually the reciprocation of a service for a gift. What, in fact, is the object of this type of negotiation? It can be the size and nature of the bribe or the size and nature of what you get in return for the bribe. In a survey of corruption in Kharkiv, Ukraine at the end of 1999, bargaining over the bribe price was clearly evident.[22] Of those citizens who said they paid a bribe, they indicate paying 28% less than what was requested by the government official! Ten percent of the respondents indicate clearly that they try to negotiate with officials to avoid paying bribes or, at least, to reduce the price.

A survey of households, businesses and public officials in Romania conducted in early 2000 emphasizes the quid pro quo between officials and citizens.[23] To obtain health care services, bribes are essential to getting better service or to getting any service at all. Likewise, in the educational field, bribes are a determining factor in getting children placed in school and in getting better grades. Among public officials, 37% said they were offered small bribes over the last 12 months; 11% said they were offered expensive gifts or bribes. But 30% indicate that while bribes were given and accepted, they were not necessary; if you have patience, they say, you can get what you want without paying bribes. But when business people responded, 75% indicate that they spend over 6% of their working hours negotiating with government bureaucrats, increasing the opportunities for bribe-giving and bribe-taking. From the business person's perspective, their involvement in the corruption negotiation was not voluntary. Forty-one percent indicate that government officials told them a bribe was expected – to speed the delivery of services or get favorable treatment. A much smaller number of business people, 18%, indicated that they were the primary initiators of the corruption negotiation, offering bribes to officials.

Whether or not the negotiation situation is acceptable to either of the parties is also a question. The victim may be able to resist the bribe-request by waiting or seeking an alternative channel to obtain the desired service. The proposed bribe-taker might be able to resist the offered gift or favor by appealing to the rule of law or indicating that the risk of accepting the bribe is just too great. In both these cases, each party can be said to have a BATNA, a best (or preferred) alternative to a negotiated agreement.

Several negotiation process elements are important to consider in corruption negotiations – the secrecy of the transaction, tolerance for the transaction, the reliability of each side, and the development of dependencies. *Secrecy* in the negotiation enables the transaction to thrive. If the process were conducted in the open, it would cease to exist due to the very illegality of the transaction. The widespread emergence of e-government applications to replace face-to-face negotiations between citizens and government officials effectively removes the secrecy element from the negotiation equation. When citizens or businesses need to access government services, they can get them directly online in a fully transparent way.

Tolerance for the practice of corruption is another factor that perpetuates it. Victims, while damning the tradition of bribery and fraud, typically practice it actively.[24] Whether willing or grudging in their acceptance of corruption, they continue to practice it, not being able to conceive of any way out. In the four country survey mentioned earlier, researchers found that between 62% and 91% of the citizens in those countries needed to pay a bribe or use a special contact to get something from government that they were entitled to by law for free.[25] Some suggest that only when tolerance turns to frustration and frustration to outrage with the practice of corruption will that acquiescence cease and the required political will to make reforms to control corruption will emerge.[26]

The *reliability* of the transaction is one of the uncertainties of corruption negotiations. Will the promised reciprocation actually occur if the bribe is provided? Will you get what you pay for? Is there trust among thieves? Trust in the other party is required for the negotiation to proceed. In the Kharkiv survey, 50% of the respondents indicate that they believe that giving the bribe guarantees quicker and better service.[27] Of these respondents, the younger the person, the more they believe the reliability of the negotiation transaction. Correspondingly, if you do not give a bribe, it is believed that service will not be provided quickly (52%) or at all (38%). Thirty percent of respondents were unsure of the reliability of the corruption negotiation, but these people tended to have less direct and personal experience with corruption transactions.

Once a bribe is given and the expected service rendered, *dependencies* may develop between the corrupting agent and the victim over time, yielding a situation that requires further bribery to get any services whatsoever. The resulting post-agreement negotiation process may see an escalation of the extortion involved, bidding up the price for services unless an alternative source for those services is found.

Strategy

How is power used among bribery negotiators to achieve their objectives? It is often the government official who has what the citizen or business person wants and can extort bribes or favors to provide the service or permission. Some officials view their positions, not as servants of the people, but as rent seekers who have the right to steal and plunder during their tenure. Survey researchers found that officials who merely ask for a bribe actually receive the bribe in most cases; extortion works.[28] More so, if officials cause unnecessary problems, delays, and administrative complications for citizens, the rate of bribe-giving increases; citizens are responsive to pressure.

From the citizen's perspective, it is a popular belief that corruption and promoting corruption can be good for business. It greases the skids and enables business to operate effectively – licenses can be obtained more readily and inspections can be "passed" at just a small cost relative to the actual regulated cost of satisfying regulations and standards. In fact, some have indicated that when it comes to the health care system in many Eastern European and former Soviet Union countries, if unofficial payments were eliminated, the entire structure of health care provision would collapse. So, under such circumstances, citizen/business strategies to initiate corrupt transactions may be viewed as positive elements. On the other hand, citizens who are pressured to give bribes often acquiesce easily and tolerate the transaction. They often fear retribution or worse inconveniences if they do not pay the bribe, and see no way out of the problem that is within their power. Like coercive diplomacy, government officials can seek to impose additional difficulties on citizens to encourage or force them to pay the bribe.[29] Coercion works because citizens feel trapped, with no BATNA or fallback position.

Deconstructing corruption negotiations

If negotiation is a primary process channel by which bribery manifests itself, it follows logically that deconstructing negotiations – making negotiations difficult or impossible to conduct – may be an efficient means to reduce corruption. How can perverse bribery negotiations be deconstructed? One way would be to disrupt the building blocks of effective bribery negotiation encounters. Another way is to inhibit the situational factors that facilitate effective negotiation and bring parties together to the bargaining table. Specific initiatives that draw on both of these approaches are described below.

Reduce self-interest in negotiation

Self-interest that stimulates negotiation can be tempered. This will inhibit negotiation motives. For example,

Reduce reliability in the negotiation dynamic. If the expectation that a bribe will not necessarily guarantee the desired service – if permission or blind eye is less than 100% – negotiators may seek alternative means to achieve their goals.

Provide better alternatives to a negotiated agreement (BATNAs). If officials believe that accepting a bribe will mean certain arrest and severe punishment, they are likely to avoid engaging in the corrupt transaction. If citizen victims find that they can hold out and still get their service or permission from government officials in a reasonable amount of time, they may desist from paying requested bribes.

Re-engineer the negotiation situation

It may be possible to modify the situation within which bribery negotiations usually are conducted to reduce their likelihood. We can draw on the negotiation research literature that evaluates situational hindrances and determinants.[30] For example,

Increase transparency. If all government operations, including negotiations between government agents and citizen clients, are conducted in the open – if there are standard "sunshine laws" in place – then it will be difficult, if not impossible to offer bribes or extort citizens.

Increase independent monitoring of government officials. Internal investigative and audit units within government departments can be established to monitor the activities of officials. Alternatively, independent nongovernmental watchdog groups can be formed to ensure the accountability of officials through the use of social audits, citizen report cards, dashboard cameras, and mystery shopping mechanisms. These groups would open government activities to public scrutiny and reduce the opportunities for secretive bribery negotiations. Citizen and business coalitions to monitor government operations would increase the power position of civil society vis-à-vis the government. By equalizing and leveling the playing field, such coalitions would become less vulnerable to harassment and abuse.

Reduce direct personal contact. If it is possible to reduce direct face-to-face contact between officials and citizens, there will be fewer opportunities for negotiation. This could be accomplished by using the postal system and the internet to renew routine licenses and to obtain registrations, for example. E-government solutions are becoming increasingly feasible in many countries. Developing one-stop centers where citizens/business people can get all necessary approvals from a single administrator, rather than going from office to office, would also serve a similar purpose.

Reduce discretion for bureaucrats. If the implementing regulations for laws are made more precise, there will be less for bureaucrats to interpret as they fulfill their functions. Administrative procedures will become more predictable and clear, both to the official and the citizen/business person. As a result, there will be less to negotiate about. Several countries have used a process called "regulatory guillotine" where old, duplicative or contradictory regulations are eliminated, resulting in a simplified, straightforward, and easily understandable set of rules to implement laws and processes.[31]

Remove mutually hurting stalemate. Negotiations often occur because all parties believe that it is the only way to achieve their mutual objectives, having reached deadlock using all other means. If officials and citizens can get what they desire using ordinary prescribed methods, deadlocks will not be encountered and everyone will achieve their goals. For example, if laws, regulations, and procedures for typical government services are clearly written, detailed, and well-publicized, there should be little need to discuss, let alone negotiate, about how they are implemented.

Reduce familiarity between officials and citizens. Negotiators who are familiar with each other are more likely to be able to reach agreement. But if officials are rotated on a frequent basis, citizens will be less likely to interact with the same bureaucrat to obtain the permissions and services on a repetitive basis. As a result, bribery negotiations are less likely to commence.

Expected results

No country has found a reliable way to escape from the problems of corruption. However, some have found ways to reduce the opportunities for corruption from emerging. Deconstructing negotiation – a central dynamic in bribery transactions – seems to be an appropriate and direct way of reducing the opportunities for the emergence of corruption.

Changing incentives will reduce corruption negotiations. The predictability of risk and cost for bribery negotiations are essential in changing the incentive structure. Parties have to know that there are negative consequences that will not serve their self-interests.

Changing processes and situational factors will reduce bribery negotiations. The negotiation literature has identified situational factors that are generally favorable to promoting and sustaining effective negotiations. It is possible to use this information to re-engineer the situation so that unfavorable negotiation conditions make bargaining unlikely. Processes can also be re-engineered so that the typical elements that make negotiations effective are not present.

Changing structures and institutions will reduce corruption negotiations. Certain institutions and structures can be established that change power relationships and open the processes within which negotiations usually take place, making them more unlikely to emerge.

What can be done from a research perspective? Simulations can be conducted in the laboratory to test the effects of deconstructing negotiations on bribery. Such simulations can seek out new ways of undoing the natural dynamic toward negotiation by controlling for different situations and conditions. In addition, practical experiments in the field can be attempted to stop perverse bribery negotiations. Donor agencies can launch pilot projects in the field to determine if the reduction of negotiation is a viable approach to bribery control. Such pilot efforts can be accomplished within broader administrative reform or streamlining programs.

Many decades of hard work have been spent experimenting with various approaches to reduce corruption and its effects. Some approaches have been effective, others not. But to date, no clear path has been identified to fight corruption. Tinkering with the negotiation process to make it less interesting to potential participants in the corrupt transaction seems to be a simple and direct way of controlling the problem that attacks its root causes in human behavior. It merits further examination and experimentation.

As this negotiation deconstruction strategy is implemented in various ways, measurement and monitoring can be conducted to assess the results and impacts of this strategy. This could include testing of civil servants using scenarios to determine their changed motives as a result of more limited transactional procedures with citizens, reduced discretion for government staff, and greater transparency in their decisions and actions.

Notes

1 This chapter is an updated version of a chapter that was originally published by the author in *Conflict Management and African Politics*, edited by Terrence Lyons and Gilbert Khadiagala. London: Routledge, 2008. The copyright for the original chapter is held by the author.

2 I. William Zartman (2000). "Ripeness: The Hurting Stalemate and Beyond," in Paul C. Stern and Daniel Druckman, editors, *International Conflict Resolution after the Cold War* (pp. 225–250). Washington, DC: National Academy Press.

3 Susan Rose-Ackerman (1978). *Corruption: A Study in Political Economy.* New York: Academic Press; John M. Kramer (1999). *Anti-Corruption Research Concerning Eastern Europe and the Former Soviet Union: A Comparative Analysis.* Arlington, VA: Management Systems International.

4 World Bank (2000a). *Anticorruption in Transition: A Contribution to the Policy Debate.* Washington, DC: The World Bank; World Bank (2000b). *Helping Countries Combat Corruption: Progress at the World Bank Since 1997.* Washington, DC: The World Bank (PREM), June; USAID (1999). *A Handbook on Fighting Corruption.* Technical Publication Series. Washington, DC: Center for Democracy and Governance, Bureau for Global Programs, US Agency for International Development; OECD (2000). *No Longer Business as Usual: Fighting Bribery and Corruption.* Paris: Organization for Economic Cooperation and Development; Kimberly Elliott, editor (1997). *Corruption and the Global Economy.* Washington, DC: Institute for International Economics; Vinay Bhargava and Emil Bolongaita (2004). *Challenging Corruption in Asia: Case Studies and a Framework for Action.* Washington, DC: The World Bank; Bertram Spector, editor (2005). *Fighting Corruption in Developing Countries: Strategies and Analysis.* Bloomfield, CT: Kumarian Press.

5 Daniel Kaufmann (2003). "Rethinking Governance: Empirical Lessons Challenge Orthodoxy," Working Paper Series, Washington, DC: World Bank Institute.

6 Jeremy Pope (1997). *The TI Source Book, Second Edition*. Berlin: Transparency International; USAID (2005). *USAID Anti-corruption Strategy*. Washington, DC: US Agency for International Development.

7 Management Systems International (2004). *Public Opinion of Corruption in Vladivostok*. Washington, DC: MSI.

8 Daniel Druckman (1993). "Situational Levers of Negotiating Flexibility," *Journal of Conflict Resolution* 32, 2: 236–276 (June); I. William Zartman (1989). *Ripe for Resolution*. New York: Oxford University Press; Janice Stein, editor (1989). *Getting to the Table: The Processes of International Prenegotiation*. Baltimore, MD: The Johns Hopkins University Press; Bertram Spector (2001). "Negotiation Readiness in the Development Context: Adding Capacity to Ripeness," in Ho-Won Jeong, editor, *From Conflict Resolution to Peace Building* (pp. 80–102). New York: Macmillan.

9 Zartman (2000), op.cit.

10 Mushtaq Khan (1996). "The Efficiency Implications of Corruption," *Journal of International Development* 8, 5: 683–696.

11 Management Systems International (2004), op.cit.

12 John McMillan and Pablo Zoido (2004). "How to Subvert Democracy: Montesinos in Peru," Unpublished. Stanford University. At: https://papers.ssrn.com/sol3/papers.cfm?abstract_id=520902.

13 Joel Hellman, G. Jones, and D. Kaufmann (2000). "Seize the State, Seize the Day: State Capture, Corruption and Influence in Transition," World Bank Policy Research Working Paper No. 2444. Washington, DC: World Bank Institute (September).

14 Management Systems International (2004), op.cit.

15 Zartman (1989, 2000), op.cit.

16 World Bank (2012). *Fighting Corruption in Public Services: Chronicling Georgia's Reforms*. Washington, DC: The World Bank.

17 Victor Kremenyuk, editor (1991). *International Negotiation*. San Francisco: Jossey-Bass.

18 Edward Banfield (1975). "Corruption as a Feature of Governmental Organization," *Journal of Law and Economics* 18 (December): 587–605; Rose-Ackerman (1978), op.cit.; Robert Klitgaard (1988). *Controlling Corruption*. Berkeley: University of California Press; Robert Klitgaard, R. Maclean-Abaroa, and H. Lindsey Parris (2000). *Corrupt Cities: A Practical Guide to Cure and Prevention*. Oakland, CA: ICS Press.

19 William L. Miller, Åse B. Grødeland and Tatyana Y. Koshechkina (1999). "What Is to Be Done about Corrupt Officials? Public Opinion in Ukraine, Bulgaria, Slovakia and the Czech Republic," *International Review of Administrative Sciences* 65, 2: 235–249.

20 William L. Miller, Åse B. Grødeland and Tatyana Y. Koshechkina (1998). "Are the People Victims or Accomplices: The Use of Presents and Bribes to Influence Officials in Eastern Europe," *Crime, Law and Social Change* 29, 4: 273–310.

21 Management Systems International (2016). *Technical Assistance Services for the eTender Initiative in Kyiv, Ukraine (Phase II), Final Informational Report*. Washington, DC: USAID.

22 Management Systems International (2000). *Integrity Survey in Kharkiv, Ukraine*. Washington, DC: USAID (Conducted by Kiev International Institute of Sociology, November–December 1999).

23 Management Systems International and the World Bank (2000). *Diagnostic Assessment of Corruption in Romania*. Washington, DC: USAID and the World Bank (July).

24 Miller, et al. (1998), op.cit.
25 Ibid.
26 Bertram Spector (2000a). "Building Constituencies for Anti-Corruption Pro-grams: The Role of Diagnostic Assessments," Paper presented at the Regional Anti-Corruption Conference, Bucharest, Romania, March 30; Bertram Spector (2000b). "Anti-Corruption Program Feasibility Study in Russia: Tomsk and Sa-mara," Final Report, October. Washington, DC: USAID.
27 Management Systems International (2000), op.cit.
28 Miller, et al. (1998), op.cit.
29 Alexander George (1991). *Forceful Persuasion*. Washington, DC: United States Institute of Peace Press.
30 Druckman (1993), op.cit.; Daniel Druckman (1994). "Determinants of Compro-mising Behavior in Negotiation: A Meta-Analysis," *Journal of Conflict Resolu-tion* 33, 3: 507–556.
31 Scott Jacobs (2005). *The Regulatory Guillotine Strategy: Preparing the Business Environment in Croatia for Competitiveness in Europe*. Washington, DC: United States Agency for International Development. At: https://pdf.usaid.gov/pdf_docs/PNADG614.pdf.

Part III

Practical implementation

Developing and testing new behavior change strategies is a critical step toward curbing corruption effectively. But *how* these reform initiatives are implemented more broadly in a country will determine if they are appropriate to the socio-political context, whether they will have the intended impact, and if they can be sustained. Conclusions based on research and recommendations for real-world action can help practitioners make the right choices.

DOI: 10.4324/9781003241119-13

11 What's next? Assessments, strategies, and implementation

Previous chapters have examined the wide range of reform programs that have been attempted over the years to address the corruption problem in countries around the world. We have certainly learned many lessons from these initiatives, but the corruption problem persists. One conclusion that researchers and practitioners have drawn is that each country faces different forms of corruption within different contexts.[1] As a result, a reform program that works well in one location may not yield similar results in another. There are no ready-made, cookie-cutter approaches to fighting corruption.

To ensure that anti-corruption interventions are more likely to succeed, they must be customized to the specific context within which they will be applied. The best way to do this is to first conduct a detailed and targeted assessment of the country and sector where the intervention will take place so that the appropriate reform programs can be selected and tailored to the situation on the ground. One needs to consider the status of relevant legal and institutional factors, the political-economic context, and cultural and social norms that serve to motivate citizens and leaders in the society. Especially, with the discussion in previous chapters of individual and group drivers of corruption, this type of assessment is even more critical. Based on such an assessment, customized reform approaches can be identified and implementation can be planned appropriately.

First, it is essential to tailor anti-corruption reforms to the political-economic context, to make sure that there is sufficient political will, resources, and capacity to carry through on the initiatives. Second, since corruption manifests itself differently across sectors, such as education, health, energy, environment, and agriculture, for example, it is important to consider the processes, opportunities, and constraints present in each sector to plan for anti-corruption reforms that are most likely to have an impact. And third, as we discussed in earlier chapters, we need to assess the situation through ethical, social psychological, and negotiation lenses to identify reform approaches that are most likely to motivate and drive individual and group behavior in new directions away from corruption. There is a lot to assess and consider.

DOI: 10.4324/9781003241119-14

Assessing different drivers

There are many entry points for anti-corruption reforms. As a result, corruption assessments need to go beyond an understanding of the legal-institutional framework and the political-economic context to examine the drivers of corrupt behaviors. As discussed earlier, through an *ethical lens*, we want to understand the extent to which government officials are motivated by the rule of law and/or principles of fairness, justice, morality, and conscience versus self-interest. Are they driven to work for the benefit of the public which they serve? In line with the ethical lens, reform programs can target strengthened recruitment systems for civil servants that screen out those with unethical leanings. Greater emphasis can be place on occupational training of existing civil servants to resocialize these officials toward a more ethical set of practices that are in the public interest. Other programs can seek to promote more empathy among government workers toward the plight of ordinary citizens and those in particular need of help and support from the government. Local cultural and religious leaders can be brought in to help civil servants think about their jobs in a more ethical way, and especially from the perspective of the recipient of their services, resulting in a more compassionate orientation that is free from corrupt transactions.

From a *social psychological frame*, we want to understand what motivates individuals to act corruptly or not. Do they rationalize corrupt behavior to make it appear acceptable? Do they do so because they want to conform to social norms or their familial or community groups? Do they avoid corrupt behavior to avert "naming and shaming" if detected? Reform programs that seek to change the way officials rationalize corrupt behavior are critical. They need to see corruption for what it really is: an abuse of their position of power. Citizens who are complicit with corrupt officials in the transaction must also be helped to view corruption as a hindrance to their rights, not just a way to get what they want from government. Investigative reports about the realities and impacts of corrupt acts and expanded public awareness can be helpful in changing how and why people justify being corrupt.

Another approach is to counter social norms and group conformity that has developed around corrupt interactions. In many societies, corrupt behavior is so engrained, that it has become the common way of conducting business. Employing a quid pro quo is the traditional way that people interact with government. If you want to fit in with others in your community or social network and be accepted by them, you do what your role models do: act corruptly. But these types of negative reinforcing behaviors can be turned around. When prominent and respected leaders in the community have the political will to oppose corruption or when the negative implications of such behavior are publicly exposed, bad social norms can be diminished, replaced by new and positive ethical approaches.

And another important opening to reduce corruption is to make the risks of committing corruption more real. People are typically risk averse, but they will behave this way only if they believe that there is a very high probability that they will be caught and punished. Strengthening active oversight and supervision of government officials – both within government (through audits, inspectors general, review boards, and stricter management, for example) and outside government (through citizen monitoring, social audits, crowdsourced complaint systems, etc.) – can make the risk of being named and shamed very real, thus averting the corrupt behavior in the first place.

The third perspective that we need to assess closely is the extent of *negotiating opportunities* between government officials and citizens when engaged in a transaction concerning the delivery of public services and the expenditure of public funds. One approach to doing this is to reduce the need for direct face-to-face contact; perhaps using e-governance applications. Another approach is to reduce the opportunity for bureaucratic discretion. This might be done by enhancing monitoring and oversight of such transactions via social monitoring, audits or stricter supervision and management controls. Increasing transparency of the processes by which government authorities and citizens transact will also reduce corrupt opportunities. When citizens are more aware of the process rules by which transactions should be conducted under the law, the intervention of corrupt actions is less likely. Also, if civil servants are paid decent salaries, comparable to what someone with the same skills and experience would make in the private sector, there is less likelihood that they will be interested in committing fraud or abuse and potentially getting in trouble.

As described in earlier chapters, isolated pilot tests to address some of these entry points have been tried with some success. But in most cases, they have not been sustained interventions and they have not been rolled out extensively throughout the country. As well, they may only be appropriate in certain contexts, in certain sectors or at certain levels of government. What is needed when considering how to adopt these new entry point reforms effectively is a comprehensive assessment to understand what might work and might be best suited to the situation.

Multifaceted assessments to frame new initiatives

There is a clear recognition that new approaches need to be taken by governments, their civil society and business communities, and international donor organizations to address corruption as a serious obstacle to development. Corruption is both the product and the cause of numerous governance failures, economic dysfunctions, and political shortcomings. To develop effective anti-corruption programs, a wide range of factors must be evaluated to avoid the trap of tackling only the symptoms and leaving the underlying disease untreated.

A first step toward implementing improved anti-corruption programs is to conduct a comprehensive assessment of how corruption manifests itself in a particular country, the array of factors that drive it, and the effectiveness of existing laws, institutions, and control mechanisms meant to reduce a country's vulnerability to corruption. A tailored anti-corruption assessment framework can be designed that is sufficiently detailed and targeted to produce prioritized recommendations for practical programming.[2] The framework should be guided by international best practice, theory, and research. It needs to examine at least three major components: (a) *foundational factors* – dealing with the state of the legal-regulatory-institutional framework that addresses corruption, (b) *the context* – examining the political-economic dynamics that define the given parameters of opportunities and constraints for potential reforms, and (c) *the drivers and motivators* – analyzing the individual and social factors that can incentivize or deter people from responding positively to anti-corruption initiatives, such as the ethical, social psychological and negotiation drivers of corruption. By offering a basic approach by which these factors can be assessed and understood, anti-corruption strategies can be improved and programs made more effective and appropriate to different country conditions.

The main objective of proceeding through an assessment approach is to assure that we cast a wide enough analytical net to capture the breadth of factors that may affect corruption and anti-corruption prospects in a country and then provide a clearly justified and strategic rationale for programmatic recommendations. The guidance provides assessment teams with tools for diagnosing the underlying causes of corruption by analyzing both the status of laws and institutions, as well as the social-political-economic context and dynamics of a country. It is especially important to also assess what norms, traditions, and incentives motivate corrupt and anti-corrupt behaviors in the country, so that reform programs are properly targeted. By understanding these country-specific drivers of corruption, assessment teams should be able to develop reasonable insights on government sectors and functions that are most vulnerable to corruption and the types of initiatives that are likely to be successful in reversing or controlling these problems. The framework described below also provides a rationale for setting priorities, choosing some approaches and rejecting others.

This assessment approach does not offer automatic cookie-cutter conclusions. The assessment team will have to assimilate and analyze information from a variety of sources to reach conclusions and recommendations. The framework facilitates this process by providing organizing concepts, information gathering tools, and corruption categories that can help in diagnosing the targeted country, prioritizing key sectors and functions in need of remediation, and developing an overall strategic plan for anti-corruption programming. Each assessment team may want to adapt, expand, or alter these approaches based on the needs of the final users and/or the specifics of the country being assessed.

Principles underlying assessments

Anti-corruption initiatives need to target and account for the existing legal and institutional foundations already established in a country, the current political-economic context, and the prevailing social and individualistic drivers and motivators of corrupt behavior. Assessments of these factors are essential in the design and implementation of appropriate reforms that can have positive effect. While there may be anti-corruption laws and agencies, detection and enforcement may be weak or nonexistent, and institutions underfunded. At the same time, analysis of the political economy may reveal useful entry points, opportunities, or constraints for reform programs that can be promoted by reform champions or frozen by spoilers; possible interest or resistance to change from political parties; and the inclusion or exclusion of active civil society groups, the mass media, and the private sector that can spur demand for change.

If appropriate controls are not in place or well-enforced and officials believe they can act with impunity – in other words, if misuse of office is seen as a low-risk, high-gain activity – corruption can progressively degrade a country's governance structures and its ability to deliver services to citizens. It can also undermine the rule of law and legitimacy of government, and thwart financial growth and investment along with a country's overall development objectives.

Over the past few decades, international research and practice have demonstrated that there are several major features of corruption that must be accounted for in any reform program. This assessment approach is premised on understanding all of these factors.

Foundational principles

All corruption is not the same. Corruption may manifest itself in similar ways across countries, but the underlying drivers can be different and the areas that corruption attacks can vary across geographic region and over time. The assessment framework is built to help governments, donors, and other interested parties identify different types of corruption (grand and administrative corruption, as well as state capture and predation), and the sectors and functions that are vulnerable to corruption in particular locales or points in time. By providing a better understanding of the nature of the problem and its root causes, this framework supports development of a comprehensive strategic outlook that can offer a customized approach to controlling corruption.

All countries do not possess the same proclivity toward the same types of corruption. Based on different foundational factors, patterns of development, and social-political-economic dynamics, countries manifest differing corruption tendencies and vulnerabilities. The assessment methodology incorporates a way to distinguish among countries along these dimensions that may help provide new perspectives on the types of programs that would be appropriate and effective in different settings.

Prerequisites. It is important to determine if certain preconditions for anticorruption programs exist or if they need to be implanted early in a comprehensive strategy. These prerequisites or essential building blocks include:

- The basic legal framework needed to fight corruption (such as an effective criminal and civil code, conflict of interest laws, meritocratic hiring rules, freedom of information laws, sunshine laws, asset disclosure rules, codes of conduct, and whistleblower protection),
- Effective law enforcement and prosecution,
- Adequate government oversight institutions,
- Accountable and transparent public finance processes, and
- Active nongovernmental advocacy and oversight of government operations.

While anti-corruption programs can proceed and sometimes thrive in the absence of some of these elements, fighting corruption is made more difficult if they are missing or not fully implemented. The assessment approach, through this legal-institutional analysis, will not only identify the existence of these laws and institutions but also how adequate they are and how well they are implemented. Inconsistencies between words and deeds can create major barriers to reform.

Contextual principles

Countries with similar political-economic conditions may have similar corruption dynamics. Patterns of corruption and responses to legal and regulatory incentives differ across societies in ways that reflect deep and long-term development processes and political-economic conditions. By understanding the underlying factors that influence these patterns – that is, the way people pursue, use, and exchange wealth and power in particular societies – it may be possible to identify the kinds of corruption problems a country is likely to have and, thereby, better diagnose its basic difficulties and devise appropriate countermeasures, not just treat its symptoms. Thus, it is important to recognize that countries with similar political-economic conditions are likely to have similar, though not necessarily identical, corruption dynamics.

Corruption is multisectoral. Corruption is both a governance and economic problem, and it is manifested in all development and service delivery sectors.[3] Its occurrence is facilitated by the absence or insufficiency of financial controls, performance monitoring for both personnel and programs, transparency, and mechanisms of accountability. Its consequences are often manifested in poor governance and economic distortions and stagnation.

While fighting corruption has traditionally been viewed as a democracy and governance task, it is also critical to address corruption vulnerabilities in each domain of a development portfolio. Often, service delivery sectors (education, health, electricity, etc.) are where people encounter corruption most visibly or frequently and where its impact can reduce the effectiveness of any number of other development initiatives.

Looking at the problem through a governance lens primarily focuses the analyst on determining if government institutions have the capacity and follow-through potential to deliver efficient, transparent, and accountable services within the law. Some of the key factors relate to adequacy of the legal and institutional framework, administrative complexity, capacity and professionalism of staff, and internal control and oversight mechanisms. A second important aspect of the governance equation is the role of the public in advocating, monitoring, and sanctioning. Key issues in this regard include access to information, freedom, the capacity of civil society and the media, and the effectiveness of elections as sanctioning mechanisms.

Essentially, corruption can be viewed as a governance problem within each sector. There may be some common approaches that can address corruption across sectors – related to budgeting and procurement, for example. But there are also sector-specific approaches that will be needed to deal with corruption vulnerabilities particular to certain sectors. Empirical analyses have shown that improvements in governance can have positive impacts on reducing corruption abuses, as can programs that directly attack corrupt practices.[4]

Looking at corruption through an economic lens puts the focus primarily on the extent of government intervention in the economy and its consequences on corrupt activities. Key factors from this perspective include overregulation, government control or rationing of resources, subsidies, procurement, revenue administration, and public expenditures, among many others.

Corruption affects multiple levels of government. Corruption can be found at all levels of government – from the central to the regional to the local levels. Preventive and control programs at the central level may have only limited reach and effectiveness down to the subnational levels of government. To be effective, initiatives are typically required from the top-down and from the bottom-up simultaneously. A strategic anti-corruption assessment needs to access information at all levels to understand differences in the nature of the problem and in programming requirements. This is accomplished through probing diagnostic questions within key sectors and functions, and special efforts to examine the phenomenon and impact of corruption at all levels.

All countries are not at the same level of anti-corruption readiness. The political will and commitment of governmental and nongovernmental leaders defines only one aspect of a country's readiness to deal effectively with the problem of corruption. The capacity to act effectively is the other element that determines a country's readiness level. Thus, there needs to be a basic framework of anti-corruption laws, regulations, and institutions in place that serve as the prerequisites or preconditions for all initiatives. As well, government officials and civil society, the mass media, and business leaders must have the training, resources, and capacity to act effectively and with meaningful resolve over the long haul if anti-corruption initiatives are to be adequately implemented.

Corruption is strongly influenced by situational factors. The types and levels of corruption in a society are largely affected by both situational opportunities and obstacles. The major factors at play include:

- *Institutional Capacity.* There may be motivation but little capacity and experience to fight corruption effectively. Training, technical assistance, and financial support can be used to strengthen the capacity of governmental and nongovernmental groups in the areas of advocacy, oversight, ethics, investigation, prosecution, awareness building, prevention, transparency, and accountability. No country needs to invent such programs from scratch; there is a wealth of international experience and a growing body of best practices that can be shared. Institutional capacity is analyzed during the sectoral-functional diagnostic phase of the assessment.
- *Culture and Tradition.* In many countries, the use of public office for private gain is viewed as a matter of their tradition and cultural heritage. It is often difficult to toss off approaches to the use of wealth, power, and influence that have become accepted and commonplace. Often, these practices can exist side-by-side with legal structures which prohibit them. While difficult, it is possible to reverse such cultural/traditional tendencies. Popular champions of reform and more modern institutions can emerge to promote rule of law, accountability and transparency, and exercise power responsibly.
- *International Actors, Influencers, and Initiatives.* International organizations and donors can strongly influence and promote anti-corruption programs. In some cases, such as with the US Millennium Challenge Corporation and World Bank, grants and technical assistance related to anti-corruption programs are conditional on meeting certain corruption index thresholds or the creation of new anti-corruption institutions. Donors require serious demonstration of a country's actions and intentions in fighting corruption as a prerequisite for larger loans and grants. Conversely, international actors can undermine anti-corruption programs by sending mixed messages. Coordination and consistency among donors (as well as among various countries' diplomatic, development, and commercial actors) regarding intentions and priorities can make the difference between leveraging common objectives and contradictions that undermine anti-corruption investments. Other initiatives, such as the United Nations Convention Against Corruption

(UNCAC) and similar regional treaties, establish agreed standards for anti-corruption efforts; some involve review mechanisms to evaluate a country's progress in meeting those standards. Industry-based efforts like the Extractive Industries Transparency Initiative (EITI) also establish standards for anti-corruption efforts in specific sectors, though the voluntary nature of all these initiatives means they do not guarantee adherence by all countries who sign on.

Motivational principles

Actors and political will. There will be little hope for meaningful and sustainable change if critical stakeholders are not actively committed to reform. Important actors can operate in government, civil society, business, and the media. Anti-corruption programs can be initiated in whichever development sector is ready for change and willing to take a stand. Champions for change and ethical leadership may exist or can be nurtured. If there are none, it still may be possible to mobilize civil society groups, the media, or business leaders to advocate for reforms and exert external pressure on government.

There can also be political will *against* reform – vested interests who want to maintain the system of corruption in place as is. It is important to identify who these interests are and understand their incentives and their power. With accurate assessment of these forces, it may be possible to propose ways of diminishing or bypassing such opponents of good governance. Overall, this framework evaluates stakeholders – both pro and con – in the context of the priority sectors and functions that are diagnosed.

Corruption impacts multiple levels in society and each level responds to corruption differently. Administrative or petty corruption is typically characterized as an everyday, low-level abuse of power that citizens and business people encounter – for example, requests for small bribes or gifts, speed money, influence peddling, and turning a blind eye to circumvent the rules or to get things done that should have been free or part of expected public service delivery.

Grand corruption involves higher-level officials and larger sums of money, and typically includes, for example, kickbacks to win large public procurements, embezzlement of public funds, irregularities in political party and campaign financing, and political patronage and clientelism. Grand corruption can sometimes come in the extreme forms of (a) state capture – where economic elites effectively dictate policies to suit their private interests or (b) state predation – where political power is used to extract financial benefits from a country's economic resources.

There is no clear line between administrative and grand corruption, and the two are often linked, but the distinction is nonetheless important for assessing problems and developing programmatic responses. If high-level corruption is endemic, for example, it may be much less likely that political leaders will be able to implement meaningful reforms, even if those reforms are only targeted at lower-level officials.

At the same time, administrative corruption in a particular ministry or agency may be addressed if the leadership of that agency is not entangled in webs of corrupt exchanges. The assessment framework encourages the team to examine all levels of corruption and develop appropriate remedies. While it is not always possible to implement, international experience suggests that it is preferable to address all types in a comprehensive program – the high-level influence peddling, the low-level administrative corruption, the collusive state capture relationships and the outright ravaging of the economy by political leaders. The logic of such an approach is that the combined impact of addressing all levels of corruption will increase the probability of detection and change corruption into a high-risk, high-cost activity across the board and reduce popular tolerance for corrupt practices.

Conducting the assessment

Traditionally, corruption has been assessed primarily as a problem of weaknesses in *legal and institutional arrangements*. But to avoid government and donor responses that only treat the symptoms of corruption, it is essential to take a more strategic perspective that assesses the underlying *political-economic context* and *the deeper socio-ethical-negotiation drivers and dynamics* that have influenced the evolution of corruption in a country. We offer a way to combine these factors and help users move from a *general understanding* of corruption issues to *problem definition* and then to *programming* (see Figure 11.1). The assessment framework presented in detail in the Appendix is applicable across all development sectors, not simply in democracy/governance or economic growth program areas.

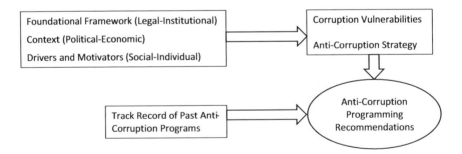

Figure 11.1 Assessment Approach: From understanding to problem definition to programming.

Foundational assessment issues

Corruption is facilitated or inhibited by the legal and regulatory framework, how it is put into practice, and how it is enforced or monitored through governmental institutions. This section of the assessment is meant to be conducted by legal experts who are well-versed in the current status of laws, regulations, and institutions that are typically considered to be the prerequisites of a comprehensive anti-corruption regime. The key questions include categories addressed in the UN Convention Against Corruption (UNCAC). These factors:

- Describe the formal provisions of laws and provide brief, factual responses as to the nature and content of the laws, regulations, and institutions that exist, at least on paper.
- Provide insight on how these provisions are implemented in practice and insight into the operations, effectiveness, and adequacy of the legal/regulatory provisions and institutions in reality.
- Identify the categories or subcategories that are the weakest or present the greatest vulnerability to corrupt practices.

The results of the analysis should be summarized at the beginning of the Assessment Report by highlighting the weaknesses and gaps in the formal legal-institutional framework, as well as in the provisions put into practice.

Contextual assessment issues

While knowledge of the strengths and weaknesses of laws and institutions is necessary for diagnosing corruption problems and proposing solutions, it is not sufficient. Understanding the dynamics of political and economic power that shape these factors is equally essential for developing a realistic strategy to address the problem. The questions in the Context section of the assessment focus on political economy factors: how power and wealth affect corruption. Power looks at the roles of political networks, and influence and wealth look at the roles of economic networks.

The readiness of stakeholders to promote and implement anti-corruption reforms is a function of their political will and capacity to act. It is important to examine the major stakeholder groups in terms of those that are likely to demonstrate a commitment to reforms and those that are likely to oppose them. While this analysis will present only a snapshot in time of the readiness/opposition of groups to deal with anti-corruption reforms, it can provide a useful early assessment of opportunities and problems that future anti-corruption programs may encounter – who may be called on as champions for change, who needs to be nurtured, who is ready to advocate, and who has vested interests in maintaining currently corrupt systems. This information is extremely valuable for informing decisions on where to focus reform initiatives.

At the heart of the anti-corruption assessment are in-depth analyses conducted "where corruption lives" in particular government sectors and functions. In many heavily corrupted societies, the problem is found almost everywhere; in order to decide what to do first, the assessment exercise must identify where corruption hurts the most and where the best opportunities exist to remedy these problems. The assessment examines several questions to identify an initial set of sectors, functions and institutions with the greatest corruption risks that are most ripe for resolution. In this regard, the Context section of the assessment focuses on analyzing questions about institutional capacity, transparency, accountability, and stakeholder interest in priority sectors and functions. The following are the sets of questions:

• Describe actor dynamics, focusing on reform champions and potential spoilers within government, as well as outside of government – civil society organizations, the mass media, businesses, and political parties. How do they use their power and influence? What is their political will and commitment, their readiness to act, and their capacity?
• Identify and examine key sectors and functions that are most vulnerable to corruption. What is the degree of transparency and accountability in their operations? What are the pathways, entry points and obstacles for reform in these sectors and functions? Develop detailed diagnoses of these risky sectors and functions. The assessment team can draw upon a library of 19 sectoral and functional Diagnostic Guides that provides probing questions to understand these critical sector/function-specific corruption weaknesses.[5]

Assessment issues concerning drivers and motivators

In this section of the assessment, questions examine the drivers and motivators of corrupt behavior. The focus is on both group and individual levels of analysis – what are the detailed enablers and inhibitors of corrupt behavior. Among the issues to be evaluated are:

• Analyzing social and organizational norms that promote or inhibit corruption. Involved here is the pressure to social conformity if corruption is acceptable behavior. It is important to understand the incentives and deterrents to comply with these norms. How widespread are rationalizations and excuses for corrupt behavior within the social frame? Do these excuses produce a culture where it is acceptable to behave corruptly with impunity?
• Examining what is considered to be ethical behavior within society. What is considered immoral? How is attention to self-interest versus ethical and empathetic behavior considered? To what extent are ethical versus unethical perspectives socialized in society?

- Understanding the extent to which individuals are motivated by risk averse behaviors.
- Assessing the opportunities for negotiating corrupt transactions between citizens and officials. For which of these transactions do these face-to-face interactions occur? Are there ways to eliminate such direct interactions?

These drivers and motivators must be targeted properly in the assessment – at a sufficiently practical and granular level – so that they can support development of appropriate programmatic options. If the assessment is conducted at a broad national level, it may not be possible to focus these driver/motivator questions to capture what is really incentivizing corruption at an individual or group level. So, it is recommended that the assessments be conducted in a more concise and targeted way: at a sector level (to understand the drivers in the health, education, or agricultural sector, for example), at a local government level (to understand the drivers in a more precise socio-political context), or at a stakeholder level, from the perspective of government officials, business people, CSO leaders, and ordinary citizens.

Past track record

The past experience of anti-corruption reforms in the country needs to be analyzed as well to learn lessons from what worked, what did not, and why. Best practice in other countries may not apply to the country under assessment, but previous attempts locally might offer valuable insights on what types of initiatives to try again and which to avoid.

Anti-corruption strategy

Examination of all the data described above should yield customized approaches for the given country that are likely to be effective. Even if some initiatives are successful, experience shows that a whole-of-government/whole-of-society strategy is needed to reduce corruption from spreading to other domains and sectors.

Based on the previous steps of this assessment, there should be sufficient insight into the country's corruption problems and anti-corruption opportunities to sketch out an anti-corruption strategy that can guide the development of recommended reform initiatives. The strategy will provide a plan of action for sustained efforts against the underlying causes shaping a country's particular pattern of corruption. The strategy will provide the basis for a set of working hypotheses that can be pilot tested and confirmed.

Analysis of the legal-institutional framework and the state of its implementation should have provided an understanding of what are usually considered the prerequisites for effective anti-corruption programs, including the gaps and deficiencies in the current context. From the political-economic analysis, information should have been generated about the dynamics of key stakeholders, the underlying vulnerabilities in particular institutions and sectors, and suggestions about anti-corruption approaches that are likely to be helpful in developing a meaningful near- and long-term strategy. From the assessment of motivational drivers, specific ideas for programming opportunities should emerge that can work within the existing social norms, ethical environment, and transactional setting surrounding corruption.

Together, these analyses provide the team with a wealth of information for an initial integrated strategy development. The strategy outline should include discussions of the following:

- The *Core Problems* represent the underlying causes of corruption that have emerged from the initial assessment. This ensures that the assessment does not deal merely with the visible symptoms of corruption but seeks to remedy problems that can have a more positive and long-lasting impact on the country. Core problems are usually described broadly and might include, for example, poor political accountability and competition, colonization of the civil service bureaucracy by political party loyalists, poor tax collection, weak governance institutions or economic and political opportunities plundered by the elite few.
- The *Strategic Goals* should be geared to specifically address the Core Problems. They propose broad basic approaches to remedy the identified problems. Core problem areas and key strategic directions can include, for example, strengthening property rights, developing stronger boundaries between the state and business, decreasing the state's role in the economy, establishing systems for credible political competition and elections, generating systems of incentives for civil servants to work for the public good not political patrons, developing an independent judiciary, and promoting an independent mass media.
- *Working Hypotheses* should be formulated that reflect these core problems and strategic goals in a way that they can be tested – validated, refuted, or adjusted – by the information and insights collected during implementation and monitoring activities. These hypotheses should get to the heart of why corruption plagues the targeted country and what broad approaches are likely to have positive impacts.

Recommended reforms

Ultimately, recommended reform initiatives to reduce or eliminate corruption vulnerabilities and corrupt behaviors should emanate from the strategy. These need to be a series of practical initiatives that fit within the larger scope of the strategy and tailored to the country's foundational factors, context, and active drivers. The recommended reforms should be prioritized and shown to fit into the overall strategic logic of the assessment's analysis – addressing the core problems and strategic goals in the Strategic Plan. The final product of this task should be a well-considered integrated program for anti-corruption action. Recommendations should be designated as short-, medium-, or long-term priorities. Each recommendation should be described briefly, major stakeholders and counterparts listed, potential obstacles to success recognized, anticipated impacts on corruption identified, and likelihood of success estimated.

* * * * * *

Such an anti-corruption assessment was carried out in late 2005 in Ukraine, a year after the Orange Revolution which summoned in a change of government that was bolstered by an anti-corruption platform. The key analyses and findings of this assessment are provided in the next chapter as an example of the targeting, detail and level of recommendations that a corruption assessment – using the model presented in this chapter – can offer to policymakers and practitioners to guide their implementation of new reform programs.

Notes

1 See R. Hanna, S. Bishop, S. Nadel, G. Scheffler and K. Durlacher (2011). *The Effectiveness of Anti-corruption Policy: What Has Worked, What Hasn't, and What We Don't Know–A Systematic Review*. Technical report. London: EPPI-Centre, Social Science Research Unit, Institute of Education, University of London; Jesper Johnson, Nils Taxell and Dominik Zaum (2012). *Mapping Evidence Gaps in Anti-corruption: Assessing the State of the Operationally Relevant Evidence on Donors' Actions and Approaches to Reducing Corruption*. U4 Issue No. 7, October. Bergen, Norway: U4 Anti-Corruption Resource Center; Alina Rocha Menocal and Nils Taxell (2015). *Why Corruption Matters: Understanding Causes, Effects and How to Address Them: Evidence Paper on Corruption*. London: Department for International Development (DFID); Stefano Migliorisi and Clay Wescott (2011). *A Review of World Bank Support for Accountability Institutions in the Context of Governance and Anticorruption*. IEG Working Paper 2011/5. Washington, DC: World Bank; Norwegian Agency for Development Cooperation (2011). *Joint Evaluation of Support to Anti-corruption Efforts 2002–2009, Synthesis*. Oslo, Norway: NORAD; Organisation for Economic Co-operation and Development (2016). *Anti-corruption Reforms in Eastern Europe and Central Asia Progress and Challenges, 2013–2015*. Paris: OECD; Svetlana Winbourne and Bertram Spector (2014). *Analysis of USAID Anticorruption Programming Worldwide (2007–2013), Final Report*. Washington, DC: USAID.
2 The following sections of this chapter draw upon Bertram Spector, Michael Johnston and Svetlana Winbourne (2009). *Anti-corruption Assessment Handbook, Final Report*. Washington, DC: USAID. At: https://pdf.usaid.gov/pdf_docs/pa00jp37.pdf.
3 See Bertram Spector, editor (2005). *Fighting Corruption in Developing Countries: Strategies and Analysis*. Bloomfield, CT: Kumarian Press; J. Edgardo Campos and Sanjay Pradhan, editors (2007). *The Many Faces of Corruption: Tracking Vulnerabilities at the Sector Level*. Washington, DC: The World Bank.
4 Daniel Kaufmann (2003). *Rethinking Governance: Empirical Lessons Challenge Orthodoxy*. Washington, DC: World Bank, March 11. At: http://ssrn.com/abstract=386904.

5 For these Diagnostic Guides, see Appendix 4 in Spector, Johnston and Winbourne (2009), op. cit., At: https://pdf.usaid.gov/pdf_docs/pa00jp37.pdf. Included are probing questions for the following governmental sectors, institutions and functions, stakeholders, and cross-cutting issues: Judiciary, Legislature, Public Institutions/Civil Service, Supreme Audit Institution, Anticorruption Agencies, Regional and Local Government, Law Enforcement Institutions, Electoral Commission and Election Process, Political Parties, Taxation System, Customs, Healthcare, Education, Private Sector, Civil Society, Media and Access to Information, Budget and Financial Management, Public Procurement, and Privatization.

12 Case study

Ukraine assessment (2005)

In late 2005, the United States Agency for International Development wanted a comprehensive assessment of corruption conducted for Ukraine to help it plan for future technical support programs.[1] The objectives of this assessment were twofold. First, it was meant to provide a broad analysis of the state of corruption in Ukraine – taking into account the political-economic context that facilitates or inhibits corruption, the legal/regulatory/oversight framework that can control corrupt tendencies, the constituencies for and against reform, ongoing anti-corruption programs, drivers and motivators of corrupt behavior in Ukraine, and entry points for appropriate anti-corruption initiatives. In accordance with USAID's Anti-Corruption Strategy,[2] this assessment was to examine multiple levels of corruption (petty, grand, and state capture) and the key sectors and functions where corruption has impaired governance capacity and the achievement of development objectives.

Second, the assessment was supposed to reach certain conclusions and provide particular guidance to the USAID mission in Ukraine concerning programmatic options it might consider to deal with corruption vulnerabilities. The resulting report was to offer suggested programs, sector-by-sector and function-by-function, that the mission could use to design its anti-corruption strategy and promote targeted anti-corruption activities in its existing programs, as well as new initiatives. Cross-cutting recommendations that apply to several sectors were intentionally included in each relevant section of the final report so that the sectoral discussions could be complete unto themselves.

The assessment was conducted in the field in November 2005, guided by the corruption assessment methodology described in the previous chapter and the series of question presented in the appendix of this book.[3] As a result, the facts, judgments, and conclusions discussed in the assessment's findings that follow reflect the state of corruption and anti-corruption efforts as of 2005. While many new political changes and dynamics have occurred in Ukraine since this assessment was conducted, it is still a meaningful historical example that occurred at a critical pivot point in Ukraine's recent history, and is valuable in demonstrating the type of assessment that

DOI: 10.4324/9781003241119-15

can support the design and implementation of effective anti-corruption reform programs in the future.

Overview of corruption in Ukraine

The fight against corruption in Ukraine received a welcome boost between late November 2004 and January 2005 as a result of the Orange Revolution. The Revolution and the election campaign leading up to it clearly highlighted the new leadership's interest in dealing with the long-standing problem of corruption in Ukraine. The rhetoric of the revolution raised expectations and provided an outlet for massive citizen frustration concerning official abuse and weak rule of law. The installation of the Viktor Yushchenko government elevated the hopes of many, both domestically and internationally, that the traditional systems of Ukrainian corruption would be drastically changed, quickly and decisively. However, a year later, only a little had been accomplished – and in a disorganized and not so visible fashion – to actualize the anti-corruption promises of the campaign, and public disappointment and cynicism had grown.

Corruption in Ukraine still remains one of the top problems threatening economic growth and democratic development. Administrative corruption is widespread and visible in the everyday lives of citizens and business people, and grand corruption is also widespread, though not as visible, in the higher levels of government where large sums of money and political influence are at stake. Without significant changes in the incentives faced by these elites and a significant strengthening in the capacity of civil society and the business community to effectively demand accountability from public officials, little is likely to change in this corruption environment.

Ukraine can be categorized as a *closed insider economy*[4] – a country strongly influenced by elite cartels. Top political and business figures collude behind a façade of political competition and colonize both the state apparatus and sections of the economy. Immediately after independence, these influential elite and their organizations grew into major financial-industrial structures that used their very close links with and influence over government, political parties, the mass media and the state bureaucracy to enlarge and fortify their control over the economy and sources of wealth. They used ownership ties, special privileges, relations with government and direct influence over the courts, law enforcement and regulatory organizations to circumvent weaknesses in governmental institutions to their own private advantage. Their tactics and their results can be viewed as a clear exercise of *state and regulatory capture*. At the same time, there is a high tolerance for corrupt practices throughout society, facilitating a trickle-down effect that allows petty, administrative corruption to flourish.

Can the Yushchenko government rebuild with a responsive, accountable and professional bureaucracy? While the situation may have appeared to the Western eye as an incipient competitive market economy, the system still operates largely in a collusive and opaque fashion, subverting the rule of law, and with apparent disregard for the public good.

The Orange Revolution signaled the beginning of a new transformation in Ukrainian social, economic, and political life. During this transformation process, many transparency, accountability, and integrity issues emerged at the same time that laws, rules, institutions, procedures, and incentives changed and Ukrainians at all levels, both in and out of government, sought to develop truly democratic governance, a fair market economy and equitable delivery of essential public services. During such times of major upheaval and change, corruption can sometimes be both tolerated and nurtured – to get necessary things accomplished in the short run under uncertain conditions. However, the extensive distortions generated by past corruption to the social, economic, and political fabric of Ukraine needed to be counteracted quickly to avert permanent damage and a deceleration of development objectives. Certainly, the pronouncements of the Yushchenko government to fight corruption and its pledge to work toward European Union accession were positive signals that needed to be translated into implementable programs that yield visible results.

Foundational factors

Fighting corruption was highlighted among the top three objectives of the Yushchenko administration in its governmental program, *Towards the People*. However, after almost a year in office, no significant, consistent, and visible actions were accomplished. The legal framework remained incomplete, in particular in the corruption prevention area, though some laws and amendments had been drafted. Implementation of laws remained a critical problem. There was no governmental institution empowered to lead anti-corruption efforts in the country. National policy and priorities were not defined. Rhetoric about fighting corruption at the highest level was not translated in a clear message and into visible deeds. Several agencies were drafting different versions of a national anti-corruption strategy with limited coordination. Few agencies had developed or were implementing internal anti-corruption programs. On the other hand, the government had signed or ratified several international conventions, committing itself to join the Council of Europe's Group of States Against Corruption (GRECO) and implement its recommendations, and reactivating its cooperation under the OECD-sponsored Anti-Corruption Network for Transition Economies (ACN).

Status of national anti-corruption policy

Until the end of 2005, the "Concept on Fighting Corruption for 1998–2005" served as the principal policy document directing national efforts in fighting corruption. The Concept outlined major strategic directions, but did not provide benchmarks and specific terms. Year after year since 1997, the government drafted Plans of Action to Fight Organized Crime and Corruption and year after year, parliamentary hearings on their implementation concluded that their enactment was unsatisfactory. Typically, Soviet-style in their format and evaluation procedures, these Plans proved to be ineffective and often harmful. Since its adoption, the Concept had never been revised to align it with changing situations or international guidance. There had been a number of presidential decrees, cabinet of ministers ordinances, and legislation issued over ten years to patch gaps in the deficient institutional and legal framework. The Presidential Coordinating Committee on Combating Corruption and Organized Crime, an institution that was supposed to assume responsibility for coordinating and monitoring implementation of the national policy, was not effective either.

Failure to achieve meaningful results in implementing the Concept or the annual plans can be explained: the government never spelled out clear objectives, did not establish benchmarks, never revisited its policy, did not identify results indicators, and did not establish a credible monitoring system. According to the Ministry of Justice, the Plan of Anti-Corruption Actions for 2004 approved by a Cabinet of Ministers Decree produced a review of the national legal framework and developed a concept for a corruption monitoring system. Since documents describing the results of these efforts were not publicly available, it is impossible to determine their effectiveness or utility for the future.

A decree of President Yushchenko, "On urgent measures to deshadow the economy and counteract corruption," was the first policy document by the new Administration calling for strengthened measures in several corruption areas: defining corruption and the subjects of corruption, public monitoring of corruption, conflicts of interest and financial disclosure, separation of business and public duties, securing privatization, and defining political appointees versus civil servants, among other items. While the decree touched upon a number of important issues, the measures appeared rather random and disconnected. Some of the measures were being developed in the form of draft laws or amendments, but the decree could be viewed as a demonstration of the president's commitment to address the corruption problem.

By 2006, there were at least three new draft national anti-corruption strategies and concepts that employed a cross-sectoral approach developed by three separate agencies: the Parliamentary Committee against Organized Crime and Corruption (CAOCC), the State Security Service (SBU), and the Ministry of Justice (MOJ). Although the government seemed to be aware of these dispersed efforts, little had been done to reconcile and consolidate these drafts into one document, though each party appeared to be in favor of joining forces and were ready to start a dialogue. These parties agreed that the National Security and Defense Council would serve as the coordinator of anti-corruption reforms within the Government of Ukraine (GOU).

Recommendations. The Government needed to define its priorities for preventing and fighting corruption and to formulate them in a systematic single national strategy supplemented with plans of action. In view of Ukraine's intention to join the European Union, the priorities should be harmonized with EU standards. Adopting and implementing GRECO principles, EU Conventions, and other EU legal instruments should be major benchmarks in the strategy. OECD's ACN recommendations and the UN Convention could serve as additional sources to help define the strategy.

The Strategy should establish benchmarks and milestones. Indicators of results and a system of monitoring and evaluation should be developed. This is very important to assess progress. The Strategy should be a dynamic document and subject to review on an annual basis along with the action plans.

The Strategy should have short- and long-term priorities. The short-term priorities should be highly visible and have an impact on the broad public and its most insecure sectors. Activities and results should be broadly publicized.

New opportunities for Ukraine came about in November 2005 when the United States Millennium Challenge Corporation approved Ukraine for participation in its Threshold Country Program, making it eligible for intensive technical support in implementing anti-corruption efforts. Some of this assistance could be focused on designing, gaining consensus for and implementing a national anti-corruption strategy.

Status of anti-corruption enforcement legislation

Ukraine's anti-corruption legislation remained incomplete and inconsistent. The principal legal enforcement documents that directly address corruption are the Law of Ukraine on Fighting Corruption and the Criminal Code (Part 17, in particular). The Law of Ukraine on Fighting Corruption was passed in 1995 and went through nine insignificant amendments since then. Most experts and practitioners agree that this law needs further modification or replacement with a new law to harmonize it with today's international legal standards and requirements.

There are several recent draft amendments in the parliament (Rada). The latest one was submitted on 15 April 2004 by the Parliamentary Committee on Fighting against Organized Crime and Corruption to extend applicability of the law to high-level officials in the executive branch, including the prime minister, vice prime ministers, and ministers. This draft was being prepared for its second reading. On 14 July 2004, a draft Law on the Basis for Preventing and Fighting Corruption was submitted to the Parliament. The Main Scientific-Expert Department reviewed the draft and recommended some changes prior to submitting it to the first reading. This draft law was supposed to replace the current Law of Ukraine on Fighting Corruption. The government referred to it at several international forums and in official reports and statements. There are several other draft laws at different stages of development.

Implementation of this anti-corruption enforcement legislation is generally problematic. It has been used against low-level public officials and bureaucrats for small and often questionable offenses; higher level officials generally are untouched. Sometimes the law is used as political retribution or as an instrument of suppression. After the Yushchenko administration came to power, many investigations into high profile corruption allegations were initiated, but there have been few court hearings.

Recommendations. Rapid adoption and implementation of new law enforcement legislation can be a useful addition to the government's overall anti-corruption program. Donor pressure can be placed on the administration to bring some high profile cases to court. While "frying big fish" is not effective as a sustainable anti-corruption program by itself, it can be a useful and dramatic demonstration of the Yushchenko government's determination to crack down on high-level abuse of office.

Status of corruption prevention legislation

Several pieces of important corruption prevention legislation were under consideration in late 2005.

Conflicts of Interest and Codes of Conduct. There has been no particular law on conflicts of interest (COI), though COI provisions can be found in the Civil Service Law and the Main Rules of Civil Servant Conduct (both are applicable to career civil servants and local public officials, but not to officials at the ministerial level), the Ukrainian Constitution, the Law on Public Deputies of Ukraine, and some other pieces of legislation. These provisions generally interpret conflicts of interest in a very limited fashion. They prohibit public officials and civil servants from being involved in any business activities or holding any other office and restrict them from supervising or being supervised by a family member. There are no policies or procedures for resolving conflicts of interest once detected. Rather, current provisions stipulate that these conflicts should be dealt with prior to taking public office, otherwise the official will be subject to the Law of Ukraine on Fighting Corruption or other enforcement laws.

As for high-level public officials in the executive branch, the only law that regulates them is the Constitution. The Law on Public Deputies of Ukraine has a very brief article on Deputies' ethics. All existing legislative documents are very sketchy about COI provisions and not very practical. A Draft Code of Conduct of Public Officials was developed by the Ministry of Justice and was posted on their website for public comments. This draft discussed, with some specificity, the conduct of public officials, conflicts of interest, employment upon retirement, and other issues. In addition, the Draft Law on Administrative Procedures was being developed by the MOJ and was supposed to define the administrative procedures and responsibilities of public officials and civil servants clearly.

Public Hiring and Appointments. Hiring is regulated by the Civil Service Law and regulations developed by the Main Department of the Civil Service of Ukraine. The Department has issued guidance on hiring procedures, but nepotism and favoritism remain a common practice to fill open positions. A new Draft Civil Service Law was drafted and discussed with the international community at a June 2005 conference and with the public via discussions at the administration's Public Collegia. The principal objective of this new law was to bring Ukraine in harmony with EU standards. However, the problem lies not so much in the law but in the way it was implemented.

Asset Disclosure. Several laws require financial disclosure for candidates and holders of public office and for civil servants and their immediate families. Only information on candidates running for elected office is available to the public. Financial disclosure information for public officials and civil servants is not publicly available due to privacy and personal safety restrictions. However, there is much skepticism about how these requirements are implemented in practice and how they can be used to control corruption.

Access to Information. There are several laws, presidential decrees, and other legislative acts that regulate information availability to the public, among them the Law on Information, the Law on Providing Information about the Government to the Media, the Law on Television and Radio, the Law on the Press, the Presidential Decree on Further Measures to Ensure Openness in Government, and the Cabinet of Ministers Order on Measures to Develop a System of "Electronic Government." Although all of these pieces of legislation discuss different aspects of how information is provided to the public, implementation of these laws by different governmental institutions is very uneven and the level of detail and the format in which information is provided are generally not adequate for meaningful use by citizens or organizations.

For example, the annual budget that is published on the government's website is 50 pages long and provides information at only the highest levels of generality. Governmental institutions, even those that have the most informative websites, publish press releases and information on legislation, but do not post reports and analysis of their performance. Studies conducted by several NGOs on governmental transparency at the central and local levels have revealed frequent abuses of citizen rights related to information access. On the other hand, civil society rarely demands better and more detailed information.

Citizen Complaint Mechanisms and Whistleblower Protection. There is a law that regulates citizen inquiries and complaints submission and handling procedures by governmental agencies. Every governmental institution is obligated to have mechanisms to collect and respond to citizen complaints. In addition, almost every governmental agency introduced telephone and web-based hotlines. But most studies of the effectiveness of these mechanisms identify the public's general frustration and skepticism. To strengthen these options or provide an alternative, Presidential Public Reception offices were opened in all oblasts and report a mounting number of complaints. It is too early to say if this new initiative is helping to improve the situation.

On the other side of the coin, there is no particular law that provides protection for public officials or civil servants who report on corruption or misconduct in their offices. Some general provisions are included in existing laws that ostensibly protect any citizen. For example, the Law on Citizen Inquiries prohibits retribution against citizens and their family members who submit complaints or criticize any governmental or private institution or officials. In the Criminal Code, persons who report paying extorted bribes are not liable for the crime if at the time they report it there was no open case against them.

Sunshine Law (laws requiring that meetings of boards or commissions must be open to the public) and Citizen Participation. Sunshine laws do not exist in Ukraine. However, parliamentary sessions are broadcast on TV in full and there are no particular restrictions for civil society groups to attend parliamentary committees (if they know when they are convened). As for the executive branch, there are no regulations and there is no practice to allow citizens to attend its meetings. On the other hand, a recent presidential decree obligated all governmental institutions at the central and local levels to establish public councils or collegiums to involve civil society in policy development and decision-making processes. A new Draft Law on Openness and Transparency of the Government was drafted by the Ministry of Justice and posted on the Ministry website for public comment.

Recommendations. Technical assistance can be provided to develop meaningful legislation in these areas in harmonization with EU and international standards. Support should include not only comparative analysis of laws and legal drafting but assistance in implementation of the laws once adopted. This could take the form of establishing an Office of Governmental Ethics, development of web technology for information access, and expansion of the role of the Ombudsman's office, for example.

The context

Predominant corruption syndrome

A country's political-economic dynamics strongly influence the degree and nature of corruption in that country. The way corruption manifests itself differs from country to country depending upon the ways that people seek and use wealth and power, the strengths or weaknesses of the state, and political and social institutions that sustain and restrain these processes. Differences in these factors give rise to several major syndromes of corruption.[5] On the basis of Ukrainian expert evaluations that were supported by interviews with additional specialists in Ukraine, our analysis characterizes corruption in Ukraine as fitting into the *Elite Cartels* syndrome.

In Elite Cartel countries, such as Ukraine, top political and business figures collude and take over the state apparatus and key sectors in the economy. From the early 1990s, powerful officials in government and politics acquired and privatized key economic resources of the state. As well, shadowy businesses, allegedly close to organized crime, became powerful economic forces in several regions of the country.[6] Over the course of the past decade, these business groupings – or clans – as they became called, grew into major financial-industrial powerhouses that used their links and influence over government to strengthen their control of the economy. Their actions can be identified as state capture.

A report by the World Bank[7] refers to this clan-based Elite Cartel syndrome in Ukraine as a "closed insider economy" that can be an obstacle to future sustainable economic growth and integration into the EU and world economy. It hinders fair competition, encourages under-the-table deals and collusion between state officials and business, promotes rent-seeking behaviors, discourages foreign investment, and decreases adaptability over time.

In more recent years, several Ukrainian clans have grown and subdivided, increasing the number of clans that compete with one another for wealth and power, and establishing what appears to the Western eye as an incipient competitive market economy. Sometimes, for convenience, these clans coalesce on political issues.

After the Orange Revolution, the network of "bosses" within the government bureaucracy that could "make things happen" for the clans was partially destroyed by Prime Minister Tymoshenko, resulting in instability and uncertainty and a slowdown for major businesses. It lies in the hands of the Yushchenko government to take hold of this current opportunity to create new administrative procedures and institutions that are based on fair and equitable rules and a professional, meritocratic, and disciplined bureaucracy. Ukraine appears to be at a crossroads – from a clan-based Elite Cartel system to a more Western market economy based on transparency, the rule of law and fair competition, and patterns of good governance.

To move Elite Cartel countries, such as Ukraine, away from corruptive clan practices, state, political, and social institutions need to be strengthened, and existing trends toward increasingly open political and market competition must continue on a gradual path. The behind-the-scenes collusion, favoritism, and the colonization of bureaucracies and economic sectors that mark Elite Cartel corruption suggest that the "consensus package" of liberalization, improved public management, and enhanced transparency may be productive, as long as change is accompanied by institution-building in the political, economic, and social realms. The Yushchenko government professes these to be their goals. If directed action follows the words of this government, the political-economic habits that characterize Elite Cartel societies may change quickly in Ukraine. Otherwise, it may take a series of genuinely competitive elections, and alternations of power, to reduce their corruptive impact. But if citizens can reward effective government and punish the most corrupt over time – as evidenced by the thousands that staged demonstrations in Independence Square in 2004 – strong disincentives to collusion will have been created.

Key stakeholder institutions and groups

The enactment of anti-corruption reforms requires active promotion and mobilization by multiple constituencies and stakeholders that want to see greater transparency, accountability, and integrity. Government and non-government actors need to be activated. The principal institutions and groups that are likely to be involved and may need support from donors are described below. Among these actors are the current and future champions of Ukraine's anti-corruption programs.

Governmental institutions

Until recently, there was no single institution in the executive branch or any interagency institution that was responsible for fighting corruption in a comprehensive cross-sectoral fashion in Ukraine. Although the functions of the former Coordination Committee on Combating Corruption and Organized Crime that existed under the Presidential Administration since 1993 were transferred to the National Security and Defense Council (NSDC) by one of the very first decrees of the new president in January 2005, NSDC did not take any significant step to assume this responsibility.

According to the Secretary of the NSDC in an official statement on 25 November 2005, an Interregional Commission against Corruption is supposed to be established soon to coordinate the anti-corruption-related activities of the Security Service of Ukraine, Ministry of Internal Affairs, prosecutor general, and representatives of the court system. It is planned that the Commission will also include representatives from the legislature and civil society organizations, but it is unclear if it will represent other agencies from all branches of government.

The other institution that may play a very substantial role in anti-corruption efforts is the recently established Presidential Commission on Democracy and the Rule of Law chaired by the Minister of Justice. The major objective of the Commission is to align Ukrainian policy with the Copenhagen criteria toward joining the EU and to implement an EU-Ukraine Action Plan. Under the Action Plan, there are a number of activities that directly or indirectly relate to fighting and preventing corruption.

The recent agreement establishing the NSDC as anti-corruption coordinator within the GOU is the starting point for real dialogue among governmental agencies on how an interagency anti-corruption institution should be organized, under whose auspices, with what membership, and with what responsibility and authority.

There are several governmental institutions whose mission it is to oversee the executive branch and some of them are directly involved in overseeing corruption abuses. The *Parliament* has conducted oversight over issues of corruption since 1992 when the first Temporary Parliamentary Commission was established. Since 1994, the Parliament has a permanent Parliamentary Committee against Organized Crime and Corruption. The Committee is very active in promoting anti-corruption policies and initiating new legislation. Among other functions, it reviews governmental and other annual reports on corruption. Recently, the Committee drafted an Anti-Corruption Strategy on its own initiative. According to the Committee head, they wanted to set an example and push the executive branch to develop and implement a national anti-corruption policy.

The *Ombudsman* does not play a significant role in fighting or preventing corruption. While it collects thousands of citizen complaints, it does not analyze this information to identify problem trends but rather acts on a case-by-case basis and rarely passes this information to the offending governmental institutions to bring their attention to abuses and violations. The Ombudsman's Annual Report to Parliament primarily contains statistics on complaints and complainers but no systematic analysis or recommendations for reform.

The *Accounts Chamber* is an independent governmental oversight institution that is empowered to conduct performance and financial control and analysis of all governmental programs and institutions, as well as review how legislation is implemented. In 2004, the Chamber uncovered the misuse or ineffective use of budget and extra-budget funds totaling over US$1.5 billion. The Chamber is proactive in its efforts to reach out to governmental institutions to improve legislation and practices. It cooperates with the Prosecutor's office and monitors the further development of cases it passed to them for investigation.

The *Main Control and Revision Office of Ukraine* under the Ministry of Finance conducts financial audits of budget expenditures. It conducts such audits for over 15,000 organizations and agencies funded from the public budget throughout the country on an annual basis. During the first 9 months of 2005, it audited over 11,000 organizations and uncovered the unlawful use or misappropriation of public funds in the amount of about US$ 200,000 and recovered about US$ 71,000.

Most of Ukraine's law enforcement agencies (police, tax police, prosecutor's office) that have responsibility to fight corruption are typically rated in public opinion surveys as being the most corrupted governmental institutions. Law enforcement reform is currently under development, but it is too early to tell how it will affect internal controls and law enforcement effectiveness in fighting corruption.

In March 2005, the president issued an order to establish a working group to draft a concept to establish a National Bureau of Investigation with responsibilities to investigate high profile crime and corruption. Such an institution is not a new idea in Ukraine. An attempt to establish such a bureau in 1997 failed, in part, because of a disagreement among law enforcement agencies about the role of the bureau and the division of responsibilities. Since then, there have been at least seven drafts to establish a new bureau. The current idea is being forcefully debated and many experts believe that strengthening and reforming existing agencies would be more effective.

Many governmental institutions could be instrumental in preventing corruption, but are not significantly involved. Some would rather maintain the status quo. A brief overview of some of these institutions follows.

The *Main Department of Civil Service of Ukraine* became very active in 2005 in issuing guidance to prevent and detect corrupt behavior, for example, guidance for state and local self-governance institutions on setting up corruption prevention frameworks, guidance on drafting professional responsibilities for public servants to prevent abuses, and guidance on monthly compliance reporting with anti-corruption regulations. All of these documents attempt to establish better control over corrupt practices in the civil service system at all levels and jurisdictions. However, there is no evident attempt to establish indicators to measure the effectiveness of these measures and to monitor implementation.

The *Tax Administration* adopted an Anti-Corruption Action Plan for 2004–2008. According to this plan, a Code of Ethics was adopted, a special Anti-Corruption Department was established in addition to the Internal Control Department, and regulations on job responsibilities are being drafted. The Anti-Corruption Department issues monthly reports on internal investigations and results. These reports are posted on its website. According to the latest summary report for the first eight months of 2005, regional branches conducted 2,259 internal investigations, among which about 30% were triggered by citizen complaints, resulting in administrative sanctions against 1,078 employees including 142 that were fired. The Department also conducts preventive measures through training of Administration staff and public outreach programs.

The *Customs Administration* aggressively pursues a campaign against corruption and abuses of power in its operations. Over the past year, it removed or rotated executive staff members, conducted about 100 internal investigations resulting in over 200 dismissals and administrative sanctions, opened a hotline for citizens, imposed a set of rules and restrictions for its personnel, and limited cash that officers are allowed to have while on duty. The Customs Administration introduced a One-Stop Shop for processing freight customs clearance to reduce business-government interactions and opportunities for bribe-taking. The Customs Administration also issued a "Stop-Card" that businesses can use against customs officers who create unjustified delays or other barriers during customs procedures. Officers that receive these cards will be investigated by internal control units.

Civil society organizations

Civil society organizations and business associations are potential sources of important demand pressure on government to reform. The number of NGOs in Ukraine has been increasing, from 25,500 in 2000 to approximately 40,000 in 2004, of which about 10% are active.[8] Many of these operate on the demand side: helping their constituencies voice their concerns and interests and advocating for change with official bodies that will help their constituents. According to a 2003 report, the largest percent of Ukrainian NGOs are involved in advocacy and lobbying, training and information dissemination.[9] However, despite the incredible force they exerted during the Orange Revolution, Ukraine's civil society and business do not present a cohesive and mature front for change vis-à-vis the government. In general, there are few strong advocacy groups, few strong watchdog groups, uneven access to information about government operations and decisions, and limited experience in using information as a valuable tool in forcing government action. Their deficiencies are attributed to the fact that many have stayed away from highly political policy debates, they have minimal management capacity, and they are overly dependent on foreign donors. The business community is also poorly organized into associations (only about 25% of businesses belong to associations). Most businesses are very skeptical about their associations' willingness and capacity to provide services to members and represent member interests.

That said, there are many local and national NGOs and business groups that conduct very effective advocacy and watchdog functions related to anti-corruption reforms. For example, the All-Ukraine Network for People Living with AIDS gathered difficult-to-access cost data on pharmaceutical procurements conducted by the Ministry of Health (MOH) and compared them with similar procurements conducted in Ukraine by the Global Fund. They uncovered extremely wide cost differentials – procurements by the MOH as high as 27 times the cost of Global Fund procurements for the same medications. Apparently, collusion and special deals between the MOH procurement commission and the vendors were producing extremely unfavorable results and greatly endangering the public at large which is being deprived of necessary drugs. The Network presented their results to the MOH, the Ombudsman, the Prosecutor's Office, and international donors. Further investigations are now under way to validate their findings.

Other groups, such as the Laboratory for Legislative Initiatives, conduct very professional watchdog monitoring activities of Rada deputies. They maintain a website that contains deputy campaign promises, complete voting records of deputies that reveal if campaign promises were kept, and deputy linkages to business interests.

Among business associations, the Coordinating Expert Center of the Entrepreneurs' Union of Ukraine that currently unites over 60 business associations has been successful in promoting business-friendly legislation. Another strong voice for business interests is the Council of Entrepreneurs, the advisory body to the Cabinet of Ministers. Although it is established under government decree, it has recently become very active and vocal in monitoring regulatory reform implementation and serving as a channel for direct dialogue between government and the business community.

Mass media

While there are certainly many exceptions, the mass media in Ukraine as of 2005 was generally deficient in investigative reporting, a major channel by which journalists can serve as effective public watchdogs. The media suffers from a lack of public access to government information and from a poor understanding of the linkages among the law, the judicial system, and corruption. Since the revolution, the strong control of media outlets by clans/cartels has lessened and repressive actions against them have been relaxed.[10]

Recommendations

Government Institutions. Several key anti-corruption institutions are in transition or under development. If they are established and visibly demonstrate early commitments, donor support and technical assistance can be offered for implementation of programs. Encouragement should be given to government agencies to coordinate their efforts and develop partnerships with civil society groups. Monitoring and evaluation programs should be developed to measure and track progress of these government institutions toward achieving their anti-corruption objectives; those institutions that achieve their results can be rewarded through additional technical assistance programs.

Civil Society, Business Associations and Media Organizations. Capacity building programs should be supported to upgrade civil society organizations and business associations as effective advocacy and watchdog groups. Training in investigative reporting skills and competitions can be supported for journalists. Freedom of information and public access to information law reforms can be supported as well. Additional assistance can be provided to support the establishment of anti-corruption coalitions across NGOs and business associations, and among journalists to bolster their activities, facilitate sharing of experiences, and promote a single voice demanding reform.

Sectoral corruption

Many government sectors and functions were assessed to determine their vulnerabilities to corruption, the foundations and drivers of that corruption, and the status of any reform activities. Three of the sectors that were considered to be the most corrupt are presented here: the judicial, health, and education sectors.[11]

Judicial sector

The judicial system usually scores as one the most highly corrupted institutions in public opinion surveys in Ukraine. It is supposed to offer citizens access to fair and equal justice, but as currently configured its operation falls short of necessary independence from the Executive branch of government, it suffers from excessive discretion on the part of judges and court administrators, it lacks sufficient internal controls to effectively reduce abuse of power, and it is not as transparent in its procedures and decisions as it ought to be.

While many of these problems stem from inadequate legal, regulatory, and institutional frameworks, the chronic underfunding of the judicial budget certainly does not help. Several draft laws are under consideration in the Rada that would fix some of these problems. Adoption of these laws, followed by meaningful and rapid implementation, will demonstrate the government's political will to reduce corruption in the judicial sector in a visible way. A recent positive step is the enactment by the Rada of a new law establishing a registry of judicial decisions. Based on passage of these prospective reforms, additional donor support programs to fully implement change activities will be warranted.[12]

There are planned and ongoing USAID programs to strengthen commercial law, administrative courts and criminal judicial reform, through both implementing partner programs and the work of the US Justice Department's Regional Legal Advisor. Other US Government agencies also offer support to reform initiatives in the judicial area, from the State Department, the Federal Bureau of Investigations, and others. The OSCE has been providing assistance to help establish the new Administrative Court. The World Bank is just starting to plan a judicial reform program that is likely to focus heavily on court facility rehabilitation. European Commission/TACIS in conjunction with the Council of Europe are supporting judicial training, court administration, and procuracy reform to bring the Ukrainian practice into harmony with European approaches.

Corruption vulnerabilities

The principal components of the judicial sector are each severely vulnerable to corruption.

Judicial Selection. Despite a thin veil of merit-based competition for judicial recruitment and appointments, there are extensive corruption-prone problems in the selection process. Patronage from the Heads of Court (who are appointed by the president) is essential to get appointed to a court seat.

In larger cities, where competition is greatest, seats allegedly can be bought from the Head of Court for US$ 2000 for the general jurisdiction courts. The process of testing in the Qualification Commissions is not transparent. The Presidential Secretariat, which has no role in the appointment process by law, has inserted itself into the process and can pull or insert judicial candidates. The result of these problems is a judiciary that is plagued by favoritism, nepotism, and political influence.

Judicial Discipline. There is minimal monitoring and oversight of judicial conduct. Disciplinary investigations, hearings, and punishment are very infrequent. In this atmosphere, judges are likely to believe that they can act with impunity.

Court Procedures and Administration. Interference in judicial decision-making by the executive and parliamentary branches, higher level judges, and business people is common. As a result, the law is not applied equally or without excessive discretion. The Heads of Court are responsible for case allocation, vacation vouchers, bonuses, and equipment and facility budgets; there is little control over their discretion on these matters. Open trials are not common in Criminal Court and oral hearings are not common in Commercial Court; as a result, there is little transparency in these proceedings. Moreover, court decisions are not published. Oversight of court clerks is minimal. The State Judicial Administration, whose head and deputy are appointed by the president, is responsible for the court system's budget, facilities, and logistics; this arrangement places the judicial system into an overly dependent position relative to the executive branch. As a result of these factors, the incentives for corruption in the judicial process are increased.

Enforcement of Judicial Decisions. Enforcement of judicial decisions is in the hands of the Ministry of Justice's State Enforcement Department, which is not extremely effective and allegedly subject to corrupt practices.

Opportunities and obstacles

Some recent actions bode well for meaningful judicial reforms. A major salary increase for all judges will go into effect on 1 January 2006. The intention of this raise is to eliminate the excuse of low wages for taking bribes. In addition, the Rada Committee on Legal Policy is a key actor that appears to be ready to support judicial reform. A working group of this committee is synthesizing 15 draft laws into a single draft that will be proposed to amend the existing 2002 Code on the Judicial System. It is hoped that this integrated draft will be discussed and adopted by the Rada immediately after the legislative elections in 2006.

The Rada has just approved a new law to establish a registry of judicial decisions. As well, the establishment of the new Administrative Court offers a new venue to deal with citizen-government problems. However, the court is operating without an Administrative Procedures Code, its planned regional and appellate division expansion is not sufficiently funded, and its judicial selection procedures suffer from the same problems as the other jurisdictional courts.

The current minister of justice is seen as a genuine reformer and now leads a national commission to develop a strategy to tackle rule of law and judicial reform issues. The Council of Judges, a self-governing body of judges, is an entity that can be called upon to handle several of the executive independence issues that currently plague the judiciary.

There are certainly many obstacles confronting effective judicial reform. The continuing problem of extreme case overload is in large part due to the fact that over 1500 judicial positions are currently vacant. The budget for the court system is wholly inadequate. It barely covers salary costs and there is extensive leakage of funds in the distribution of the budget to the courts. Many judges are inadequately trained for their jobs. The Criminal Procedure Code is an outmoded holdover from Soviet times and needs to be modernized. Excessive political and economic influence over judges is difficult to control.

Recommendations

Contingent upon the adoption by parliament of effective judicial reform laws, the following programming options would be useful in support of Ukrainian implementation of those reforms. USAID programs should be carefully integrated with the activities of other donor organizations already working in this sector in judicial and procuracy reform, including the World Bank, OSCE, and EC/TACIS-Council of Europe. Specific initiatives are identified below within each component area.

To address problems in the *judicial selection process*, provide technical assistance for the Qualification Commissions to design criteria, improve testing procedures, develop merit-based assignment procedures, and conduct training programs at the Academy of Judges. Develop control mechanisms to reduce the influence of the Heads of Court in the selection process. As well, support development and training for an electronic registry to track judicial candidate processing and support assignment and placement of judges.

To address problems in the *judicial discipline process*, there needs to be support that emphasizes prevention, including randomization of case allocation and strengthening of the Code of Judicial Conduct with associated monitoring and enforcement of the Code by the self-governing body of judges (the Council of Judges).

To address problems in *court administration procedures*, there needs to be technical assistance to transfer the State Judicial Administration under the authority of the Supreme Court, supporting design of its internal regulatory framework, and providing organizational and budgetary training.

Support the *systematic publication of court decisions* on the web. This will make judges more accountable for their decisions. Support further development and adoption of Alternative Dispute Resolution mechanisms to reduce case overload. Provide support to clarify and strengthen court administration procedures and make them more transparent. Support training of court management staff. Support development and adoption of civic education programs for high schools that include, among other topics, the workings of the judicial system.

To address problems in the *execution of judicial decisions*, there needs to be technical assistance to reinforce the bailiff function and develop stronger control and oversight mechanisms.

Health sector

While Ukraine faces fast-growing HIV and tuberculosis epidemics, government health expenditures are low (ranging between 3% and 5% of gross domestic product as compared to a European Union average of 8.5%), and equity and access to health care services are problematic.[13] The ratio of doctors to population is very high – 4.5 doctors per 1,000 population in Ukraine versus 2.9 doctors per 1,000 in Germany, for example – but these medical staff are disproportionately concentrated in urban areas.[14] Moreover, expert teams have called for a major reorganization of the Ukrainian health system, indicating that accountability by authorities to initiate changes required to meet looming health crises is lacking, management capacity in the health system is weak, and governance practices in health care provision need to be improved.[15]

Corruption vulnerabilities

Many of the common health care corruption problems found in other countries exist in Ukraine: abuses in public procurement tenders, leakage in budget resources from the center to the facilities, small bribes to obtain services that are supposed to be provided for free, and lack of transparency in the provision of services. Other problems that are often found elsewhere apparently are not major issues for Ukraine. These include the presence of ghost workers that draw salaries but do not provide services, and conflict of interest situations for health care providers who are both on the public payroll and operate private services at the same time (the private health care market is still very small).

Studies have found that in 66% of cases, the patient knows it is necessary to make an under-the-table payment to receive proper services, while in 25% of the cases, health care providers ask for payment outright.[16] In a cash-strapped health system, several schemes have been observed:[17]

- *Charity:* State hospitals that cannot accept cash legally for medical care provided request charitable contributions, which may accrue to the hospital or be pocketed by the staff.

- *Local coverage:* Local hospitals have been known to offer their own insurance policies to patients that provide holders with special privileges.
- *Virtual clinics:* Doctors or hospital administrators establish private clinics illegally within their hospitals and ask patients to pay.
- *Special hospitals:* Clinics or hospitals administered by government departments or ministries other than the Ministry of Health receive extra payments from private insurance companies.
- *Barter:* Private companies have been known to pay off the debts of public hospitals in return for free health care for their employees.

Opportunities and obstacles

Health care providers and citizen groups at a local level are both motivated stakeholders for anti-corruption reform: an increase in transparency, a reduction in budget leakage, and a decline in procurement abuses would provide immediate and visible returns to both providers and consumers. The All-Ukrainian Network for People Living with AIDS, for example, is an excellent example of an NGO that has mobilized its resources to become an effective citizen watchdog of health care pharmaceutical procurement. Another example is a health care provider in Donetsk that is working under a USAID grant and found solutions to overstaffing in the hospital maternity ward: reorganization and reengineering of existing institutions and procedures are likely to reduce costs extensively and release funds that can be used to provide basic services.

On the positive side, the salaries of health care providers have recently been increased, diminishing wage levels as an excuse for extracting bribes from citizens seeking services. President Yushchenko has recently stressed his intention to establish a national health insurance fund soon, in part to help solve the problem of illegal payments in the health care system.[18]

As to possible obstacles to anti-corruption action, it has been alleged that popularly considered reformers within the Ministry of Health have recently been dismissed. Obviously, the powerful stakeholders that benefit from procurement kickbacks are likely to oppose reforms.

Recommendations

The recommendations listed here are illustrative of anti-corruption initiatives that would promote greater accountability and transparency across several basic health care components. First, there are several program options available to strengthen the public procurement of pharmaceuticals and medical supplies/equipment, including:

- Support for strengthening the procedures and controls used by the Tender Commissions. This would include enhanced transparency measures in their procedures.

- Support for citizen and business watchdogs to monitor and oversee public procurements.
- Support for establishing a Procurement Audit Unit within the Ministry of Health to oversee tenders.

Leakage from already inadequate health care budgets reduces the quality and quantity of service delivery in this sector. Several program options can help detect and stem these leaks, for example:

- Support a study that tracks budget expenditures from the Ministry of Health budget plan to the oblast, rayon, and city levels to detect leakage.
- Train health providers and managers at the local level (for example, hospital and clinic administrators) on how to monitor the flow of budgetary resources from the center to their facilities, and then how to track the expenditure of those funds. This effort can help improve the transparency and accountability of the health budget.
- Support the establishment of Community Health Review Boards, involving the participation of citizens, NGOs, business groups, and health service providers at a community level, to monitor the expenditure of health resources and detect misuse.

Support can be provided to the Ministry of Health in formulating a national health insurance fund that will deal effectively with problems of corruption and control for informal payments, while providing for fair and equal access to health care services for all.

The health care system and health care facilities, in particular, are in need of organizational, management, and institutional reform. There is evidence from USAID programs that some health care facilities or departments may be overstaffed, while others are understaffed. There is a concentration of doctors in urban areas and sparse resources in rural areas. In addition, small bribes and informal payments for health services that are supposed to be free have become customary in Ukraine, allegedly to compensate for low salaries. These imbalances can produce deteriorating effects on health care delivery, especially in situations where budget resources are inadequate. As a result, several program options are desirable:

- Support technical assistance in several pilot health care facilities to reassess and reengineer staffing plans to bring them in line with the demand for services. This can include downsizing of staff, beds, and hospitals; overall reorganization and redeployment of resources in relation to usage; and the introduction of family doctors to manage health care services at the local level.
- Support several pilot tests introducing official "fee for services," where the fees are openly posted and the revenues accrue to the health care facilities' coffers.

Education sector

The Ukrainian educational system is still in need of major reform and over-haul. As with many Ukrainian state structures, the Education Ministry lacks transparency and accountability at many levels. There is little involve-ment of national CSOs in the Ministry's work, but the education system touches most families in the country and civil society is involved at local levels. With corruption widely perceived as rampant from the classroom on up, education is one area that motivates many families to care and be concerned.

Widespread acknowledgement of low teacher salaries lends some cred-ibility to the practice of students making payments under the table at schools. Payments of special fees and bribes are quite prevalent for grad-uation and entrance exams. The pervasiveness of corruption in this sector poses three serious development concerns: (1) a further financial strain on families with children in school, (2) an attendant increase in frustration with Government's inability to deliver promised services, and (3) the further in-stitutionalization of bribe payment as an acceptable norm for young people attending schools.

Corruption vulnerabilities

A number of issues plague the education sector in Ukraine which contrib-utes to a serious problem of corruption at all levels in the school and higher education systems. From procurement to grading to entrance examinations, corruption is currently fused into Ukraine's education system.

Centralized financing without transparency to show the allocation and spending of funds down to the local school level has resulted in what ap-pears to be misappropriation and misallocation of monies and has fre-quently resulted in shortfalls at the local level. The lack of involvement and participation of CSOs in various school and Ministry processes also inhibit transparency and accountability. Some officials may seek to sell grades and passing scores for higher school placement.

Opportunities and obstacles

The president has mandated that computerized higher school entrance ex-ams be administered nationally to reduce corruption and provide equal op-portunities. The period prior to the elections has enabled parties, politicians and CSOs to address the need for higher wages and reform of testing stand-ards nationally, while combating corruption as a cross-cutting issue. Edu-cation reform has powerful salience among voters and is not an extremely divisive issue among politicians. Current government officials see reform in this sector as achievable.

First and foremost, parents are constituents for reform; they seek better educational opportunities for their children and more responsiveness from the government on this matter. Most academics are opposed to and even shamed over the need to take bribes.

There also appears to be a willingness to reform in the Ministry itself, but this is at least partially tied to policy issues as well. Many government officials and parliamentarians are sensitive to the frustrations of families and feel this is a safe issue to tackle. Even corrupted politicians do not generally feel threatened by reform in this area. Administrative practice and bureaucratic intransigence appear to be the major stumbling blocks to reform, in addition to those who may benefit from the status quo system.

Recommendations

Meetings between CSOs and budget watchdog groups with teacher organizations should be promoted to work on common strategies to solve corruption issues in schools and the Ministry. They should target transparency in the expenditure of budget and extra-budget funds. Assistance on standardized testing remains a serious entry-point opportunity to have an immediate impact on families and show progress in the fight for reform. The US Embassy's Public Affairs Section has piloted standardized testing at three sites. In addition, programs that enhance legal literacy among students should be promoted in order to build a broader, more educated constituency for anti-corruption behavior and reform.

Drivers and motivators

What are the particular factors that facilitate the spread of corruption throughout a wide range of sectors and government functions in Ukraine? Many of the legal and institutional preconditions for dealing effectively with the problem of corruption have yet to be put in place. A year into the revolution, the existence of demonstrated political will among the new leadership to control corruption is still questionable and the government's capacity to actually manage such a considerable adjustment to Ukraine's widespread and pervasive corruption – even in the presence of strong rhetorical political will – is debatable.

Incentives that promote corrupt behavior

Ukraine's major anti-corruption vulnerabilities and factors that promote corruption include the following:

Inadequate Legal Framework. The legal framework as it relates to corruption, transparency, accountability, and integrity requires major revisions, amendments, and additions. According to some counts, more than 28 laws need to modified and/or adopted anew. Drafts of many of these legal changes have been on hold in the Parliament for years. Public discussion on these needed reforms has been uneven.

Selective Enforcement of Law. Enforcement of existing laws and regulations is selective, subject to political and business influence and corrupt practices. Excessive discretion is exercised by public and elected officials at all levels.

Excessive Regulation of the Economy. There is excessive regulation by the state of the economic sphere which yields many opportunities for corrupt behavior.

Excessive Executive Control. The executive branch exercises control and influence over the judicial branch, reducing its independence and its capacity to provide equal and fair justice to all citizens. The legislative branch conducts minimal oversight of executive power.

Business-Government Ties. There are strong ties between the political and economic elite in Ukraine. Many political leaders have extensive business interests. And business leaders seek to enhance their wealth through their close connections with the state. Despite the goals of the Orange Revolution, vested interests – both political and economic – do not want to see these relationships fade.

Manipulation of the Bureaucracy. The activities of the civil service are subject to political manipulation. This situation is fostered by clan influence in hiring, low salaries, and the minimally adequate candidates for bureaucratic positions due to low salaries. The absence of a strong ethic of professionalism and enforced performance standards within the bureaucracy, along with unclear regulations and poor procedures, create opportunities for excessive discretion and abuse of office.

Low Capacity in Civil Society. Civil society organizations are numerous, but lacking in the capacity and experience to oversee government operations effectively or in exercising firm pressure on government to reform itself.

Weak Accountability Mechanisms. The government has few effective accountability mechanisms and external guarantors of accountability are very limited. Internal and external audits and inspections are not conducted frequently enough and are insufficiently funded, and if abuses are identified, there is minimal follow-up authority within the judicial or administrative systems. Supervision and management within the civil service is generally ineffective. Citizen watchdog groups that monitor and oversee government departments and their use of the public budget rarely exist. Investigative journalists, often natural watchdogs of government operations, have not been a major force for transparency and accountability.

Uneven Transparency. Transparency in government decisions and activities is uneven. Public accessibility exists to some information, but not all. Even where there is public access, citizen awareness is low and the ability to use the information effectively is inadequate for advocacy activities.

Resistance to Decentralization. Government operations and decisions in Ukraine are highly centralized, which helps to maintain collusive practices among political and economic elite. The movement toward devolving power and resources to regional and local levels, a goal of the current administration and a possible tool in breaking corruptive networks, has already been derailed, at least temporarily.

Impunity for Corrupt Behavior. Abuse of power, rent-seeking behaviors, and other corruption actions are viewed as low-risk events for public officials. Management and supervision, internal and external audits, and checks and balances are relatively weak in most sectors and functions of government. As a result, public officials believe that they can engage in corrupt activity with impunity. Moreover, the public has high tolerance for corrupt practices.

Even in this kind of environment, if political will existed at the top levels, some positive actions could be taken by executive decree at a minimum. However, many of the presidential decrees that have been put forth have primarily been rhetorical platforms and have not yielded real change. Moreover, recent presidential directives to several ministries and top-level agencies have led to a confusing situation where there are multiple uncoordinated draft national anti-corruption strategies and proposed organizational structures to manage a yet-to-be-approved anti-corruption program.

Disincentives of corrupt behavior

Despite this discouraging picture, the team identified many factors in Ukraine that have the potential to inhibit corrupt behaviors and facilitate the promotion of good governance, assuming the necessary commitment on the part of leaders.

The New Government. The Orange Revolution mobilized popular frustration about corruption and President Yushchenko has pledged to deal effectively with the problem. The recent sacking of the Cabinet, primarily over corruption problems, may be an indication of political will to follow up on these words. The president has also directed several ministries and agencies to develop a National Anti-Corruption Strategy and to formulate a new Anti-Corruption Commission.

Preventive Measures Already Taken. A memorandum issued by the Presidential Secretariat outlined successful actions to deal with the problem of corruption.[19] They include:

- Reforms in the State Customs Service that have resulted in large increases in revenues collected.
- The State Tax Administration has conducted a large number of workshops for its officers on corruption issues.
- The Central Department of the Civil Service has increased its activities to enhance the legal literacy of public officials.
- There is more stringent adherence to recruitment procedures for applicants into the civil service.
- Enhancements to the legal framework related to corruption issues have progressed, with several new draft laws under consideration.

- There is an increasing trend in corruption cases submitted to and considered by the courts during 2004.

Proposed anti-corruption strategy

The preceding analysis of corruption and anti-corruption trends, policies, legislation, institutions and corruption drivers/motivators in Ukraine suggests several strategic directions for future government initiatives, as well as USAID and other donor support to promote anti-corruption programs. These directions address the problems associated with Ukraine's corruption syndrome – as a closed insider economy/elite cartel grouping. The core and intermediate strategies are depicted below. Specific anti-corruption program options that operationalize these strategic directions are identified in subsequent sections of the assessment.

Several major strategic themes were proposed: (a) establishing the legal, institutional, and economic conditions within which anti-corruption programs will thrive, (b) promoting capacity building within key government institutions, the civil service, and the judiciary if they demonstrate a serious political commitment to change, (c) strengthening civil society and business to advocate for change and oversee government including activities at local levels and transparency initiatives, and (d) mainstreaming anti-corruption programs so that the problem is attacked at many levels, but concentrating efforts in major sectors and promoting high-level diplomatic dialogue and multi-donor coordination.

Core strategies

Support establishment of the prerequisite conditions for effective anti-corruption programs. The legal, policy, and institutional frameworks for the government and civil society to pursue major and comprehensive anti-corruption programs are not fully established. Since the Orange Revolution, it appears as if the political will and trajectories exist to upgrade or revise these frameworks to establish a strong foundation for future activity. USAID and donor support is warranted to bring these frameworks to the required levels of competence. The US Millennium Challenge Account Threshold Program can serve as a major resource to bolster the prerequisite conditions for effective anti-corruption programs.

Support the development of strong demand-side pressure for anti-corruption reforms. The revolution clearly demonstrated the power and inclination of Ukrainian civil society and media to make their voices heard and demand for reform. More capacity building is needed, as well as organizational coordination across civil society organizations, to establish them as a permanent and forceful source of external demand on government. Support for watchdog and advocacy activities should be provided.

Support supply-side institutions contingent upon visible demonstration of their political will. There is much rhetoric by government leaders about their desire to reduce and control corruption, but little demonstrated action or progress. The recent selection of Ukraine to participate in the Millennium Challenge Account Threshold Program provides Ukraine with a major incentive to turn its words into deeds. In addition, USAID and major donors can be encouraged to enhance their dialogue, coordination, and messages to the government. Moreover, they can develop a set of clear benchmarks and initiate a monitoring and evaluation program by which positive actions and results demonstrating the government's sincere commitment to anti-corruption goals can be measured and tracked. If demonstrated progress can be presented, then the government should be rewarded with appropriate technical assistance and resources.

Mainstream anti-corruption activities throughout the portfolio of donor programs. USAID and other donors should seek ways to inject anti-corruption objectives and activities into all their programs in Ukraine – across all sectors and functions. This mainstreaming approach will yield a more comprehensive and visible assault against corruption. Moreover, USAID and other donors should encourage the Ukrainian government and civil society groups to do the same. Technical assistance to USAID implementing partners to incorporate anti-corruption elements in their projects can be helpful.

Intermediate strategies

Support implementation of transparency initiatives. Many Ukrainian laws and regulations mandate transparency, publication of government information, and openness in government operations. However, implementation of these requirements does not always meet the necessary standards. USAID and other donors should apply pressure to government agencies to achieve their transparency objectives quickly. Where technical assistance is reasonably required to meet these goals, it can be offered. Demand from civil society for improved government transparency should be generated and supported.

Support nongovernmental programs that address social psychological drivers of corruption. Given widespread social norms that accept corrupt behavior in Ukraine, provide training and support to local CSOs to establish legal offices that will bring citizen complaints about corrupt transactions to light and employ administrative resolution techniques with government managers to eliminate corrupt procedures and avoid public naming and shaming. Also, support investigative journalists in pursuing corruption cases and publishing their reports in traditional and social media.

Reduce face-to-face negotiations about bribes and kickbacks. Technical support can be provided to CSOs and to government to develop e-governance applications that can be used by citizens and businesses when they need to get permits, licenses, registrations, and other services, and when government conducts public procurements. These IT solutions can reduce opportunities for direct interactions that often result in requests for bribes or kickbacks.

Support programs at the central and local levels. While the drama of the Orange Revolution and political pronouncements against corruption occurred in Kyiv, much can be done to deal with the problem at the regional and local levels, where the effects of corruption are felt most personally. As a result, USAID and other donor programs should be targeted at both central and subnational levels to allow for trickle down and trickle up effects.

Promote an independent judiciary and improve access to information. Support programs for court reform that ensure separation of powers that will reduce executive interference in judicial decision-making. A major objective of donor support should be not only to strengthen public and media access to information but to build the capacity of civil society, business, and the media to *use* the information that they gain access for effective monitoring and oversight of government functions.

Promote a professional and ethical bureaucracy. Emphasize efforts to shore up administrative quality, autonomy, and professionalism in the civil service, and sustain them over the long run. In line with promoting ethical drivers, develop and expand periodic ethics training for civil servants at all levels of government and follow-up with monitoring exercises to ensure that ethical values are actually applied by government staff. Strengthen recruitment practices for the civil service by instituting new screening tests to assess levels of ethical socialization at an early stage.

Support economic competition. Strengthening and expanding ongoing programs to enhance economic competition will reduce opportunities for state capture by monopolistic forces. The subdivision of business-administrative groups into competing units is a positive sign that will dilute the influence of each particular elite group. Promoting economic and political competition at all levels will reduce the extent of state capture by economic elite over time.

Promote anti-corruption programs in key sectors and functional areas. This and other assessments have shown that corruption in Ukraine is widespread and affects almost all government sectors and functions. However, it is not reasonable to expect USAID and other donors to direct their anti-corruption efforts against *all* sectors and functions. As a result, this assessment identifies key areas where corruption weaknesses are high, but opportunities to deal with the corruption problems are available and strong. These areas include the judicial, health, education, and private sectors; the public finance function; and the institutions of the parliament, political parties, and municipalities.

Promote high-level diplomatic dialogue and multi-donor pressure. Since the revolution, anti-corruption has risen on the Ukrainian political agenda to the highest level. To capitalize on this status, high-level diplomatic dialogue and multi-donor pressure is needed, along with anti-corruption donor programming, to mobilize Ukrainian counterparts and ensure that there continues to be strong movement forward. It is important to maintain diplomatic and donor pressure on the top leadership so they stay the anti-corruption course and that they maintain pressure, in turn, on their mid-level managers. There is a need to maintain pressure to mobilize Parliamentary leaders as well, so that they adopt major pieces of legislation that have been languishing in committee. NGOs need to know that donors are strongly behind their activities – both in terms of financial and moral support. This is especially important due to the sensitive and dangerous nature of corruption issues that they deal with.

Recommended actions

While USAID has supported major anti-corruption programming in the past, increased attention to reinvigorate and expand these initiatives is now essential. The assessment recommends priority programs in various sectors and functional domains, as well as in several cross-sectoral areas, to fight and control corruption in Ukraine. Included here are programs that were deemed important not only for the three most corrupt sectors that were examined above but the longer list of sectors and government functions that were analyzed in the full assessment report.

Cross-Sectoral and Prerequisite Conditions. Many activities need to be conducted that will establish the basic foundation upon which continued anti-corruption programs across all sectors can be launched. These include supporting the design and execution of a national and coordinated anti-corruption strategy, supporting the passage of missing anti-corruption legislation and the establishment and strengthening of anti-corruption institutions in government, and improvements in public procurement procedures and institutions. In addition, the demand-side of fighting corruption needs to be enhanced: advocacy skills of citizen, business and media groups must be strengthened, citizen oversight/watchdog groups must be formed, and civic education programs related to corruption must be supported. To facilitate these activities and encourage the inclusion of anti-corruption elements into existing programs, an anti-corruption mainstreaming workshop should be conducted for USAID program officers, as well as implementing partners.

Judicial Sector. Key activities must be supported to reform the judicial selection process and bring it into line with modern meritocracies. In addition, reforms in court administration and procedures need to be promoted to increase transparency.

Health Sector. Major remedies need to be promoted to make the procurement of pharmaceuticals more transparent and accountable. In addition, it is critical to develop tracking systems to monitor and oversee budgetary expenditures to stem leakages. Overall, organizational, management, and institutional reforms are needed to improve the efficiency and effectiveness of health care delivery and reduce mismanagement which can encourage corrupt practices.

Education Sector. It is important to support CSO budget oversight initiatives to put external pressure on the educational system to be accountable for its use of public funds and to encourage greater transparency. Continued expansion of standardized testing procedures for higher school entrance exams is merited.

Public Finance. Support should be given to ensure effective implementation of new procurement laws and ongoing tax reform initiatives. In addition, the accounting chamber and the Chief Control and Auditing Administration should be strengthened, especially in the enforcement of their findings and recommendations. Finally, budget and expenditure oversight – internally and externally – should be promoted.

Private Sector. The business community needs to be mobilized to advocate for conflict of interest and transparency laws, and to support regulations that promote the business environment and eliminate administrative barriers. Expanded support should be given to private sector associations to conduct continuous monitoring of the implementation of business laws and regulations.

Parliament. Continued pressure and support needs to be applied to the Rada to promote adoption of an adequate anti-corruption legal framework. MPs need to be made more accountable to their constituents and various monitoring and transparency programs can be supported. Legislator skills training and resources need to be provided to improve legislative drafting, coalition building and negotiation/compromise skills.

Political Parties. Programs are needed to build more transparency into party financing.

Subnational Government. Local government institutions need to be strengthened so that they can deliver services in a transparent and accountable fashion. CSO advocacy and watchdog capacity building at the subnational level is also a major requirement to control corrupt tendencies.

Where to start

Logically, it is important to begin a comprehensive anti-corruption program by ensuring an adequate foundation – an acceptable legal and institutional framework that is sensitive to corruption issues – on which other reforms can be built. Such activities should certainly be started immediately. However, it must be understood that these prerequisites often take time to establish and they should be considered as medium- to long-term efforts. At the same time, it is essential not to wait until these fundamentals are in place to start other initiatives that could yield early and visible successes. In this regard, strengthening demand-side capacity is critical to sustain the pressure on government and for the public to believe that progress is being made. As well, an additional early step should involve conducting mainstreaming workshops and providing one-on-one technical assistance to current USAID implementers to help them incorporate targeted anti-corruption elements quickly into their projects. Here are some suggested starting points:

1 Mainstream anti-corruption goals in all ongoing and future government- and donor-sponsored projects
2 Establish the Prerequisites
   - Promote passage of key corruption-related legislation in the Rada
   - Promote better implementation of current corruption-related laws
   - Support design and implementation of a comprehensive national anti-corruption strategy
   - Begin activities to reform the judiciary
3 Support Demand-Side Capacity Building
   - Establish civil society monitoring and watchdog groups in key areas, such as budgeting, procurement, the courts, and the legislature
   - Establish constructive civil society-government dialogues
   - Support a network of Citizen Advocate Offices that provide citizen victims of corruption with legal services to act on grievances
4 Target a Key Government Sector. Select a major public service delivery sector, such as health, and initiate a comprehensive anti-corruption program there to serve as a model for other future efforts.

Notes

1 This chapter is an adaptation and expansion of the author's assessment report: Bertram Spector, Svetlana Winbourne, et al. (2006). *Corruption Assessment: Ukraine, Final Report (February).* Washington, DC: USAID. At: https://pdf.us-aid.gov/pdf_docs/PNADK247.pdf.
2 Adopted in 2005, the USAID Anti-Corruption Strategy addresses four broad actions: (1) confront the dual challenges of grand and administrative corruption, (2) deploy Agency resources to fight corruption in strategic ways, (3) incorporate anti-corruption goals and activities across Agency work, and (4) build the Agency's anti-corruption knowledge. USAID (2005). *Anti-corruption strategy*, PD-ACA-557. At: https://www.usaid.gov/sites/default/files/documents/1868/200mbo.pdf.
3 Bertram Spector, Michael Johnston and Svetlana Winbourne (2009). *Anti-Corruption Assessment Handbook, Final Repo*rt. Washington, DC: USAID. At: https://pdf.usaid.gov/pdf_docs/pa00jp37.pdf.
4 World Bank (2004). "Ukraine: Building Foundations for Sustainable Growth, A Country Economic Memorandum: Volume 1 (August)." Washington, DC, The World Bank.
5 Michael Johnston (2005). *Syndromes of Corruption: Wealth, Power, and Democracy.* New York: Cambridge University Press.
6 Roman Kupchinsky (2003). "Analysis: The Clan from Donetsk," RFE/RL Poland, Belarus and Ukraine Report (January 12).
7 World Bank (2004), op.cit.
8 Vera Nanivska (2005). *NGO Development in Ukraine.* Kyiv: International Center for Policy Studies, 2001; United States Agency for International Development (2004). *NGO Sustainability Index for Central and Eastern Europe and Eurasia, 8th Edition.* Washington, DC: USAID.
9 Counterpart Creative Center (2004). *Civil Society Organizations in Ukraine: The State and Dynamics (2002–2003).* Kyiv, 2004.
10 *Nations in Transit* (2005). Washington, DC: Freedom House.

11 See Spector, Winbourne, et al. (2006), op.cit., for assessments of additional government sectors.

12 See assessments of the judicial system by J.T. Asscher and S.V. Konnov (2005). *Ukraine Justice System Assessment Report*. Brussels: European Commission, TACIS, June; and David Black and Richard Blue (2005). *Rule of Law Strengthening and Anti-Corruption in Ukraine: Recommendations for USAID Assistance*. Washington, DC: USAID, May, for more detailed reviews of the judicial sector and potential reform options.

13 World Health Organization (2005). *World Health Report*. Geneva: WHO; Guy Hutton (2002). *Equity and Access in the Health Sector in Five Countries of Eastern Europe and Central Asia: A Brief Review of the Literature*. Geneva: Swiss Agency for Development and Cooperation, November; World Health Organization (2004). "Summary Country Profile," July, Geneva: WHO.

14 US Foreign Commercial Service/US State Department (2001). *Ukrainian Market for Health Care Services*. Washington, DC: US State Department.

15 United Nations Country Team (2004). "Common Country Assessment for Ukraine," October, New York: United Nations.

16 Hutton (2002), op.cit.

17 John Marone (2005). "Ukraine's Health Care System: Finding the Right Cure," *The Ukrainian Observer*, Issue 208.

18 V.A. Yushchenko (2005). "Current State of Ukraine's Medical Sector: One of the Most Disturbing Problems," *Presidential Radio Address*, November 12. At: www.president.gov.ua/en.

19 Presidential Secretariat (2005). *General Information on Measures on Combating Corruption in Ukraine in 2005*. Kyiv: Presidential Secretariat.

13 Additional implementation issues to consider

This chapter addresses important issues that affect how well anti-corruption reforms can be implemented to achieve their desired impacts. One critical issue that needs to be considered is how men and women are impacted differently by corruption and anti-corruption reforms. Another issue relates to special corruption problems that must be tackled when countries respond to crisis or emergency situations, taking the COVID-19 worldwide pandemic context as a case in point. Third, we examine the important role and problems faced by international and regional donors that can significantly impact the effectiveness of anti-corruption implementation.

Gender and corruption

Corruption impacts men and women differently. This is due to social and cultural norms that affect how people interact with each other and with government, and how they obtain public services. It is also a function of laws and policies – or the absence of both – that lay out principles of gender equality for a society.[1]

To understand the linkage between gender and corruption, we must examine the corruption phenomenon both from the perspective of the perpetrator and the victim. In terms of promoting corruption, experimental research shows that men and women are equally prone to behaving corruptly. Therefore, women who are in positions of power in government should be no less corrupt than men. However, context matters. Women who hold positions of governmental authority tend to do so in more democratic societies, where there is a free press, robust rule of law, and free and fair elections. Due to greater oversight, accountability, and transparency in a democratic context, these women leaders tend to be less corrupt than men who are more likely to be in positions of power in both democratic and authoritarian situations.

At the same time, women and girls are more typically the victims of corruption than are men. As traditional caregivers, women have greater exposure to corruption when accessing basic social services for themselves and their families. Men are disproportionately the providers of these services.

DOI: 10.4324/9781003241119-16

On a direct basis, women are often confronted with requests for bribes and sexual extortion when seeking services, such as health care and education. On an indirect basis, they are often the recipients of poor quality schools and health care as a result of government funds that are stolen by corrupt officials.

What can be done? Laws and policies to increase gender equality can reinforce anti-corruption efforts. For example, laws that mandate equal pay for men and women are likely to disrupt corrupt networks in the private sector. Gender-sensitive whistleblower protection laws will reduce the fear of reprisals and thereby motivate more whistleblower reports. Promoting anti-corruption policies that address the vulnerabilities faced by the less powerful in society, including women and the poor, can yield greater access to quality public services. And gendered perspectives can be added to almost all anti-corruption reforms.

Case study: women in parliament

USAID's Assistance for Afghanistan's Anticorruption Authority (4A) project in Afghanistan (2010–2013) worked closely with a newly established women's caucus – the Parliamentary Anti-Corruption Caucus (PACC) – in the lower house of parliament, the *Wolesi Jirga*.[2] Sixteen women members of the *Wolesi Jirga* originally created this caucus with the goal of ensuring that future legislation at the national and provincial levels would sufficiently address sorely needed anti-corruption reforms.

The 4A Project started by organizing a series of workshops to train the PACC members on a number of substantive issues that are important to parliament. The American University of Afghanistan (AUAF) was called upon to conduct four all-day workshops on legislative oversight of the extractive industries, the role of parliament in curbing corruption, financial oversight, and global anticorruption efforts. While male members of parliament were invited to join PACC, it remained woman-led and emphasized the need to address women's vulnerabilities to corruption on an everyday basis.

4A served as an interface between PACC and the Global Organization of Parliamentarians against Corruption (GOPAC) to expedite PACC's membership in the global group and become a member of the South Asian Parliamentarians against Corruption (SAPAC) as well. 4A provided PACC with a parliamentary research assistant who conducted research and prepared briefing books on agenda items debated on the floor of the parliament. 4A and PACC's most notable work was a successful outreach to several provincial councils, convincing them to establish anti-corruption commissions within their provincial assemblies. They also had meetings and conducted workshops with CSOs and university faculties in these provinces on key anti-corruption issues. Media coverage was extensive, especially because of this unusual women's leadership initiative in Afghanistan.

Pandemic response and corruption

Humanitarian and natural emergencies are special contexts that are particularly vulnerable to corrupt activities. Large sums of money get transferred and spent over short periods of time to mitigate these crises and rebuild, introducing opportunities for fraud and abuse. Starting in early 2020 and probably continuing for many decades to come, the COVID-19 pandemic became a worldwide platform for corruption to thrive. In late 2020, United Nations Secretary-General Antonio Guterres issued a statement[3] in which he made an urgent call for more robust systems of accountability, transparency, and integrity:

> Corruption is criminal, immoral, and the ultimate betrayal of public trust. It is even more damaging in times of crisis, as the world is experiencing now with the COVID-19 pandemic. The response to the virus is creating new opportunities to exploit weak oversight and inadequate transparency, diverting funds away from people in their hour of greatest need. Governments may act in haste without verifying suppliers or determine fair prices. Unscrupulous merchants peddle faulty products such as defective ventilators, poorly manufactured tests, or counterfeit medicines. And collusion among those who control supply chains has led to outrageous costs of much-needed goods, skewing the market and denying many people life-saving treatment. We must work together to stop such thievery and exploitation by clamping down on illicit financial flows and tax havens, tackling the vested interests that benefit from secrecy and corruption, and exercising utmost vigilance over how resources are spent nationally. Together, we must create more robust systems for accountability, transparency, and integrity without delay. We must hold leaders to account. Business people must act responsibly. A vibrant civic space and open access to information are essential. And we must protect the rights and recognize the courage of whistleblowers who expose wrongdoing. Technological advances can help increase transparency and better monitor procurement of medical supplies. Anti-corruption bodies need greater support and empowerment. The United Nations itself continues to prioritize transparency and accountability, in and beyond the COVID-19 response. For many people in all regions, corruption has been a longstanding source of distrust and anger against their leaders and governments. But corruption in the time of COVID-19 has the potential to seriously undermine good governance around the world and to send us even farther off-track in our work to achieve the Sustainable Development Goals. I urge all governments and all leaders to be transparent and accountable and to use the tools provided by the United Nations Convention against Corruption. As an age-old plague takes on new forms, let us combat it with new heights of resolve.

One year into the pandemic, investigative reporters in the Global South identified many instances of corrupt behavior.[4] This includes the coverup of data in many countries, and underreporting of cases and deaths. This suppression of information and lack of transparency serves as a denial of the pandemic and leads to public mistrust of government. Another rampant form of corruption takes place when countries bypass public procurement regulations due to the emergency situation. Direct awards are made for medical and personal protective equipment with no competition. Companies with no relevant experience win contracts. Price gouging is widespread for available vaccines. All of this corrupt behavior results in misallocation of resources, weaker and lower quality health care facilities, and growing mistrust of government.

This type of behavior is not restricted to developing countries. In the United Kingdom, an investigative study by Transparency International UK has revealed gross mishandling of public procurements of personal protective equipment and other COVID-19 response contracts.[5] In the emergency, anti-corruption safeguards were suspended. As a result, many contract awards were made without competition, awards were made to companies with no obvious track record providing such medical goods and services, and there has been limited recordkeeping of these procurements, allowing for massive fraud and abuse. Approximately 20% of COVID-19-related contracts awarded by the UK government in 2020 – amounting to US $5.25 billion – raised red flags for investigators for possible corruption. It was obvious that companies with strong political linkages had preferences and a fast lane to these public awards.

As well, a Brookings Institution report[6] developed early in the COVID-19 response in the United States compiled information about many clients of lobbyists connected to President Trump who were awarded up to US $10.5 billion in public contracts. Beneficiaries of US government COVID spending included extensive nepotism involving President Trump's family, business associates and political allies. More than 100 companies operated by major donors to President Trump's election campaign were awarded almost $300 million in public awards. And waivers have been issued to ethics requirements concerning conflicts of interest for administration staff.

The UN secretary-general offers some useful approaches to address the problem, but what does research tell us ought to work, especially under such difficult conditions? Here are two powerful tools.

Vigorous oversight

It is important for corruptors and their victims to know that someone is watching them and that they will not be able to get away with their fraud and abuse. But this oversight needs to be real and pervasive, because corrupt officials have long figured out ways to avoid detection. If a substantial and integrated program is put in place incorporating continuous oversight, attempted corruption can be detected and stopped, and evidence of corruption can be collected and suspects indicted and convicted. Such a program would likely include activation and coordination among inspectors general, external auditors, internal auditors, social auditors and citizen monitors, investigative journalists, parliamentary overseers, ombudsman offices, complaints handling agencies, access to information commissions, and whistleblowers.

In our COVID-19 environment, such monitoring and oversight can play powerful preventive and enforcement purposes if they are incorporated in a significant way from the very beginning in government planning for its pandemic response. Knowing that oversight has been beefed up and focused on the use of public funds can make potential corrupt officials think twice about pursuing fraudulent activity. The oversight efforts will give citizens a greater sense of empowerment to stand up for their rights and report corruption threats. The existence of strengthened oversight will also build citizen trust in government's response to the pandemic. And detection of corrupt behaviors through monitoring and oversight can lead to legal action being taken against the corruptors.

In response to this intense need for vigorous oversight of pandemic-related public spending, four oversight bodies have been established in the United States.[7] The pandemic-related Congressional Oversight Commission is empowered to assess how effectively funds (US $500 billion) are being spent that were lent to businesses and state and local governments to stabilize the economy. The Pandemic Response Accountability Committee (PRAC) consists of 21 inspectors general from across the federal government and is established to detect and prevent fraud, waste, and abuse in pandemic-response public contracts and awards through detailed audits and reviews. The special inspector general for pandemic recovery (SIGPR) assesses and audits loans and investments made by the government for the pandemic response to ensure companies are eligible and the expenditures are appropriate. And the US House of Representatives established a Select Subcommittee on the Coronavirus Crisis, meant to provide its own oversight of spending and other matters. It reports on the efficacy, equity, and transparency of taxpayer funds used for crisis response.

Reinventing government

Vigorous oversight efforts can try to put a stop to corrupt practices by creating negative incentives for corrupt officials, but a more positive and preventive approach is to eliminate the opportunities for corrupt transactions from occurring in the first place. Many countries have implemented programs to streamline and simplify their administrative procedures, specifically removing old or obsolete steps and requirements, and eliminating processes that facilitate government officials taking advantage of citizens seeking government services they are entitled to.

Before the COVID-19 pandemic, the European Commission established the Regulatory Fitness and Performance Program (REFIT) in 2013 to guide participating countries to simplify laws and regulations, improve coordination between government agencies, and streamline what were inconsistent and duplicative procedures that promote corrupt practices. The goals of REFIT are to speed up administrative procedures, decrease public expenditures and reduce opportunities for corruption in the public sector.

Earlier, in the United States, the National Partnership for Reinventing Government (NPR) operated between 1993 and 2000 with the objectives of simplifying government processes to generate efficiencies in bureaucratic operations. To achieve this, NPR promoted deregulation initiatives and information technology solutions to reduce the size of the bureaucracy, generate administrative streamlining for those seeking public services, and reduce opportunities for corruption. These types of initiatives have had positive and documented impacts on speeding up and reducing the cost of public services, at the same time as reducing corrupt transactions in many countries.

In the pandemic environment, reenergizing such streamlining initiatives can be very useful in delivering health care services to citizens more efficiently, but only if the oversight mechanisms are also invigorated to make sure that corruptors don't take advantage of the situation. One-stop shops and e-governance apps, for example, can be implemented rapidly to make COVID testing and vaccinations more efficient and available, procure medical supplies quickly, and receive and deal with complaints about potential abuses of power.

Here is a final thought on the "do no harm" principle while seeking to reduce corrupt behaviors in a crisis context. Citizens, investigative reporters, and civil society organization that mobilize themselves to monitor, oversee, and advocate for anti-corruption reforms put themselves in potential danger of retaliation if they expose corruption or point at government agencies that abuse their authority. Implementing programs over the past 25 years, my group has experienced a few situations where active citizens and groups pursuing anti-corruption goals have been subjected to arrest, imprisonment, and conviction as payback for their vigilant work to fight corruption in their countries. When tracking down and seeking to reduce corruption, it is critical for activists to get security training so they remain alert to potential dangers and do not put themselves into overly risky situations.

Donors and how they respond to anti-corruption efforts

Starting in the early 1990s, international donors became increasingly interested in supporting developing countries to reduce corruption, following in the footsteps of the World Bank. In the early stages, the belief was that corruption could be reduced primarily through legal and institutional reforms. It was assumed that effective anti-corruption strategies could be formulated with a list of laws and regulations that needed to be adopted or adjusted, the establishment of national anti-corruption commissions, and strengthened enforcement. The World Bank and the International Monetary Fund for many years would not release loans or provide technical assistance unless a national anti-corruption commission had been developed, whether or not it was adequately funded or trained to do its job. As discussed in earlier chapters, despite many years of implementing such programs, corruption was not reduced significantly and better approaches needed to be sought.

While each donor operates in different ways, there are some basic similarities in terms of their priorities, programming, constraints, and problems faced in implementing anti-corruption assistance. As described below, the implications of these decisions often yield unfortunate results.

- To a large extent, technical support provided by donors ranges from capacity building and training of government staff to grants awarded to local nongovernmental organizations. These efforts tend to yield minimal outcomes as they are short term, do not actively engage participants, and do not provide in depth mentoring that can last.
- Assistance is usually fairly short term, only up to five years. As most donor agencies need to report back to their legislatures to demonstrate that funding was used effectively, activities are often programmed to end too quickly. Especially in the anti-corruption arena, it has been learned that reform efforts need to operate for many years to change embedded traditional and cultural norms of corrupt behavior.
- Despite the short lifespan of many programs, measurable impact and sustainability are expected. This, again, is due in part to donor agencies needing to account to their legislatures. Demonstrating the impact of anti-corruption reform programs and long-term durability of those results is something that often can only be presented over several generations. In addition, impact is usually measured using generic indicators, such as the Transparency International or World Bank corruption indices, rather than program-specific measures. While these indices provide some indication of movement in corruption levels, they often have a built-in lag of several years and can be influenced by many factors not associated with particular donor programming.
- Donors often initiate their anti-corruption programs through identified reform champions. The assumption is that these champion-partners will enthusiastically carry forth the program's initiatives. But in many cases, these champions are not on the scene for the long term. With elections and changing sociopolitical circumstances, these individuals typically are not in their special positions for too long, and the impact of the donor initiatives may falter as a result.
- Donors have learned that cookie-cutter approaches to anti-corruption programming are not appropriate. While some anti-corruption initiatives may work well in one country, they may not be appropriate in

other countries. That is why donors have largely adopted the use of assessments early in the programming process to determine where the major corruption risks lie, the socioeconomic conditions that promote or constrain these risks, and which reform approaches might work best. However, donors tend to be conservative in their choice of strategies and not inclined to try new and untested initiatives, even if they appear to be appropriate to the country context.

• Donors have learned that it is important to design reform programs that attack the corruption problem from a multiactor, multisector, and multitechnique approach. Thus, coordination with other donors and government, and with civil society stakeholders in implementing anti-corruption initiatives is a useful tactic. As well, if you can attack the problem across multiple sectors simultaneously, that has been shown to yield better results. And if you can deal with the corruption problem using coordinated enforcement, prevention, and public education methods, such multitechnique approaches are typically more effective. However, this type of integrated programming and coordination is difficult to achieve over the short term of most donor interventions.

Overall, international donors have made incredibly important contributions in the fight against corruption, but the nature of their funding and policy constraints have resulted in problems to their effectiveness. These complications are not insurmountable. Based on lessons learned over the past 30 years and new perspectives on how to proceed, their efforts can yield greater and more long-lasting results.

Notes

1 United Nations Office on Drugs and Crime (2020a). *The Time Is Now: Addressing the Gender Dimensions of Corruption*. Vienna: UNODC. At: https://www.unodc.org/documents/corruption/Publications/2020/THE_TIME_IS_NOW_2020_12_08.pdf; United Nations Office on Drugs and Crime (2020b). *Mainstreaming Gender in Corruption Projects/Programmes: Briefing Note for UNODC Staff*. Vienna: UNODC. At: https://www.unodc.org/documents/Gender/20-05712_Corruption_Brief_ebook_cb.pdf; Frédéric Boehm and Erika Sierra (2015). "The Gendered Impact of Corruption: Who Suffers More – Men or Women?," *U4 Brief No. 9*, Bergen, Norway: Chr. Michelsen Institute. At: https://www.u4.no/publications/the-gendered-impact-of-corruption-who-suffers-more-men-or-women.pdf.
2 Management Systems International (2013). *Assistance for Afghanistan's Anti-corruption Authority (4A) Project, Final Report*. Washington, DC: USAID.
3 Official Statement of the United Nations Secretary-General Antonio Guterres, October 15, 2020, United Nations, United Nations Official Website. At: https://www.un.org/en/coronavirus/statement-corruption-context-covid-19
4 Syriacus Buguzi, Fiona Broom, Joel Adriano and Aleida Rueda (2021). "COVID-19, Lies and Statistics: Corruption and the Pandemic," (7 April). At: https://www.scidev.net/sub-saharan-africa/scidev-net-investigates/covid-19-lies-and-statistics-corruption-and-the-pandemic/.

5 Transparency International UK (2021). *Track and Trace: Identifying Corruption Risks in UK Public Procurement for the COVID-19 Pandemic*. London: Transparency International UK. At: https://www.transparency.org.uk/sites/default/files/pdf/publications/Track%20and%20Trace%20-%20Transparency%20International%20UK.pdf.

6 Aryeh Mellman and Norman Eisen (2020). *Addressing the Other COVID Crisis: Corruption*, 22 July. Washington, DC: Brookings Institution. At: https://www.brookings.edu/research/addressing-the-other-covid-crisis-corruption/.

7 Ibid.

14 Sustaining anti-corruption reforms

It happens over and over again. Anti-corruption reforms are implemented and appear to have positive effects. Incidents of corruption are prevented or moderated and public perceptions of corruption are reduced. Then there is a change in government or the international donor that funded the reforms ends their program under the assumption that the problem has been resolved. That is when the plug gets pulled from the computers running the e-governance applications that reduced face-to-face transactions between citizens and officials. That is when oversight committees get dissolved and government audits are minimized.

Despite all the hard work and innovative thinking that went into anti-corruption reform initiatives, they can easily disappear if funds, resources, staff, institutions, and, most importantly, political will are pulled out. Even if the group and individual drivers and motivators of corruption are addressed directly targeting critical behavioral changes that are necessary to ensure reductions in corrupt actions, as discussed in previous chapters, all progress can be erased if continuous attention, commitment, and resources are not applied to sustain these reforms. So, in addition to some of the novel approaches to motivate behavioral change that were discussed in earlier chapters, there needs to be a lot of thought given on how to sustain anti-corruption advances.

One of the key problems plaguing sustainability is that anti-corruption reforms are typically isolated one-off attempts that are relatively easy to erase. There may be a few reform efforts launched in the education or health sectors, and a few new laws or institutions established, but no integrated whole-of-government strategy that ensures that anti-corruption initiatives are implemented in a planned, cohesive, and forceful way that can endure major changes in a country's political-economic dynamics. As well, reforms may be carried out at a central government level but not at a subnational level, or vice versa, leaving many opportunities for corrupt practices to creep back in to disrupt anti-corruption efforts.

One approach to promote sustainability of established anti-corruption reforms – at all levels – is to embark on scaling up and scaling out campaigns to ensure that all sectors and functions are impacted, that all levels

DOI: 10.4324/9781003241119-17

of government implement programs, and that all stakeholders in society are included and engaged in the reforms. Another approach is to rally and engage the potential victims of corruption – the public – to maintain their commitment and social momentum to demand change. Both are discussed below.

Scaling up

Scaling up is the "process of expanding, adapting and sustaining successful policies, programs, or projects in geographic space and over time to reach a greater number of people."[1] Especially for critical programs implemented under difficult circumstances, there is a dual need to expand successful pilots effectively so they can have greater reach throughout society, while promoting coordination of essential resources and stakeholders to make sure the reforms are sustained. Scaling up incorporates a range of actions based on strategies to accelerate the spread and endurance of good practices.[2] The goal is to move away from a piecemeal, short-term, and uncoordinated approach to change.

The initial steps in a scaling up strategy include assessing the viability of spreading reforms widely, developing a plan, and pilot testing it.[3] Then, it is critical to establish the preconditions for scaling: identifying and enhancing political will for scaling up among leadership and within society to ensure the legitimacy of these actions, and mobilizing the resources needed to make it happen effectively. Third, steps must be taken to organize and coordinate the scaling up activities necessary to keep the reforms going and expanding, in addition to tracking performance over time and adapting initiatives as needed. The scope of scaled up activities must be expanded beyond the pilot and outward to all parts of the countries at all levels, getting other actors and communities involved in adopting the initiatives. To do this, it is essential to increase the social bonds of cooperation and partnership among institutions, sectors, central and local levels of authority, and citizens and government. Linkages must be forged between these entities and stakeholders, encouraging the pooling of their capacities and bridging any divisions. Overall, scaling allows for better organization and alignment of resources and resource distribution, the building of networks, pooling of multiple donor resources, mechanisms to share expertise and lessons learned, public communications campaigns about results and impacts, and the empowering of multiple communities.

In the end, the effectiveness of policy change initiatives is assessed not only by whether they are targeted at the right drivers – the factors that are most likely to motivate behavioral change – but also whether those changes are likely to endure the test of time. Scaling up is an essential element in this equation.

Case study: Indonesia

An example of scaling up of anti-corruption efforts over a 10-year period (2011–2021) can be found in Indonesia via USAID-sponsored programs. Indonesia has a population of 275 million, making it the fourth largest in the world. It is composed of 17,000 islands spread out over 3,200 miles from east to west. It is the 14th largest country by land area. Given these statistics, scaling up any kind of reform program is likely to face problems over an extended period of time.

The strategy to achieve greater reach, spread, and speed for anti-corruption reform programs, mostly piloted in the capital, Jakarta, employed the use of information technology in many ways to engage government officials, citizens, businesses, and the mass media in all provinces and across many sectors.

Complaint handling

In early 2014, the USAID program, in close coordination with the Indonesian government, completed a new data management system that allowed the Ombudsman office to manage, control and supervise the processing of public complaints at its central office and its 33 local branches throughout the country.[4] All regional offices were required to use the new system. Between 2014 and 2016, the Ombudsman received more than 13,000 citizen complaints and nearly 4,800 were resolved quickly. This is a dramatic increase from the number of complaints that were received and resolved between 2011 and 2012.

The USAID program also significantly improved the Indonesian National Complaint Handling System.[5] In addition to a web-based system, it was developed to operate easily on smartphones to increase its reach throughout all regions. Complaint systems run by 12 local and provincial governments were integrated into the national system to ensure better transparency and accountability of government agencies in handling public services. These developments were publicized throughout the country to attract new users by holding events on university campuses in many provinces, and e-learning applications were implemented to ensure that administrators of the system would be best equipped to handle large influxes of complaints through the system. By the end of 2020, 34 ministries, 102 agencies, and 520 local governments were connected to the unified complaint handling system.[6]

To ensure that the complaint system met the needs of all of these government agencies, the project conducted assessments and pilot tests on various adjustments to the system. Extensive coordination and collaboration across agencies and across provinces were needed to make the system accessible, operable, and used by the public. During 2020 alone, the system received

123,731 complaints from all platforms. In comparison to the previous year, the system received an increase of 86% more registered complaints, demonstrating its popularity throughout the country.

Recruitment screening

One of the most important components of a well-functioning government is its civil service. The civil service's ability to successfully support the government depends heavily on its effectiveness and integrity. In 2014, Indonesia undertook legislative reform of its civil service to make its recruitment more open, accountable and increasingly transparent through open competition. In order to decrease subjectivity in the hiring of public servants, the Ministry for State Apparatus and Bureaucratic Reform introduced a mandatory computer-assisted test (CAT) as part of the 2014 civil service recruitment process.

The USAID program supported this effort by increasing trust by applicants in the new recruitment procedures.[7] Events were conducted in 14 provinces to explain the test and its purpose in reducing corruption in civil service recruitment. In subsequent years, the program was extended to participation by the Civil Service Commission, many ministries and local governments.[8]

The program also worked directly with the Civil Service Commission on an IT application to monitor the competitive recruitment processes for high-ranking officials.[9] Between 2017 and 2019, this system was used by approximately 719 agencies throughout the country, consisting of all 34 ministries, 29 non-ministry agencies, 34 provincial governments, 514 city and district governments, and 108 nonstructural agencies, to manage the recruitment of high-ranking officials. By the end of 2019, the system had been used for a total of 2,446 recruitment processes.

E-learning

E-learning modules were designed and deployed in coordination with many government agencies that provide online professional development training and public outreach solutions to overcome constraints imposed by geographic distance, time expended, and large numbers of staff in need of training.[10] With more than 4.3 million civil servants in Indonesia, e-learning tools provide a unique mechanism to extend the reach of training programs far beyond what could be done in face-to-face training.

During 2019, the USAID program worked with the Supreme Court to pilot e-learning modules for Anti-Corruption Judges Certification Training. The e-learning module is expected to free up classroom sessions for more interactive and substantive discussions, based on prerequisite reading/lessons, and reduce the preparatory burden for lecturers/trainers, who are typically senior Supreme Court figures.

Working with the supreme audit institution, the program developed e-learning modules to conduct training of auditors to monitor the utilization of state funds. Along with the Financial Intelligence Unit, the program built a new e-learning tool to assist frontline banking staff to recognize red flags for money laundering and terrorism financing. Government officials and staff from across 114 commercial banks in Indonesia completed the e-learning course and qualified for certificates.

The Civil Service Commission supervises the implementation of basic civil service norms, codes of ethics and codes of conduct, as well as the application of a merit system for personnel. Training the large number of civil servants on these topics across the country can be very costly. The program worked alongside the Commission to create an e-learning system to train local government staff, selection committees, and central government staff across all ministries.

Indonesia's Corruption Eradication Commission (KPK), together with the USAID program, launched an online learning center for civil servants throughout the country in 2012 focused on the definition and proper handling of gifts and gratuities.[11] This e-learning module was developed in light of the limited understanding of gratuities and gift-giving regulations among civil servants. Many public officials across all ministries and citizens view the practice of providing kickbacks and gifts as normal despite the fact that there are laws that regulate it. The online e-learning tool was designed to educate civil servants and politicians about gratuities and their legal obligations to properly report them. While the number reporting gratuities is still insufficient, it is growing. In the January-November 2012 period alone, the KPK's gratuities working unit received 1.88 billion rupiah (US $196,251) from politicians and civil service employees that had been received in gratuities. The amount of gratuity reporting has grown significantly with the help of the e-learning module.

In 2018, the program worked together with an NGO, Indonesia Corruption Watch (ICW), to distill its expertise in conducting oversight, investigations and advocacy into an online learning platform designed for other anti-corruption activists. However, while the system was being built, ICW recognized its potential to reach a far broader segment of the public throughout the country, so additional modules were created for more general audiences. The resulting *Anti-Corruption Academy* represented a hybrid between a general mass education tool and a platform for a smaller niche of experienced anti-corruption activists. In partnership with six major universities throughout Indonesia, the Academy provided e-courses to over 2500 student, business person, and civil servant users in its first year of operation.

All of these Indonesian e-governance applications shared several key scaling up features. They vastly expanded the number of people and the number of provinces that could take advantage of the public services and anti-corruption reforms that had been pilot tested in a few locations to start with. They all allowed citizens and officials working in different government sectors and at different levels to get engaged, replicate the results of others, and adjust and adapt the systems to their own particular needs. And they all involved collaboration and partnerships across central, provincial, and local levels, and across sectors, so that corrupt behavior could be attacked from multiple platforms simultaneously. Utilizing these IT tools along with scaling up approaches resulted in these anti-corruption reforms being disseminated to more people in more places faster and with less expense.

Citizen engagement

Another way to maintain commitment and social momentum to sustain significant anti-corruption reforms is to get citizens actively engaged in demanding change. They are logical stakeholders in this regard since they are the primary victims of corrupt behavior who are forced to pay bribes to get services they are entitled to, and they suffer when public services are of poor quality or not available. Citizens are hurt when basic and essential infrastructure is not provided or maintained, and when the overall economy suffers due to rampant corruption.

The most critical moment for sustainability among citizen groups is when they realize that they can indeed make a difference in promoting anti-corruption reforms. A CSO we worked with in Russia, after some training and through our insistence, held a face-to-face meeting with local authorities advocating for administrative changes that would reduce opportunities for bribe-taking when citizens and businesses seek licenses and permits. Using a cooperative approach, the CSO negotiated with the local government to make these adjustments... and they succeeded. Their interaction, which yielded positive results, was a real game-changer for the group. They never believed that they had the right, the power, or the ability to approach government officials and seek such changes, no matter how small they might be. Now, with this success under their belts, they proceeded to seek additional administrative changes – in a friendly and nonconfrontational way – to reduce opportunities for corruption. Experiencing their ability to make change, that had a direct impact on citizen's lives, strengthened the CSO's commitment to push forward and make demands in the public's interest.

Another activity that we promoted among CSOs in many countries was to both train their members on how to conduct social audits to keep government authorities accountable for their actions and to follow through with coaching and grant funding for these CSOs so that they could implement effective social audits and publicize their findings. Often, the resulting naming and shaming of government officials and agencies stemming from these audits and public campaigns had positive outcomes in terms of changes to administrative procedures, the return of bribes, and the firing of government staff. Such results also invigorated further CSO activities and citizen commitment. The Citizen Advocate Office (CAO), described earlier in Chapter 7, also was an activity carried out by CSOs through grant funding that resulted in unexpected positive results for the CSOs, largely through the impetus of naming and shaming, and produced greater citizen commitment and resolve to continue forward.

Notes

1 Arntraud Hartmann and Johannes F. Linn (2008). "Scaling Up: A Framework and Lessons for Development Effectiveness from Literature and Practice," Wolfensohn Center Working Paper No. 5, Brookings Institution. At: https://www.brookings.edu/wp-content/uploads/2016/06/10_scaling_up_aid_linn.pdf.
2 Larry Cooley and Jonathan Papoulidis (2017). "Scalable Solutions in Fragile States," November 28. At: https://www.brookings.edu/blog/future-development/2017/11/28/scalable-solutions-in-fragile-states/.
3 Larry Cooley (2016). *Scaling Up — From Vision to Large-Scale Change, A Management Framework for Practitioners*, Third Edition. Arlington, VA: Management Systems International. At: https://msiworldwide.com/sites/default/files/additional-resources/2018-11/ScalingUp_3rdEdition.pdf.
4 Management Systems International (2016). *Strengthening Integrity and Accountability Program 1 (SIAP 1), Final Report*. Washington, DC: United States Agency for International Development.
5 Management Systems International (2019). *USAID CEGAH Project, Annual Report FY 2019*. Washington, DC: USAID.
6 Management Systems International (2020). *USAID CEGAH Project, Annual Report FY 2020*. Washington, DC: USAID.
7 Management Systems International (2016), op.cit.
8 Management Systems International (2020), op.cit.
9 Management Systems International (2019), op.cit.
10 Ibid.
11 Management Systems International (2016), op.cit.

15 Making corruption fail

Sometimes taking a negative stance turns out to be the right thing to do. That is what we mean by "making corruption fail." Corruption plays havoc with citizen's rights, places restrictions on good governance, interferes with economic development, and exacerbates poverty. As we have seen, pursuing efforts to make corruption fail requires a diversity of counteractions that are contextually appropriate, address key drivers and motivators of participants in corrupt transactions, and can become sustainable over time.

Our analysis demonstrates that most countries are not doing enough to stop corruption. Other countries are actively addressing the corruption problem, but perhaps not in the most effective ways. That is not to say that all efforts implemented in the past have not been useful to some extent; it is just that they have not been enough given the inherent persistence of corrupt behavior.

Our analysis has focused on some of the major gaps in anti-corruption initiatives in the past. These efforts have primarily focused on influencing legal and institutional changes, which are important and necessary, but not sufficient. In the end, many policy practitioners and researchers have concluded that the most effective ways of making corruption fail are to target embedded human motivations to commit corruption. What is needed are targeted approaches that make corrupt behavior viewed as negative conduct – not only by the observer but by the individuals personally engaged in these acts. While some of these programs have been piloted, they have not been scaled up in a resolute way to take hold countrywide.

Addressing the social psychological drivers of human behavior – traditional socialization, social norms, group conformity, rationalizations, and risk aversion – will make engaging in corrupt transactions appear to be bad behavior to the actors themselves and will denigrate their reputation to others in society. To be accepted within your social community or network is a powerful motivator of individual choice and behavior; if corrupt behavior is viewed as negative and made public, that will be a major incentive which limits unethical temptations.

Addressing the ethical drivers of human behavior – self-interest versus social justice, and doing what may be good for you and your friends versus

DOI: 10.4324/9781003241119-18

empathy for others – raises additional conflicts in incentives at a personal level. How one views what is the right thing to do is a matter of how one has been socialized, as well as personal conscience. Clarifying what is ethical behavior and what is not is a difficult process. It can be pursued through engaging cultural and religious leadership and powerful role models, providing evidence of how unethical behavior damages the lives of others in society, and demonstrating how corruption denigrates the corruptor's personal image and standing in the community.

Another critical path that needs to be addressed to make corruption fail is to sabotage the negotiation encounter that defines corrupt transactions. Finding ways to eliminate the face-to-face interactions that facilitate the corrupt tit-for-tat dealing are essential. This works in both directions – both for government officials and for powerful citizens and business people – reducing the demand and supply sides of corruption.

The path forward for anti-corruption initiatives needs to address these important drivers that have only received preliminary testing so far. Some examples of what these initiatives might look like and how to go about implementing them were presented in earlier chapters.

Critical principles looking forward

Lessons learned from the many past attempts to make corruption fail present us with a set of essential principles that should improve the chances of transforming this chronic problem of corruption. We have discovered that just addressing a few of these factors will not be sufficient; effectiveness requires all of these elements to be activated together in a "big push" that integrates many mechanisms, policies, dynamics, and stakeholders toward the common goal.[1] The multidimensional nature of corruption requires a multidimensional attack on the factors that support and sustain such an engrained human behavior.

Establish the basic foundational factors. It is critical to ensure that the foundational legal framework that criminalizes corruption is in place and enforced. In addition, the institutions needed to put these laws, regulations, and policies into effect must also exist.

Political will and commitment. Backing up these anti-corruption foundational factors must be the political will and commitment to follow through and enforce them by political and societal leadership. Otherwise, the laws will be seen as just window dressing and subject to disregard and neglect. Governmental, societal, and cultural leaders, as well as civil society groups, must commit themselves to anti-corruption goals as serious aspirations. Change is not going to be visible immediately, so all must be willing to persevere on the quest to make corruption fail. This will require a commitment to changing what may be traditional social norms about how to behave in society, what is correct behavior, and what it means to be accepted as part of the group. Leaders must view a resulting reduction in corruption as a new norm that is worth seeking and must promote their political will for change to the public at large to reeducate them and gain their support.

Available resources. Political will must always be backed up by sufficient levels of resources and capacity to implement the reforms and keep them going. Budgets need to be adequate and available. Staff, especially in the civil service, need to be trained and educated on what a non-corrupt governmental transaction with citizens and business people looks like. Citizen groups need to be trained and experienced in advocating for reforms and conducting social audits.

Prevention. Legal proscriptions against corruption, when enforced, punish those who commit corrupt acts. Preventive policies and mechanisms stop the corruption from happening in the first place. As discussed earlier, there are many ways to try to prevent corruption from occurring; not all will work under all circumstances. Establishing and enforcing good governance processes, that focus on expanding transparency and accountability in the public and private spheres, is a positive step toward eliminating corrupt behaviors from emerging.

Prioritize Individual and Group Drivers of Corruption. Tactics that target the motivators of corrupt behavior at an individual and group level should be prioritized. These will attack longstanding cultural and social norms that legitimize corruption, make it undesirable to rationalize actions in the name of corruption, and strengthen social empathy and justice for all over excessive self-interested motives.

Reinvent social norms. What are the principal social norms that need to be altered to reduce corrupt behavior and make it fail? Training and education need to be conducted at all levels to start the process of reform. This can start at the lowest levels from kindergarten and elementary school education programs – demonstrating the negative aspects of corruption and how to avoid it. For example, ABC books on corruption have been developed to teach young children that there are ways to operate in society without using corruption, at the same time that they may see their role models practicing fraud and abuse. Teens and young adults can be engaged in youth camps, school debates, quiz shows, and social media competitions to demonstrate how they can adjust society's existing corrupt tendencies and veer away from those behaviors. Older members of society can be given new opportunities to practice anti-corruption behaviors – through crowdsourced applications where they can register complaints about corrupt transactions they have experienced or through advocacy groups where they can propose new options for anti-corruption reforms.

Contextualization. Lessons from past attempts at fighting corruption demonstrate that there are no cookie-cutter approaches. An effective tactic in one country is not necessarily effective in other countries. Reform approaches need to be customized to the social-political-economic conditions so they attack the corruption problem appropriately. Conducting assessments of the political-economic context can help in the development of reform strategies that are likely to succeed. Are the foundational factors – the legal and institutional preconditions – in place or do they need to be expanded and implemented further? Are the relevant stakeholders within government and in society prepared to take on the reform agenda and promote it? Are there other political and economic issues or dynamics that are likely to distract from the anti-corruption focus? Answers to these types of questions will help design a tailored plan of action, get actors to engage, and organize an advantageous timeline to pursue.

Go Multidimensional. To take hold and be sustainable, a big push of reforms is needed. This entails implementation of a comprehensive anti-corruption strategy that addresses how the problem impacts upon all policy sectors in government, not just a generic approach that assumes all key sectors will follow suit. All key stakeholders need to be involved including civil society, businesses, and the media, along with public sector actors. All levels of government need to be engaged, from local districts to cities to provinces to the central government, because corrupt behaviors can easily become embedded wherever social and political decisions are made. And the anti-corruption programs must be rolled out to the entire country to avoid sustaining regional pockets of corruption that can result in respreading these behaviors.

Monitoring. After reforms are implemented, oversight of reformed laws, institutions, and norms is required to determine if they are having the desired impact. This oversight can come in different forms – government audits, civil society monitoring, social audits, investigative reporting by the media, and so on. As monitoring results are analyzed, the reforms can be adjusted to achieve improved outcomes. And the results of these reforms should be publicized to build public confidence in anti-corruption efforts and their implications for everyday life and national growth.

Scaling. Engaging in many simultaneous pilot tests of potential anti-corruption reforms is essential to find the few that will work well within country-specific, political-economic conditions. When piloted reform programs prove to be effective, it is important to scale them up rapidly so that the reforms and their positive results can be experienced throughout the country.

Evolutionary transformation. Despite the need for big push efforts, making corruption fail will not proceed on a quick revolutionary path. It is typically an evolutionary transformation of long-held traditional norms and behaviors. No matter how clever, contextualized, and driver-focused the reform programs, a quick and measurable impact is not likely to emerge. It will be more like baby steps in the right direction. Once those baby steps are observed, it is critical to immediately promote the evolution from traditional corrupt practices and to reinforce those reforms at all levels of government, across all regions of the country, across all sectors, and across all age groups. Continual reinforcement of successes, scaling up what works, and strengthening social momentum behind anti-corruption initiatives are essential for sustainability.

Recommendations

The overarching argument framing this study has been that researchers and practitioners have not been targeting the right solutions to make corruption fail. They have been fixated on addressing legal, institutional, and contextual factors that facilitate corrupt behavior. Most of these reforms can be circumvented by government officials, powerful citizens and business people who are persistent and relentless in their quest for self-interest. Many other reform approaches, focused on the drivers and motivators of corrupt and non-corrupt behaviors by groups and individuals, have not been tested or if they have, have only been piloted and not implemented on a wide-enough scale. These are the initiatives that we believe will make a significant difference in stemming corruption over the longer term because they promote behavioral change at a personal and social level.

Several broad recommendations have been discussed throughout the book that are offered here to start researchers and practitioners on this improved path.

Conduct Thorough Assessments. There are no ready-made approaches; every country and every context is different and demands customized reforms. So, the planning stage for an anti-corruption strategy needs to begin with an assessment of how well the foundational factors of anti-corruption laws and institutions have been implemented, an analysis of the political-economic context, and an examination of the key drivers and motivators of corrupt behavior. The questions presented in the Appendix offer a starting point for an assessment guide that should be adapted to the country context and formulated to address relevant sectors. The findings of the assessment will reveal what is realistic, practical, and likely to be effective from reform initiatives. A tailored anti-corruption strategy with specific approaches can then be developed, implemented, adjusted over time, and sustained.

Focus on Behavioral Change Initiatives. One result of the assessment might be that the laws and institutions to fight corruption are not sufficient or have not been adequately implemented. The political-economic analysis might also suggest that various stakeholders would benefit from additional support and training so they can play important roles in the reform agenda. Beyond fixing these prerequisites, the focus of the anti-corruption strategy should be on effecting behavioral change at a group and individual level. What are the incentives and disincentives for societal groups and individuals to pursue corrupt acts? What initiatives can be implemented that might promote changes in these behaviors and attitudes toward corruption? Once groups and individuals begin to practice new behaviors and reactions to corruption – and see the rewards for doing so – they are more likely to be reinforced in their changed behaviors and will continue along these new lines.

Reduce Opportunities for Negotiation. The corruption transaction is a perverse form of negotiation. Government officials demand gifts or bribes from citizens in return for government services that they would normally receive for free. Another form of corrupt negotiation is when powerful citizens demand extra services, special attention or public contracts from government officials in return for bribes or kickbacks. There is always a tit-for-tat angle. Behavioral changes imposed on this transactional formula can have a devastating impact on the ability of corrupt officials and corrupt citizens or business people to follow-through on the tit-for-tat. For example, bureaucratic discretion can be reduced through greater oversight and supervision, required checks and balances, or increased regulation. E-governance technology can be used to reduce this discretion, at the same time it reduces face-to-face opportunities, so that corrupt negotiations will be hampered. Strengthened accountability and transparency of government actions will also reduce corruption negotiations – through increased civilian review and social audits of government, and improved complaint systems for corruption victims that pinpoint the sources of corruption. Public naming and shaming of corrupt officials will reduce the likelihood of future corrupt transactions by those who fear getting caught, outed, and prosecuted.

Scale up for Sustainability. After the reforms are implemented and they appear to work, it is important to keep up the pressure. Many reforms in the past have been short-lived. The critical efforts needed to keep reforms alive and working involve scaling them up to all sectors, all levels of government, all regions of the country, and all citizens and civil servants. Citizens also need to feel a strong commitment and social momentum for anti-corruption initiatives. Having a sustainability strategy in hand is important early on to ensure that the behavioral changes that are achieved by reform initiatives become embedded in national and cultural traditions looking forward.

* * * * *

Corruption has been a prominent feature of human behavior since the beginning. But it does not have to be with us forever. Across millennia, humans have implemented massive changes to the way we live – emerging from caves, finding ways to ensure sustenance, forming societies, creating and sustaining economies, establishing laws and governments to ensure peace, stability, and justice, and the list goes on. While corrupt behaviors have certainly been part of the equation all along, human innovation can go a long way toward eliminating them if there is the commitment, resources, ideas, and inspiration.

And I hope that when I drive down the parkway to the city in the not too distant future – and I'm traveling over the speed limit and the police stop me – it doesn't even cross my mind that the policeman is looking for a bribe.

Note

1 Mariana Borges, et al. (2017). *Combatting Corruption among Civil Servants: Interdisciplinary Perspectives on What Works*. Chicago, IL: Institute of International Education, Northwestern University. At: https://www.usaid.gov/sites/default/files/documents/2496/Combatting_Corruption_Among_Civil_Servants_-_Interdisciplinary_Perspectives_on_What_Works.pdf.

Appendix
Corruption assessment

The assessment questions presented below are broken out into three categories: the foundational framework (the legal-institutional situation),[1] the context (the political-economic situation),[2] and the drivers and motivators (the individual and group incentives).[3] These questions can be used to customize an assessment for any country and any sector.

A   Foundational framework (legal-institutional situation)

For each of the questions, identify (a) the formal provisions, (b) how these provisions are implemented in practice, and (c) major weaknesses that need to be improved upon.

1   Anti-Corruption Strategy and Plans

    1.1 Is there a formal national anti-corruption strategy/program?

    1.2 Are there governmental institutions mandated to enforce/implement this strategy/program? What are their legal authorities?

2   Anti-Corruption Enforcement Laws and Institutions

    2.1 Explicit Anti-Corruption Laws

        2.1.1 Is there legislation explicitly prohibiting or criminalizing corruption or corrupt behaviors (bribery, embezzlement, kickbacks, trading in influence, abuse of functions, illicit enrichment, bribery and embezzlement in the private sector, laundering of proceeds of crime, concealment, obstruction of justice, etc.)?

        2.1.2 Are there governmental institutions mandated to enforce/implement this anti-corruption legislation? What are their legal authorities?

    2.2 Corruption Investigations: Is there legislation regulating investigations of corruption cases? What institutions are responsible for investigations of corruption cases? What are their legal authorities?

2.3   Corruption Prosecution in Courts: Is there legislation regulating prosecution of corrupt offenses? What institutions are responsible for prosecuting corruption cases? What are their legal authorities?

2.4   Money Laundering: Is there legislation prohibiting laundering the proceeds of corrupt activities? Are there governmental institutions mandated to enforce/implement this legislation?

2.5   Asset Recovery: Is there legislation regulating recovery of assets from corruption cases (confiscation, forfeiture, return, international cooperation, etc.)? Are there governmental institutions mandated to enforce/implement this legislation?

2.6   Witness Protection: Is there is legislation that protects witnesses in corruption cases or whistleblowers who expose corruption? Are there governmental institutions mandated to enforce/implement this legislation?

3   Corruption Prevention Laws and Institutions

3.1   Executive Branch

3.1.1   Asset Disclosure: Are there laws or regulations that require disclosure of assets for senior elected officials or political candidates and their families? Are there governmental institutions mandated to enforce/implement/monitor such laws/regulations?

3.1.2   Abuse of Discretion: Are there laws or regulations that place limits on the discretion of senior government managers in making decisions about the use of government funds? Are there governmental institutions mandated to enforce/monitor such laws/regulations?

3.1.3   Gifts/Favors/Abuse of Influence: Are there laws or regulations that place limits on accepting gifts, favors or services, that control or limit how senior government managers use their influence, or that regulate conflicts of interest for executive branch managers? Are there governmental institutions mandated to enforce/implement/monitor such laws/regulations?

3.2   Legislative Branch

3.2.1   Asset Disclosure: Are there laws or regulations that require disclosure of assets for legislators or legislative candidates, and their families? Are there governmental institutions mandated to enforce/implement/monitor such laws/regulations?

3.2.2   Gifts/Favors/Abuse of Influence/Conflicts of Interest: Are there laws or regulations that place limits on accepting gifts, favors or services, that control or limit the use of influence, or that regulate conflicts of interest for legislators? Are there governmental institutions mandated to enforce/implement/monitor such laws/regulations?

3.2.3 Oversight Responsibility: Is there legislation that provides clear monitoring and oversight responsibility to the legislature to ensure executive and budgetary accountability? Are there governmental institutions mandated to enforce or implement such laws?

3.3 Judicial Branch

3.3.1 Asset Disclosure: Are there laws or regulations that require disclosure of assets for judges, senior court officials and their families? Are there governmental institutions mandated to enforce/implement/monitor such laws/regulations?

3.3.2 Gifts/Favors/Abuse of Influence/Conflicts of Interest: Are there laws or regulations that place limits on accepting gifts, favors or services, that control or limit the use of influence, or that regulate conflicts of interest for judges and senior court officials? Are there governmental institutions mandated to enforce/implement/monitor such laws/regulations?

3.3.3 Judicial Independence: Are there laws or regulations that ensure judicial independence from the executive (related to judicial selection, dismissal, and budget issues)? Are there governmental institutions mandated to enforce or implement such laws?

3.3.4 Accountability Mechanisms: Are there laws or regulations that ensure judicial accountability (including transparency of judicial records, process, and decisions)? Are there governmental institutions mandated to enforce/implement/monitor such laws or regulations?

3.4 Civil Service

3.4.1 Conflicts of Interest: Are there laws or regulations that define conflicts of interest for public officials? Are there governmental institutions mandated to enforce/implement conflict of interest legislation?

3.4.2 Asset Disclosure: Is there legislation that requires civil servants to disclose their assets? Are there governmental institutions mandated to enforce/implement asset disclosure legislation?

3.4.3 Codes of Conduct: Are there laws or regulations that establish ethics standards for public officials and civil servants? Are there governmental institutions mandated to enforce/implement codes of conduct legislation?

3.4.4 Whistleblower Protection: Is there legislation that provides protection for people who report cases of corruption? Are there governmental institutions mandated to enforce/implement whistleblower protection legislation?

3.4.5 Lobbying: Are there laws and regulations that regulate lobbying of public officials? Are there governmental institutions mandated to enforce/implement lobbying legislation?

3.4.6   Public Hiring and Appointments: Is there legislation that requires public hiring to be based on merit rather than patronage, nepotism, favoritism, personal connections and bribery? Are there governmental institutions mandated to enforce/implement public hiring and selection legislation?

3.4.7   Immunity: Is there legislation that regulates removing immunity from elected representatives or senior public officials so that investigations can be conducted into suspected corrupt offenses that they have committed? Are there governmental institutions mandated to enforce/implement such immunity-removal legislation?

3.5   Transparency and Accountability

3.5.1   Complaint Mechanisms: Is there legislation that establishes and regulates an Ombudsman office or other mechanism for reporting acts of corruption? Is an Ombudsman office established or are there other governmental institutions mandated to take reports about corruption and act on them?

3.5.2   Freedom of Information: Is there legislation that provides citizens with rights to access public documents related to government resources and decision-making? Are there governmental institutions mandated to enforce/implement freedom of information legislation?

3.5.3   Public Participation: Are there laws or regulations that require that executive, legislative and regulatory meetings, including commissions, be open to the public? Are there governmental institutions mandated to enforce/implement legislation/regulations on public hearings?

3.6   Political Parties and Elections

3.6.1   Political Party Financing: Is there legislation that requires transparency in political party funding and expenditures? Are there governmental institutions mandated to enforce/implement political party financing legislation?

3.6.2   Elections: Is there legislation that regulates the conduct and financing of elections? Are there governmental institutions mandated to enforce/implement legislation related to elections and their financing?

3.7   Public Finance

3.7.1   Financial Management Systems: Are there laws or regulations that establish and regulate an integrated financial management system? Are there governmental institutions mandated to enforce/implement this legislation/regulation?

3.7.2 Audits of Public Expenditures: Is there legislation that requires periodic auditing of public accounts, public budgets, and public expenditures? Are there governmental institutions mandated to enforce/implement public audit legislation?

3.7.3 Public Procurement: Is there legislation that regulates and promotes transparency in public procurements? Are there governmental institutions mandated to enforce/implement public procurement legislation?

3.7.4 Budgeting Process: Are there laws or regulations that require transparency in budget planning? Are there governmental institutions mandated to enforce/implement this legislation/regulation?

3.7.5 Taxation: Is there legislation that disallows the deductibility of expenses that constitute bribes for tax purposes? Are there governmental institutions mandated to enforce/implement this provision in the law?

3.7.6 Banking System: Are there laws or regulations that require transparency and accountability in the banking system? Are there governmental institutions mandated to enforce/implement this legislation/regulation?

3.8 Private Sector Regulation and Privatization

3.8.1 Business Regulations: Are there laws or regulations that establish rules for regulating business operations (including, but not limited to, accessibility of information on business requirements and fee structures, and administrative remedies to challenge decisions and fees)? Are there governmental institutions mandated to enforce/implement such business-related legislation or regulations?

3.8.2 Privatization: Is there legislation that regulates how the privatization of state enterprises should be conducted? Are there governmental institutions mandated to enforce/implement privatization legislation?

3.8.3 Business Sector Anti-corruption Actions: Are there anti-corruption actions taken by the private sector (ethics codes, anti-corruption advocacy activities, etc.)?

3.9 Nongovernmental Organizations and the Media

3.9.1 Civil Society Organizations: Are there laws or regulations that limit the ability of nongovernmental organizations to organize or advocate for reform or monitor government performance? Are there governmental institutions mandated to enforce/implement this legislation? Are there CSOs that advocate for anti-corruption reforms and/or implement anti-corruption activities?

3.9.2 Media: Are there laws that limit the media's rights to investigate corruption cases (censorship, gag, or libel laws)? Are there governmental institutions mandated to enforce/implement this legislation? Are investigations on corruption published in the media?

4   Initial Analysis of Sectors, Functions, and Institutions[4]

For example, but not limited to, Agriculture, Anti-corruption Agency, Budget, Civil Service, Civil Society, Construction and Infrastructure, Customs, Decentralization, Education, Electoral Process, Electricity, Energy, Environment, Forestry, Health, Justice, Labor and Workforce, Law Enforcement, Media, Military, Parliament, Petroleum, Pharmaceuticals, Political Parties, Private Sector, Privatization, Procurement, Public Finance, Public Service Delivery, Regional/Local Government, Supreme Audit Institution, Taxation, Transport, and Water and Sanitation. Be sure to evaluate each sector/function based on both formal legal requirements and actual practice.

- Institutional Capacity (ability to operate within the law and regulations; established internal rules and procedures; leadership ability; staff professionalism and meritocracy; availability of budget and resources)
- Transparency Status (public access to information; open hearings; open decision-making and procedures)
- Accountability Status (internal audits and controls; external oversight; conflict of interest rules; management reporting)
- Stakeholders (political will; champions; opponents; civil society; business; media)

B   The context (political-economic situation)

The questions in this section are adapted from USAID's political economy analysis approach.

1   Basics

1.1 Causes of corruption: What kinds of corruption have been most pervasive and why?
1.2 Enabling factors: What actors and structures have enabled corruption?
1.3 Key actors: What is the role of corruption in unifying or dividing people?
1.4 Response from the state: How functional is the state bureaucracy? How do capacity and resource issues affect the problem?

1.5 Response from citizenry/CSOs and the relationship between state and citizenry: What type of oversight/accountability mechanisms exist both within the state (internal and external audits and controls), as well as outside of the state (media, CSO watchdogs)?

2 Here and Now

2.1 Reform champions and spoilers: Who benefits from reforms to make government more transparent, effective and accountable? How and why? Are they organized, empowered and influential enough to drive reform? Who benefits from blocking reforms?

2.2 Pathways to change: What is the nature of policymaking processes? What factors determine whose voices are heard?

2.3 Influencers: What is the role of CSOs, private sector, media, religion, and other groups in reform? How do key actors use their influence? What influence do they have and to whom are they accountable?

2.4 What's working/what's not: Has civil society been able to hold the government accountable? What has worked/what hasn't worked?

2.5 Role of the international community: What influence does the international community have to drive reform? What are the limitations?

3 Dynamics

3.1 What are potential pathways for reform for anti-corruption (new leadership, civil service reform, institutionalization of transparency laws, collective action, etc.)?

3.2 Who is empowered to act and what help do they need to be effective?

3.3 Are there opportunities to build reform coalitions? How?

3.4 What current initiatives are working/not working and how can they be built upon effectively? Are these seen as legitimate? Do they have genuine constituencies?

3.5 What entry points for change are likely to open up?

3.6 Are there lessons learned from other countries in the region that could help?

C Drivers and motivators (individual and group incentives)

1 Social Norms/Social Psychology

1.1 Is the dominant social norm guiding how people behave that of self-interest (including for oneself, family, and close community) or that of social justice and empathy for others?

1.2 Is corruption generally viewed as a reasonable way to get public services?

1.3 Do people typically make excuses for acting corruptly in order to get what they need?

1.4 Is corrupt behavior generally acceptable in the country's traditional culture and social norms?

1.5 Are people generally risk averse? Will they hold back on committing corrupt behavior if they believe they will be publicly shamed or caught?

1.6 Are there many leaders and role models in society that are viewed as corrupt, thereby promoting corrupt norms?

2 Ethics

2.1 How widespread in society are norms to behave ethically?

2.2 Are there popular leaders or role models in society who promote ethical beliefs and behaviors?

2.3 Are there major sources of ethical training and learning in society at all levels that most people accept and abide by?

2.4 Does government screen recruits for the civil service for their ethical behavior or beliefs?

3 Negotiation

3.1 Are there mechanisms in place that make transactions between government officials and citizens more transparent and/or more closely monitored?

3.2 Do bureaucrats have too much discretion and too little supervision concerning how they act?

3.3 Do citizens have easy ways by which they can complain about corrupt officials?

Notes

1 Adapted from Bertram Spector, Michael Johnston and Svetlana Winbourne (2009). *Anti-Corruption Assessment Handbook, Final Report*. Washington, DC: USAID. At: https://pdf.usaid.gov/pdf_docs/pa00jp37.pdf.

2 See USAID Learning Lab (2018). *Applied Political Economy Analysis (PEA): Reference Materials, Sample Interview Questions and Data Collection Template.* At: https://usaidlearninglab.org/sites/default/files/resource/files/supplemental_resource_-_sample_interview_guide.docx_1.pdf.

3 See Cheyanne Scharbatke-Church and Diana Chigas (2019). *Understanding Social Norms: A Reference Guide for Policy and Practice.* The Henry J. Leir Institute of Human Security. Medford, MA: The Fletcher School of Law and Diplomacy, Tufts University. At: https://sites.tufts.edu/ihs/social-norms-reference-guide/.

4 For detailed questions for 19 government sectors and functions, see Appendix 4 in Spector, Johnston and Winbourne (2009), op.cit. at: https://pdf.usaid.gov/pdf_docs/pa00jp37.pdf.

Bibliography

Abel, R. (1977). *The Legal Profession: An Annotated Bibliography*. Los Angeles, CA: University of California at Los Angeles (mimeo).

Ariely, Dan (2012). *The (Honest) Truth about Dishonesty*. New York: Harper Collins.

Aronfreed, J. (1968). *Conduct and Conscience*. New York: Academic Press.

Asscher, J.T. and S.V. Konnov (2005). *Ukraine Justice System Assessment Report*. Brussels: European Commission, TACIS, June.

Association of the United States Army (AUSA) (1977). *Manpower for the Military: Draft or Volunteer?* Washington, DC: AUSA.

Baez Camargo, Claudia and Lucy Koechlin (2018). "Informal Governance: Comparative Perspectives on Co-optation, Control and Camouflage in Rwanda, Tanzania and Uganda," *International Development Policy | Revue internationale de politique de développement* 10: 78–100. At: http://journals.openedition.org/poldev/2646.

Banfield, Edward (1975). "Corruption as a Feature of Governmental Organization," *Journal of Law and Economics* 18 (December): 587–605.

Benequista, Nicholas (2011). "Blurring the Boundaries: Citizen Action across States and Societies," Brighton, UK: The Development Research Center on Citizenship, Participation and Accountability. At: https://opendocs.ids.ac.uk/opendocs/bitstream/handle/20.500.12413/12499/cdrc_2011_blurring.pdf?sequence=1&isAllowed=y.

Bertucci, Guido (2000). "Why Anti-corruption Crusades Often Fail To Win Lasting Victories," Presentation at the UN Anti-Corruption Summit. At: http://unpan1.un.org/intradoc/groups/public/documents/un/unpan010749.pdf.

Bhargava, Vinay and Emil Bolongaita (2004). *Challenging Corruption in Asia: Case Studies and a Framework for Action*. Washington, DC: The World Bank.

Bjorkman, Martina and Jakob Svensson (2009). "Power to The People: Evidence From a Randomized Field Experiment on Community-Based Monitoring in Uganda," *The Quarterly Journal of Economics* 124, 2: 735–769.

Black, David and Richard Blue (2005). *Rule of Law Strengthening and Anti-Corruption in Ukraine: Recommendations for USAID Assistance*. Washington, DC: USAID.

Boehm, Frédéric and Erika Sierra (2015). "The Gendered Impact of Corruption: Who Suffers More – Men or Women?," U4 Brief No. 9, Bergen, Norway: Chr. Michelsen Institute. At: https://www.u4.no/publications/the-gendered-impact-of-corruption-who-suffers-more-men-or-women.pdf.

Bolongaita, Emil (2010). *An Exception to the Rule? Why Indonesia's Anti-Corruption Commission Succeeds Where Others Don't – A Comparison with the Philippines' Ombudsman*. Bergen: Chr. Michelsen Institute (U4 Issue: 4). At: http://www.u4.no/publications/an-exception-to-the-rule-why-indonesia-s-anti-corruption-commission-succeeds-where-others-don-t-a-comparison-with-the-philippines-ombudsman/.

Borges, Mariana, et al. (2017). *Combatting Corruption Among Civil Servants: Interdisciplinary Perspectives on What Works*. Chicago, IL: Institute of International Education, Northwestern University. At: https://www.usaid.gov/sites/default/files/documents/2496/Combatting_Corruption_Among_Civil_Servants_-_Interdisciplinary_Perspectives_on_What_Works.pdf.

Buguzi, Syriacus, Fiona Broom, Joel Adriano and Aleida Rueda (2021). "COVID-19, Lies and Statistics: Corruption and the Pandemic," 7 April. At: https://www.scidev.net/sub-saharan-africa/scidev-net-investigates/covid-19-lies-and-statistics-corruption-and-the-pandemic/.

Bushey, Adam J. (2014). "Second Generation Rule of Law and Anti-Corruption Programming Abroad: Comparing Existing U.S. Government and International Best Practices to Rachel Kleinfeld's Advancing the Rule of Law Abroad: Next Generation Reform," *Houston Journal of International Law* 37: 139.

Campbell, J.L. and A.S. Göritz (2014). "Culture Corrupts! A Qualitative Study of Organizational Culture in Corrupt Organizations," *Journal of Business Ethics* 120: 291–311.

Campos, J. Edgardo and Sanjay Pradhan, editors (2007). *The Many Faces of Corruption*. Washington, DC: The World Bank.

Carlin, J. (1966). *Lawyer's Ethics: A Survey of the New York City Bar*. New York: Russell Sage Foundation.

Chayes, Sarah (2020). *On Corruption in America*. New York: Knopf.

Checchi Consulting (2020). *Legal Professional Development and Anti-Corruption Activity in Liberia (LPAC)*, Final Report. Arlington, VA: Checchi Consulting. At: https://pdf.usaid.gov/pdf_docs/PA00XFM1.pdf.

Chêne, Marie (2012). "Lessons Learned in Fighting Corruption in Post-conflict Countries," *U4 Expert Answer* 17, 355 (December). At: http://www.u4.no/publications/lessons-learned-in-fighting-corruption-in-post-conflict-countries/downloadasset/2995.

Cheyne, J. A. and R. H. Walters (1969). "Intensity of punishment, timing of punishment, and cognitive structure as determinants of response inhibition," *Journal of Experimental Child Psychology* 7: 231–244.

Cobham, Alex (2013). "Corrupting Perceptions: Why Transparency International's Flagship Corruption Index Falls Short," July 23. At: https://www.cgdev.org/blog/corrupting-perceptions-why-transparency-international%E2%80%99s-flagship-corruption-index-falls-short.

Coffey International (2019). *Pay No Bribe – Endline Survey Report*. Support to Anti-Corruption in Sierra Leone Project. London: Coffey International. At: https://www.anticorruption.gov.sl/slides/slide/endline-survey-report-186.

Cooley, Larry (2016). *Scaling Up — From Vision to Large-Scale Change, A Management Framework for Practitioners*, Third Edition. Arlington, VA: Management Systems International. At: https://msiworldwide.com/sites/default/files/additional-resources/2018-11/ScalingUp_3rdEdition.pdf.

Cooley, Larry and Jonathan Papoulidis (2017). *Scalable Solutions in Fragile States.* Washington, DC: The Brookings Institution. At: https://www.brookings.edu/blog/future-development/2017/11/28/scalable-solutions-in-fragile-states/.

Counterpart Creative Center (2004). *Civil Society Organizations in Ukraine: The State and Dynamics (2002–2003).* Kyiv: Counterpart Creative Center.

Cuadrado, Daniela Cepeda (2021). *Covid-19 Corruption in 2021: January–April Developments,* April 22. Bergen: U4 Anti-Corruption Resource Centre. At: https://medium.com/u4-anti-corruption-resource-centre/covid-19-corruption-in-2021-march-april-developments-c4a6dbee530b.

Cuéllar, Mariano-Florentino and Matthew Stephenson (2020). "Taming Systemic Corruption: The American Experience and its Implications for Contemporary Debates," (September 4). *Harvard Public Law Working Paper No. 20–29.* At: https://ssrn.com/abstract=3686821.

Darley, John M. (2005). "The Cognitive and Social Psychology of the Contagious Organizational Corruption," *Brooklyn Law Review* 70. At: https://brooklynworks.brooklaw.edu/blr/vol70/iss4/2.

De Speville, Bertrand (2008). "Failing Anti-corruption Agencies – Causes and Cures," Paper Presented at the ISCTE Conference, Lisbon.

Department for International Development (2015). "Why Corruption Matters: Understanding Causes, Effects and How to Address Them," Evidence Paper on Corruption (January), London: DFID.

Druckman, Daniel (1993) "Situational Levers of Negotiating Flexibility," *Journal of Conflict Resolution* 32 (2): 236–276.

Druckman, Daniel (1994) "Determinants of Compromising Behavior in Negotiation: A Meta-Analysis," *Journal of Conflict Resolution* 33 (3): 507–556.

Dupuy, Kendra and Siri Neset (2018). *The Cognitive Psychology of Corruption: Micro-level Explanations for Unethical Behaviour.* Bergen, Norway: Chr. Michelsen Institute, U4 issue 2018:2.

Elliott, Kimberly, editor (1997). *Corruption and the Global Economy.* Washington, DC: Institute for International Economics.

Ferraz, Claudio and Frederico Finan (2008). "Exposing Corrupt Politicians: The Effects of Brazil's Publicly Released Audits on Electoral Outcomes," *The Quarterly Journal of Economics* 123, 2: 703–745.

Freedom House (2005). *Nations in Transit 2005.* Washington, DC: Freedom House.

Gauthier, Bernard (2013). "Making Leakages Visible: Public Expenditure Tracking in Education," in Gareth Sweeney, Krina Despota and Samira Lindner, editors, *Global Corruption Report: Education, Transparency International.* New York: Routledge.

George, Alexander (1991). *Forceful Persuasion.* Washington, DC: United States Institute of Peace Press.

Hanna, Rema, S. Bishop, S. Nadel, G. Scheffler, and K. Durlacher (2011). "The Effectiveness of Anti-corruption Policy: What Has Worked, What Hasn't, and What We Don't Know–A Systematic Review." Technical Report. London: EPPI Centre, University of London. At: http://eppi.ioe.ac.uk/cms/LinkClick.aspx?fileticket=9T7IlZ7LFw8%3D&tabid=3106&mid=5783.

Hanna, Rema and Shing-Yi Wang (2013). "Dishonesty and Selection into Public Service," Working Paper 19649. Washington, DC: National Bureau of Economic Research. At: https://www.nber.org/papers/w19649.

Hartmann, Arntraud and Johannes F. Linn (2008). "Scaling Up: A Framework and Lessons for Development Effectiveness from Literature and Practice," Wolfensohn Center Working Paper No. 5, Brookings Institution. At: https://www.brookings.edu/wp-content/uploads/2016/06/10_scaling_up_aid_linn.pdf.

Heeks, Richard, (2011). "Understanding success and failure of anti-corruption initiatives," U4 Brief, No. 2 (March 2011). At: http://www.u4.no/publications/understanding-success-and-failure-of-anti-corruption-initiatives/downloadasset/206.

Heidenheimer, Arnold, Michael Johnston and Victor LeVine (1999). *Political Corruption: A Handbook*. New Brunswick, NJ: Transaction Publishers.

Hellman, Joel, G. Jones and D. Kaufmann (2000). "Seize the State, Seize the Day: State Capture, Corruption and Influence in Transition." World Bank Policy Research Working Paper No. 2444. Washington, DC: World Bank Institute (September).

Heywood, Paul (2014). "Measuring Corruption: Perspectives, Critiques, and Limits," At: https://www.ceu.edu/sites/default/files/attachment/event/9385/heywood-measuring-corruption.pdf.

Heywood, Paul and Jonathan Rose (2014). "Close But No Cigar:" The Measurement of Corruption," *Journal of Public Policy* 34, 3: 507–529.

Holmes, Oliver Wendell (1897). "The Path of Law," *Harvard Law Review* 10: 457. At: http://pdf.usaid.gov/pdf_docs/PDACG850.pdf.

Huberman, J. (1964). "Discipline Without Punishment," *Harvard Business Review* 42: 62–68.

Huntington, Samuel (1968) *Political Order in Changing Societies*. New Haven, CT: Yale University Press.

Hussmann, Karen (2007). "Anti-Corruption Making in Practice: What Can Be Learned for the Implementation of Article 5 of UNCAC?," U4 Report. At: http://www.u4.no/publications/anti-corruption-policy-making-in-practice-what-can-be-learned-for-implementing-article-5-of-uncac-2/.

Hutton, Guy (2002). *Equity and Access in the Health Sector in Five Countries of Eastern Europe and Central Asia: A Brief Review of the Literature*. Geneva: Swiss Agency for Development and Cooperation.

Jacobs, Scott (2005). *The Regulatory Guillotine Strategy: Preparing the Business Environment in Croatia for Competitiveness in Europe*. Washington, DC: United States Agency for International Development. At: https://pdf.usaid.gov/pdf_docs/PNADG614.pdf.

Janowitz, M. and R. Little (1974). *Sociology and the Military Establishment, Third Edition*. Beverly Hills, CA: Sage Publications.

Johnsøn, Jesper, Nils Taxell and Dominik Zaum (2012). *Mapping Evidence Gaps in Anti-Corruption: Assessing the State of the Operationally Relevant Evidence on Donors' Actions and Approaches to Reducing Corruption*. Bergen: Chr. Michelsen Institute (U4 Issue 2012:7). At: https://www.cmi.no/publications/file/4624-mapping-evidence-gaps-in-anti-corruption.pdf

Johnston, Michael (2000). *Controlling Corruption in Local Government: Analysis, Techniques and Action*. Arlington, VA: Management Systems International.

Johnston, Michael (2005). *Syndromes of Corruption: Wealth, Power, and Democracy*. New York: Cambridge University Press.

J-PAL (2006). "Encouraging Teacher Attendance through Monitoring with Cameras in Rural Udaipur, India," At: http://www.povertyactionlab.org/evaluation/encouraging-teacher-attendance-through-monitoring-cameras-rural-udaipur-india.

Katz, Daniel (1964). "Motivational Basis of Organizational Behavior," *Behavioral Science* 9, 2: 131–146.

Kaufmann, Daniel (1997). "Corruption: The Facts," *Foreign Policy* 107 (Summer): 114–131.

Kaufmann, Daniel (2003). "Rethinking Governance: Empirical Lessons Challenge Orthodoxy," Working Paper Series, Washington, DC: World Bank Institute.

Khan, Mushtaq (1996). "The Efficiency Implications of Corruption," *Journal of International Development* 8, 5: 683–696.

Khavronyuk, M.I. (2017). *Executive Summary of the Shadow Report on Evaluating the Effectiveness of State Anti-Corruption Policy Implementation.* Kyiv: Centre of Policy and Legal Reform and Transparency International Ukraine.

Kirchner, Lauren (2014). "The Psychology of Bribery and Corruption." *The Week* (November 20). At: https://theweek.com/articles/442692/psychology-bribery-corruption.

Klitgaard, Robert (1988). *Controlling Corruption.* Berkeley: University of California Press.

Klitgaard, Robert, R. Maclean-Abaroa, and H. Lindsey Parris (2000). *Corrupt Cities: A Practical Guide to Cure and Prevention.* Oakland, CA: ICS Press.

Kobis, Nils (2018). *The Social Psychology of Corruption.* Ph.D. dissertation, Free University of Amsterdam. At: https://www.researchgate.net/publication/322476552_The_Social_Psychology_of_Corruption.

Kohlberg, L. (1958). *The Development of Modes of Moral Thinking and Choice in Years 10 to 16.* Ph.D. dissertation. University of Chicago.

Kohlberg, L. (1964). "Development of Moral Character and Moral Ideology," in M.L. Hoffman and L.W. Hoffman, editors, *Review of Child Development Research* (Vol. 1, pp. 381–431). New York: Russell Sage Foundation.

Kohlberg, L. (1969). "Stages and Sequence: The Cognitive-Developmental Approach to Socialization," in D. Goslin, editor, *Handbook of Socialization Theory and Research* (pp. 347–480). Chicago, IL: Rand McNally.

Kohlberg, L. and R. Kramer (1969) "Continuities and Discontinuities in Childhood and Adult Moral Development," *Human Development* 12, 2: 93–120.

Kohlberg, L. and P. Scharf (1972). "Bureaucratic Violence and Conventional Moral Thinking," *American Journal of Orthopsychiatry* 42: 294–295.

Kramer, John M. (1999). *Anti-Corruption Research Concerning Eastern Europe and the Former Soviet Union: A Comparative Analysis.* Arlington, VA: Management Systems International.

Kremenyuk, Victor, editor (1991). *International Negotiation.* San Francisco: Jossey-Bass.

Kupchinsky, Roman (2003). "Analysis: The Clan from Donetsk," RFE/RL Poland, Belarus and Ukraine Report (January 12).

Kuris, Gabriel (2012). *Inviting a Tiger into your Home: Indonesia Creates an Anti-Corruption Commission with Teeth, 2002–2007.* Princeton, NJ: Innovations for Successful Societies. At: https://successfulsocieties.princeton.edu/sites/successfulsocieties/files/Policy_Note_ID211.pdf.

Kuris, Gabriel (2014). *From Underdogs to Watchdogs: How Anti-Corruption Agencies Can Hold Off Potent Adversaries.* Princeton, NJ: Innovations for Successful Societies. At: http://www.princeton.edu/successfulsocieties/content/data/policy_note/PN_id236/Policy_Note_ID236.pdf.

Lewis, Maureen (2006). "Governance and Corruption in Public Health Care Systems," Working Paper Number 78, Center for Global Development (January). At: https://www.cgdev.org/sites/default/files/5967_file_WP_78.pdf

Management Systems International (2000). *Integrity Survey in Kharkiv, Ukraine.* Washington, DC: USAID (Conducted by Kiev International Institute of Sociology, November–December 1999).

Management Systems International (2004). *Public Opinion of Corruption in Vladivostok.* Washington, DC: USAID.

Management Systems International (2009). *Community Participation and Regional Advocacy Project in the Russian Far East, Final Report.* Washington, DC: USAID. At: http://pdf.usaid.gov/pdf_docs/PDACQ845.pdf.

Management Systems International (2009). *Greater Transparency and Accountability of Government Program (GTAG), Final Report.* Washington, DC: USAID. At: http://pdf.usaid.gov/pdf_docs/PDACP996.pdf.

Management Systems International (2009). *Surveys: 2008–2009 for the MCC Threshold Country Program.* Washington, DC: USAID. At: https://sites.google.com/a/usaid.gov/drg/home/about-1/drg-center-teams/governance-and-rule-of-law/anti-corruptionmapping.

Management Systems International (2010). *Promoting Citizen Engagement in Combating Corruption in Ukraine (ACTION), Final Report.* Washington, DC: United States Agency for International Development. At: https://pdf.usaid.gov/pdf_docs/PDACR665.pdf.

Management Systems International (2013). *Assistance for Afghanistan's Anti-Corruption Authority (4A) Project, Final Report.* Washington, DC: USAID. At: http://pdf.usaid.gov/pdf_docs/PA00JP3T.pdf.

Management Systems International (2014a). *Indonesia Strengthening Integrity and Accountability Project-1, Annual Report.* Washington, DC: USAID.

Management Systems International (2014b). *Analysis of USAID Anticorruption Programming Worldwide (2007–2013).* Washington, DC: United States Agency for International Development. At: https://www.usaid.gov/sites/default/files/documents/1866/AnalysisUSAIDAnticorruptionProgrammingWorldwideFinalReport2007-2013.pdf.

Management Systems International (2015). *Practitioner's Guide for Anti-corruption Programming.* Washington, DC: USAID. At: https://www.usaid.gov/opengov/developer/datasets/Practitioner%27s_Guide_for_Anticorruption_Programming_2015.pdf.

Management Systems International (2016). *Strengthening Integrity and Accountability Program 1 (SIAP 1), Final Report.* Washington, DC: United States Agency for International Development.

Management Systems International (2016). *Technical Assistance Services for the eTender Initiative in Kyiv, Ukraine (Phase II), Final Informational Report.* Washington, DC: USAID.

Management Systems International (2019). *USAID CEGAH Project, Annual Report FY 2019.* Washington, DC: USAID.

Management Systems International (2020). *Support to Anti-Corruption Champion Institutions (SACCI) Project in Ukraine, Progress Report.* Washington, DC: United States Agency for International Development. At: https://pdf.usaid.gov/pdf_docs/PA00X39S.pdf.

Management Systems International (2020). *USAID CEGAH Project, Annual Report FY 2020.* Washington, DC: USAID.

Management Systems International and the World Bank (2000) *Diagnostic Assessment of Corruption in Romania.* Washington, DC: MSI and the World Bank.

Mann, Catherine (2011). "Behaviour Changing Campaigns: Success and Failure Factors," U4 Expert Answer, (21 February: 270). At: http://www.transparency.org/files/content/corruptionqas/270_Behaviour_changing_campaigns.pdf.

Marone, John (2005). "Ukraine's Health Care System: Finding the Right Cure," *The Ukrainian Observer,* Issue 208.

Mauro, Paolo (1997). "The Effects of Corruption on Growth, Investment and Government Expenditure: A Cross-Country Analysis," in K. Elliott, editor, *Corruption and the Global Economy* (pp. 83–108). Washington, DC: Institute for International Economics.

McGee, R. and J. Gaventa (2010). *Review of Impact and Effectiveness of Transparency and Accountability Initiatives.* Brighton, UK: Institute for Development Studies. At: https://www.transparency-initiative.org/wp-content/uploads/2017/03/synthesis_report_final1.pdf

McMillan, John and Pablo Zoido (2004). *How to Subvert Democracy: Montesinos in Peru.* Unpublished: Stanford University. At: https://papers.ssrn.com/sol3/papers.cfm?abstract_id=520902.

Mellman, Aryeh and Norman Eisen (2020). "Addressing the Other COVID Crisis: Corruption," 22 July. Washington, DC: Brookings Institution. At: https://www.brookings.edu/research/addressing-the-other-covid-crisis-corruption/.

Menocal, Alina Rocha and Bhavna Sharma (2008). *Joint Evaluation of Citizens' Voice and Accountability: Synthesis Report.* London: DFID.

Menocal, Alina Rocha and Nils Taxell (2015). *Why Corruption Matters: Understanding Causes, Effects and How to Address Them: Evidence Paper on Corruption.* London: Department for International Development (DFID).

Migliorisi, Stefano and Clay Wescott (2011). *A Review of World Bank Support for Accountability Institutions in the Context of Governance and Anticorruption.* IEG Working Paper 2011/5. Washington, DC: World Bank.

Milgram, Stanley (1974). *Obedience to Authority.* New York: Harper and Row.

Millennium Challenge Corporation (2011). "Albania Threshold Program, Stage II." At: https://www.mcc.gov/where-we-work/program/albania-ii-threshold-program.

Miller, William L., Åse B. Grødeland and Tatyana Y. Koshechkina (1998). "Are the People Victims or Accomplices: The Use of Presents and Bribes to Influence Officials in Eastern Europe," *Crime, Law and Social Change* 29, 4: 273–310.

Miller, William L., Åse B. Grødeland and Tatyana Y. Koshechkina (1999). "What is to be Done about Corrupt Officials? Public Opinion in Ukraine, Bulgaria, Slovakia and the Czech Republic," *International Review of Administrative Sciences* 65, 2: 235–249.

Moriarty, A. and P. Toussieng (1976). *Adolescent Coping.* New York: Grune and Stratton.

Murray, H. (1938). *Explorations in Personality.* New York: John Wiley and Sons.

Nanivska, Vera (2001). *NGO Development in Ukraine*. Kyiv: International Center for Policy Studies.

Norwegian Agency for Development Cooperation (2011). *Joint Evaluation of Support to Anti-Corruption Efforts 2002–2009, Synthesis*. Oslo, Norway: NORAD.

Organization for Economic Cooperation and Development (2000) *No Longer Business as Usual: Fighting Bribery and Corruption*. Paris: Organization for Economic Cooperation and Development.

Organization for Economic Cooperation and Development (2016). *Anti-corruption Reforms in Eastern Europe and Central Asia: Progress and Challenges, 2013–2015*. Paris: OECD.

Pamula, Anusha (2015). "The Social Psychology of Corruption." *The Global Anti-Corruption Blog* (August 28). At: https://globalanticorruptionblog. com/2015/08/28/the-social-psychology-of-corruption-lack-thereof/.

Piaget, Jean (1965). *The Moral Judgment of the Child*. New York: Free Press.

Pope, Jeremy (1997). *The TI Source Book, Second Edition*. Berlin: Transparency International.

Pope, Jeremy and Frank Vogl (2000). "Making Anticorruption Agencies More Effective," *Finance & Development* 37, 2 (June). At: https://www.imf.org/external/ pubs/ft/fandd/2000/06/pope.htm.

Presidential Secretariat (2005). *General Information on Measures on Combating Corruption in Ukraine in 2005*. Kyiv: Presidential Secretariat.

Roberts, Sean and Robert Orttung (2015). *Changing Corrupt Behaviors Assessment*. Washington, DC: USAID. At: https://www.usaid.gov/sites/default/files/ documents/1863/Changing%20Corrupt%20Behaviors%20Assessment%20 Oct.%202015.pdf.

Rose-Ackerman, Susan (1978). *Corruption: A Study in Political Economy*. New York: Academic Press.

Rose-Ackerman, Susan and Bonnie Palifka (2016). *Corruption and Government*. New York: Cambridge University Press.

Scharbatke-Church, Cheyanne, and Diana Chigas (2019). *Understanding Social Norms: A Reference Guide for Policy and Practice*. The Henry J. Leir Institute of Human Security. Medford, MA: The Fletcher School of Law and Diplomacy, Tufts University. At: https://sites.tufts.edu/ihs/social-norms-reference-guide/.

Seats, Ellen and Samantha H. Vardaman (2009). *Lessons Learned Fighting Corruption in MCC Threshold Countries: The USAID Experience*. Washington, DC: USAID. At: http://pdf.usaid.gov/pdf_docs/pnads603.pdf.

Sleeper, Jonathan (2003). *How USAID Safeguards against Corruption can be used by the Millennium Challenge Account*, Issue Brief #3 (PN-ACT-341). Washington, DC: US Agency for International Development (June).

Spector, Bertram (1973). *The Stages of Moral Development and their Implication for Principled Government Leadership*. New York: Center for International Studies, New York University, Seminar Paper.

Spector, Bertram (1977). *Intrinsic/Extrinsic Motivation, Ethical Values and the Legal Profession*. Arlington, VA: CACI, Inc.

Spector, Bertram (2000). "Building Constituencies for Anti-Corruption Programs: The Role of Diagnostic Assessments," Paper presented at the Regional Anti-Corruption Conference, Bucharest, Romania, March 30.

Spector, Bertram (2000). *Anti-Corruption Program Feasibility Study in Russia: Tomsk and Samara, Final Report*, October. Washington, DC: USAID.

Spector, Bertram (2001). "Negotiation Readiness in the Development Context: Adding Capacity to Ripeness," in Ho-Won Jeong, editor, *From Conflict Resolution to Peace Building* (pp. 80–102). New York: Macmillan.

Spector, Bertram, editor (2005). *Fighting Corruption in Developing Countries: Strategies and Analysis*. Bloomfield, CT: Kumarian Press.

Spector, Bertram (2011). *Negotiating Peace and Confronting Corruption: Challenges for Post-Conflict Societies*. Washington, DC: United States Institute of Peace Press.

Spector, Bertram (2012). *Detecting Corruption in Developing Countries: Identifying Causes/Strategies for Action*. Sterling, VA: Kumarian Press.

Spector, Bertram, et al. (2005). *Corruption Assessment: Mozambique*. Washington, DC: United States Agency for International Development. At: https://pdf.usaid.gov/pdf_docs/PNADF937.pdf.

Spector, Bertram, Michael Johnston and Svetlana Winbourne (2009). *Anti-Corruption Assessment Handbook, Final Report*. Washington, DC: USAID. At: https://pdf.usaid.gov/pdf_docs/pa00jp37.pdf.

Spector, Bertram, Svetlana Winbourne, et al. (2006). *Corruption Assessment: Ukraine, Final Report (February)*. Washington, DC: USAID. At: https://pdf.usaid.gov/pdf_docs/PNADK247.pdf.

Spector, Bertram, Svetlana Winbourne, et al. (2017). *Anti-corruption Dynamics in Ukraine: A Political Economy Analysis*. Washington, DC: United States Agency for International Development.

Stein, Janice, editor (1989). *Getting to the Table: The Processes of International Prenegotiation*. Baltimore, MD: The Johns Hopkins University Press.

Stein, Morris (1963). "Explorations in Typology," in R. White, editor, *The Study of Lives* (pp. 280–303). New York: Atherton Press.

Stein, Morris (1971). "Ecology of Typology," Paper presented at the Association of American Medical Colleges Conference on Personality Measurement in Medical Education, Des Plaines, Illinois.

Stein, Morris and J. Neulinger (1968). "A Typology of Self-Descriptions," in M. Katz, et al., editors, *The Role and Methodology of Classification in Psychiatry and Psychopathology* (pp. 390–403). Washington, DC: GPO, No. 1584.

Stephenson, Matthew (2014). "The Importance of Personnel Selection in Promoting Government Integrity: Some Evidence from India," *The Global Anti-Corruption Blog* (June 26). At: https://globalanticorruptionblog.com/2014/06/26/the-importance-of-personnel-selection-in-promoting-government-integrity-some-evidence-from-india/.

Taylor, Alison (2015). "The Characteristics of Corrupt Corporate Cultures." *The Global Anti-Corruption Blog* (July 2). At: https://globalanticorruptionblog.com/2015/07/02/guest-post-the-characteristics-of-corrupt-corporate-cultures/.

Teachout, Zephyr (2016). *Corruption in America*. Cambridge, MA: Harvard University Press.

Transparency International (2021). *Corruption Fighters' Toolkits*. Berlin: Transparency International. At: http://www.transparency.org/whatwedo/tools/corruption_fighters_toolkits_introduction/2/.

Transparency International UK (2021). *Track and Trace: Identifying Corruption Risks in UK Public Procurement for the COVID-19 Pandemic*. London: Transparency International UK. At: https://www.transparency.org.uk/sites/default/files/pdf/publications/Track%20and%20Trace%20-%20Transparency%20International%20UK.pdf.

United Nations (2004). *UN Anti-Corruption Toolkit, Second Edition.* Vienna: United Nations Office on Drugs and Crime. At: https://www.un.org/en/coronavirus/statement-corruption-context-covid-19

United Nations (2020). *Official Statement of the United Nations Secretary General Antonio Guterres, October 15, 2020.* New York: United Nations. At: https://www.un.org/sg/en/content/sg/statement/2020-10-15/secretary-generals-statement-corruption-the-context-of-covid-19-scroll-down-for-french-version.

United Nations Country Team (2004). *Common Country Assessment for Ukraine,* October. New York: United Nations.

United Nations Global Compact (2009). *UN Global Compact Anti-Corruption Tools Inventory.* New York: United Nations. At: www.business-anti-corruption.com.

United Nations Office on Drugs and Crime (2020a). *The Time Is Now: Addressing the Gender Dimensions of Corruption.* Vienna: UNODC. At: https://www.unodc.org/documents/corruption/Publications/2020/THE_TIME_IS_NOW_2020_12_08.pdf.

United Nations Office on Drugs and Crime (2020b). *Mainstreaming Gender in Corruption Projects/Programmes: Briefing Note for UNODC Staff.* Vienna: UNODC. At: https://www.unodc.org/documents/Gender/20-05712_Corruption_Brief_ebook_cb.pdf.

United Nations Security Council (2018). "Global Cost of Corruption at Least 5 Per Cent of World Gross Domestic Product, Secretary-General Tells Security Council, Citing World Economic Forum Data," At: https://www.un.org/press/en/2018/sc13493.doc.htm.

United States Agency for International Development (USAID) (1999). *A Handbook on Fighting Corruption.* Washington, DC: Center for Democracy and Governance, Bureau for Global Programs, US Agency for International Development.

United States Agency for International Development (2005). *2004 NGO Sustainability Index for Central and Eastern Europe and Eurasia, Eighth Edition.* Washington, DC: USAID.

United States Agency for International Development (2005). *Anti-Corruption and Transparency Coalitions: Lessons from Peru, Paraguay, El Salvador and Bolivia* (August). At: http://pdf.usaid.gov/pdf_docs/PNADD813.pdf.

United States Agency for International Development (2005). *Reducing Administrative Corruption in Ukraine: Regulatory Reform, BIZPRO.* Washington, DC: USAID.

United States Agency for International Development (2005). *USAID Anti-Corruption Strategy.* Washington, DC: US Agency for International Development. At: https://www.usaid.gov/sites/default/files/documents/1868/200mbo.pdf.

United States Agency for International Development (2006). *Anti-Corruption Interventions in Economic Growth: Lessons Learned for the Design of Future Projects.* At: http://pdf.usaid.gov/pdf_docs/pnadg601.pdf.

United States Agency for International Development (2009). *Combating Corruption and Strengthening Rule of Law in Ukraine, Final Report.* At: http://pdf.usaid.gov/pdf_docs/Pdacn921.pdf.

United States Agency for International Development (2009). *Corruption and Business Regulations in Ukraine: Construction and Land Transactions Permits. Comparative Analysis of National Surveys: 2008–2009.* Washington, DC: USAID.

United States Agency for International Development (2009). *Georgia Business Climate Reform (GBCR), Final Report.* At: http://www.chemonics.com/OurWork/OurProjects/Documents/Georgia Business Climate Reform Final Report.pdf.

United States Agency for International Development (2009). *Panama Strengthened Rule of Law and Respect for Human Rights Program, Final Report.* At: http://pdf. usaid.gov/pdf_docs/PDACW212.pdf.

United States Agency for International Development (2009). *Reducing Corruption in the Judiciary: Office of Democracy and Governance – USAID Program Brief.* At: http://pdf.usaid.gov/pdf_docs/PNADQ106.pdf.

United States Agency for International Development (2009). *Transition Initiative: Nepal, Final Report.* Washington, DC: USAID. At: http://pdf.usaid.gov/pdf_docs/ PDACQ596.pdf.

United States Agency for International Development (2009). *Ukrainian Standardized External Testing Initiative, Final Report.* At: http://pdf.usaid.gov/pdf_docs/ PDACQ648.pdf

United States Agency for International Development (2010). *Liberia Governance and Economic Management Assistance Program, Final Evaluation Report.* At: http://pdf.usaid.gov/pdf_docs/PDACR798.pdf.

United States Agency for International Development (2010). *Mobilizing Action Against Corruption in Armenia Project, Mid-term Evaluation.* Washington, DC: USAID. At: http://pdf.usaid.gov/pdf_docs/PDACR143.pdf.

United States Agency for International Development (2011). *Moldova Business and Tax Administration Reform, Mid-term Evaluation.* At: http://pdf.usaid.gov/pdf_ docs/PDACS244.pdf.

United States Agency for International Development (2013). *Anti-Corruption and Cross-Sectoral Program Mapping: Enabling Environment Programs Worldwide.* At: http://www.usaid.gov/sites/default/files/documents/1866/AnalysisUSAIDAnti-corruptionProgrammingWorldwideFinalReport2007-2013.pdf.

United States Agency for International Development (2013). *Palestinian Authority Capacity Enhancement (PACE), Final Report.* At: http://pdf.usaid.gov/pdf_docs/ PDACY026.pdf.

United States Agency for International Development (2018). *National Anti-Corruption Survey, December 5.* At: https://dif.org.ua/article/kozhna-tretya-ukrainkaets-gotovi-doluchitisya-do-organizovanoi-protidii-koruptsii.

United States Agency for International Development Learning Lab (2018). *Applied Political Economy Analysis (PEA): Reference Materials, Sample Interview Questions and Data Collection Template.* At: https://usaidlearninglab.org/sites/default/ files/resource/files/supplemental_resource_-_sample_interview_guide.docx_1.pdf.

US Foreign Commercial Service/US State Department (2001). *Ukrainian Market for Health Care Services.* Washington, DC: U.S. State Department.

US GAO (2004). "U.S. Anticorruption Programs in Sub-Saharan Africa Will Require Time and Commitment," GAO-04-506 (April). At: http://www.gao.gov/ products/GAO-04-506.

U.S. News and World Report (1977). "Lawyers — Can They Police Themselves?" (June 6).

Weisband, Edward and Thomas Franck (1975). *Resignation in Protest: Political and Ethical Choices between Loyalty to Team and Loyalty to Conscience in American Public Life.* New York: Grossman Publishers.

Winbourne, Svetlana and Bertram Spector (2014). *Analysis of USAID Anticorruption Programming Worldwide (2007–2013), Final Report.* Washington, DC: USAID. At: https://www.usaid.gov/sites/default/files/documents/1866/AnalysisU-SAIDAnticorruptionProgrammingWorldwideFinalReport2007-2013.pdf.

Winbourne, Svetlana and Bertram Spector (2019). "A Rapid Results Anti-Corruption Tool – That Builds Citizen Trust and has Lasting Impact... and Now, with World-wide Reach," *Global Anticorruption Impacts, Technical Note 12.* Arlington, VA: Management Systems International. At: https://msiworldwide.com/sites/default/files/2018-11/GlobalACImpacts_12.pdf.

Winbourne, Svetlana, Bertram I. Spector and Elena Ponyaeva (2013). *Anti-Corruption and Cross-Sectoral Program Mapping: the Europe & Eurasia Region and Business Enabling Environment Programs Worldwide.* Washington, DC: USAID.

World Bank (2000a). *Anticorruption in Transition: A Contribution to the Policy Debate.* Washington, DC: The World Bank.

World Bank (2000b). *Helping Countries Combat Corruption: Progress at the World Bank Since 1997.* Washington, DC: The World Bank (PREM), June.

World Bank (2004). *Ukraine: Building Foundations for Sustainable Growth, A Country Economic Memorandum: Volume 1* (August). Washington, DC: The World Bank.

World Bank (2008). *Public Sector Reform: What Works and Why? An IEG Evaluation of World Bank Support.* Washington, DC: The World Bank. At: https://openknowledge.worldbank.org/bitstream/handle/10986/6484/448180PUB0Box310only109780821375891.pdf?sequence=1&isAllowed=y

World Bank (2011). *Country-Level Engagement on Governance and Anti-corruption: An Evaluation of the 2007 Strategy and Implementation Plan.* Washington, DC: The World Bank.

World Bank (2011). *How Many Stops in a One-stop Shop? A Review of Recent Development in Business Registration.* Washington, DC: World Bank Group. At: http://documents.worldbank.org/curated/en/708751468149688644/How-many-stops-in-a-one-stop-shop-A-review-of-recent-development-in-business-registration.

World Bank (2012). *Fighting Corruption in Public Services: Chronicling Georgia's Reforms.* Washington, DC: The World Bank.

World Health Organization (2004). *Summary Country Profile.* Geneva: WHO.

World Health Organization (2005). *World Health Report* 2005. Geneva: WHO.

Yushchenko, V. A. (2005). "Current State of Ukraine's Medical Sector: One of the Most Disturbing Problems," Presidential Radio Address, November 12. At: www.president.gov.ua/en.

Zartman, I. William (1989) *Ripe for Resolution.* New York: Oxford University Press.

Zartman, I. William (2000) "Ripeness: The Hurting Stalemate and Beyond," in Paul C. Stern and Daniel Druckman, editors, *International Conflict Resolution after the Cold War* (pp. 225–250). Washington, DC: National Academy Press.

Index